The Beatles Acting Naturally

Rare, Unfinished and Abandoned Film and TV Projects of the Fab Four

To Graham
Thanks for all the support!

Rory x ☺

Rory Hoy

NEW HAVEN PUBLISHING LTD

Published 2021
First Edition
New Haven Publishing
www.newhavenpublishingltd.com
newhavenpublishing@gmail.com

Cover design ©Pete Cunliffe

newhaven
publishing

CONTENTS

Introduction

This book is dedicated to John, Paul, George and Ringo - the four greatest rock stars of all time. Without you, the world wouldn't be the same!

It's not an understatement to say that The Beatles were pretty much the most successful musical act to come out of the 20th century and, to this day, the most successful act in pop music history. These Liverpudlian "mop tops" have been part of the pop culture landscape since the 1960s, with no signs of their popularity slowing down. The Beatles brand will be here to stay for some time, attracting another generation of fans. Pretty much every aspect of the band, which John once infamously claimed was *"more popular than Jesus"*, has been covered at some time or another... but here's a different take, which includes the more obscure appearances and references worldwide through the wonderful art of film, television and video, some of which will make you gasp in disbelief! In this book, we will look at the history of films and TV shows that are associated with The Beatles, from their main canonical movies, such as the fictionalised documentary of *A Hard Day's Night* and the animated masterpiece of *Yellow Submarine*, to documentaries about them, biopics, parodies, and other projects that involved the Fab Four in some capacity. The Beatles didn't just revolutionise pop music, they revolutionised pop culture as a whole!

As this introduction implies, pop stars back in the day were more than just people that played music, they were multimedia "jacks of all trades". The Beatles were not just fantastic musicians, but competent actors, film directors and producers as well. George Harrison was the founder and mastermind behind the movie company Handmade Films, one of the most successful independent film companies of its time. Ringo Starr was a successful actor, who appeared in many popular movies of the 1970s and 1980s and even narrated the beloved children's TV series *Thomas The Tank Engine & Friends*. Paul McCartney has produced his own films, made cameo appearances in many successful films and TV shows, and even had his hand in children's animation; while John Lennon, with his wife Yoko Ono, experimented in the arena of arthouse cinema.

But did you know...

· In 1963, The Beatles turned down their first movie offer *The Yellow Teddy Bears*

· The boys made a film BEFORE *A Hard Day's Night*, which was only released in Australia in 1964

· John and Paul hosted a variety TV special in 1965

· Paul made experimental avant garde shorts in 1966

· In 1967, they were set to appear in a film written by Joe Orton aimed at a more adult audience

· John and Yoko made a short feature in cooperation with the parents of notorious "murderer" James Hanratty in 1969

· The same year, The Beatles were set to make their own adaptation of *The Lord Of The Rings*

· Paul McCartney appeared on the children's TV series *The Basil Brush Show* in 1972

· Also in the 1970s, McCartney wanted to make his own sci-fi films

· Ringo directed a film about the band T-Rex in 1973

· That same year, George Harrison and Carole King performed together on a novelty single

· Ringo Starr and *Star Wars* actress Carrie Fisher duetted together in a variety special in 1978

· And in 2008, original drummer Pete Best was in a film with Bradley Cooper and Emma Stone

...you didn't? Well, read on for more details on all of this and much more!

I have tried to list all the relevant projects all four Beatles have taken part in, in the fields of film and television. If I have missed anything out, it is not intentional!

So, without further ado, let's take a Magical Mystery Tour into the Fab Four's adventures in celluloid.

Rory

A Super Brief History of The Beatles

The Beatles - John Lennon, Paul McCartney, George Harrison and Ringo Starr

Believe it or not, there are a minority of young people who don't know who The Beatles are (you are sadly deprived), and have never heard a single Beatles song (shock, horror), and somebody who has just casually picked this book up may not have a clue what I'm talking about when I mention John, Paul, George and Ringo. This chapter is for those people - a super brief history of the Fab Four.

The story began in a city in Merseyside, England, called Liverpool, in the summer of 1956, when a teenager named John Lennon (born October 9th 1940) formed a skiffle band called The Quarrymen (named after John's school, Quarry Bank High School) with his friends, with John playing rhythm guitar. For those who are not familiar, skiffle is a type of "homemade" music that is a combination of jazz and blues, usually with improvised instrumentation. In July 1957, they played at the Wooltan Village Fete, and this impressed a young man named Paul McCartney (born June 18th 1942). They met backstage, they both developed a mutual bond, and not long after that Paul joined The Quarrymen. One year later, Paul's friend George Harrison (born February 25th 1943) would join the group as lead guitarist, and by 1959, many of the other members left, leaving only John, Paul and George; and their sound had gone from skiffle to rock & roll. In 1960, John's friend from art college, Stuart Sutcliffe, joined as bass guitarist (by all accounts, while being a great artist, he wasn't much of a musician), and he was the one who convinced them to rename themselves to The Beatals, then The Silver Beetles, Long John and The Silver Beatles and then finally in that summer - just The Beatles!

Me with early Beatles promoter, Sam Leach, in The Grapes pub, where they all used to meet by The Cavern in Liverpool.

Around that time, they found a full-time drummer in Pete Best, and they started a residency in the red light district of Hamburg in West Germany. They returned many times, though in 1961, Stuart left the band, and went back to being an artist, while Macca (Paul's nickname) took over on bass duties. Tragically, Stuart died in 1962 of a brain haemorrhage. Back to '61, the now four piece Beatles were promoted by, amongst others, a man named Sam Leach. They grabbed the attention of a German record producer, Bert Kaempfert, and they were asked to back up guitarist/singer Tony Sheridan for some recordings for Polydor Records in Germany. Also in the same year, at their residency at the famous Cavern Club in their hometown of Liverpool, they grabbed the attention of a local well-known businessman named Brian Epstein, who ended up becoming their manager. In January of 1962, they auditioned for Decca Records, only to be rejected, with the response *"Guitar groups are on the way out"* - oh how wrong they were! One label that did accept them was EMI's Parlophone Records, a label which primarily concentrated on comedy and novelty recordings, and here they caught the eye of a producer named George Martin (1926-2016). After a recording session in June 1962 in Abbey Road Recording Studios, Martin was not impressed with Pete Best's drumming, which unfortunately resulted in him getting the sack. He was replaced by Richard Starkey, AKA Ringo Starr (born July 7th 1940), originally from Rory Storm and the Hurricanes, and already a friend to The Beatles - now, the band evolved into the lineup we know and love.

Their official debut single 'Love Me Do 'was recorded in September of that year, and was released in the following month, doing well commercially, reaching No.17 in the UK Singles Chart. Their follow-up single, released in January 1963, 'Please Please Me', was an even bigger hit, reaching the coveted No.1 position. Their debut album of the same name was pressed on March 22nd of that year, and was recorded in a single day. It was about this time that a phenomenon emerged called "Beatlemania", a craze that resulted in teenage female fans becoming hysterical, screaming like banshees, and chasing them wherever they appeared. Three massive non-album singles emerged from this time period - 'From Me To You', 'I Want To Hold Your Hand 'and 'She Loves You' - all reaching No.1, and their even more successful second album *With The Beatles* was released on that fateful day on November 22nd 1963 when US President John F. Kennedy was tragically assassinated. Despite the horrific events, the album went straight to the top of the charts and remained there for 23 weeks.

On Boxing Day 1963, US label Capitol Records picked up their single 'I Want To Hold Your Hand 'and an even bigger wave of Beatlemania emerged in the US a year later. On February 9th 1964, they appeared on the famous *Ed Sullivan TV Show* to an audience of 73 million people (around 45% of all Americans at the time). This resulted in a trend of successful UK bands, such as The Kinks, The Who, The Hollies, Herman's Hermits, The Dave Clark Five and most notably The Beatles 'friendly rivals, The Rolling Stones, making a splash in the Atlantic, resulting in a trend dubbed "The British Invasion". Also in the same year, The Beatles made their transition to the silver screen with the black and white film *A Hard Day's Night* (a lot more on that later in the book), which was a critical and commercial success, and was accompanied by a soundtrack album of the same name. During their immensely successful tour of America, they met an up-and-coming singer-songwriter named Bob Dylan in the Delmonico Hotel in Manhattan (a massive star in his own right) and he introduced them to... well, let's just say her name is Mary Jane - it apparently had a big impact later on. The year ended with them releasing their fourth album *Beatles For Sale* and guess what - it was again a massive hit (no surprises there!).

In 1965, the Beatlemania phase reached its peak. The year saw Her Majesty the Queen award the band with MBE honours (Member of the British Empire), and in that summer they released their second film *Help!*, which was allegedly made somewhat under the influence of the "wacky baccy" and was in colour. While not quite as successful as the first film, it was still a huge hit, and resulted in a soundtrack album of the same name, which contained probably their most famous song,' Yesterday '- a song so good that it is the most covered pop song of all time. The year also saw them return to America, and on August 15th they did their legendary show at Shea Stadium in New York to a huge crowd of 55,600, which was a massive success, despite nobody being able to hear a thing! September saw the transmission of a cartoon series based on the band for ABC TV in America, and in December they released their sixth album *Rubber Soul*, an LP that took them in a more mature direction.

1966 saw the first threat to their career. In March, John Lennon was interviewed by Maureen Cleave in *The Evening Standard* newspaper in the UK and said that the Beatles were *"more popular than Jesus"*. In the UK, nobody took any notice, but in America, some took deep offence, taking everything out of context, leading to protests and record burnings, and even threats from a very well-known extremist group. Lennon had to later clear things up, and reluctantly apologised, and after that, all systems were go... but the boys were getting less enthusiastic about performing live, and in that year, they gave up touring altogether with their final concert (for now) being at Candlestick Park in San Francisco in America. August saw them release their seventh album, *Revolver*, which was the start of them going in a direction that would jumpstart the psychedelic rock movement, now sounding a little more left field than the teenybopper stuff they did three years earlier. The album received universal acclaim, with many critics saying it was one of the greatest albums of all time (they were right!).

1967 saw the release of probably their most famous album, *Sgt. Pepper's Lonely Hearts Club Band*, in May of that year - another album to receive the acclaim of being *"the best ever"*, and it was even more "out there" than *Revolver*. It also pioneered the idea of the concept album. June saw them perform to a record-breaking audience of 350 million people with their hit single 'All You Need Is Love 'via the first ever global television link. Despite being a fantastic year for the band, there was the extremely tragic news of the passing of their manager, Brian Epstein; he was only 32. The future was uncertain, and for a bit of light relief, with Paul trying desperately to keep the band together and working, they made probably the most expensive home movie ever, *Magical Mystery Tour*, for BBC Television. It was their first critical and commercial failure at the time, but on the positive side, the soundtrack EP to it was phenomenal and was again a massive success.

1968 saw them travel to India to get spiritual guidance from a guru named Maharishi Mahesh Yogi, who they had befriended a year earlier. It was during this time that Lennon started dating a Japanese conceptual artist named Yoko Ono, who he had met earlier in 1966. This resulted in him leaving his previous wife Cynthia and son Julian. In May 1968, The Beatles launched a company named Apple (no not THAT company), which was a business venture that specialised in music, films, and even had a shopping boutique. July saw the release of the animated film *Yellow Submarine* which was based on their music, and the band had real life cameos in the end of the film. It was a big hit and is beloved to this day. October 1968 saw the release of their self-titled album simply called *The Beatles* but now better known as *The White Album*, as it came in a plain white sleeve. This two record epic was certainly their most eclectic album, schizophrenically switching genres, from music hall ('Honey Pie') to hard rock ('Helter Skelter') to ska ('Ob-La-Di Ob-La-Da') to "what the hell is this?" ('Revolution 9'). It was another outstanding success.

The start of 1969 saw the beginning of the end of The Beatles, and the mood was getting more apathetic (something that they had been leading up to since Epstein's death). Paul wanted the band to do live gigs again, and the others were reluctant. During rehearsals, tensions only got worse, and the idea of them touring again fell through. The 30th January saw them perform their final concert - an impromptu show on the roof of the office of Apple Headquarters, with guest keyboard work from George's friend, Billy Preston. It was during this time that they recorded an album entitled *Get Back*, later renamed *Let It Be*, which didn't get released until 1970. It was then that the band went their separate ways, with Lennon quietly leaving in September. It was also in that month they released their grand finale album *Abbey Road* - another massive hit, with an iconic album cover of them walking across a pedestrian crossing outside the Abbey Road studios in London (then known as the EMI Studios), which is emulated by millions of people to this day. Despite mixed reviews at the time, it is now considered a masterpiece, and a fitting finale to The Beatles 'career (even though *Let It Be* was released later, it was recorded earlier - strange isn't it?) In April 1970, the band officially announced their breakup, and May of that year saw them eventually put out *Let It Be*, with a documentary film released in cinemas to accompany it. Even though the news of The Beatles 'disbandment was tough, they all had successful solo careers.

On December 8th 1980, John Lennon was tragically murdered outside his apartment in New York. 1995 saw the remaining Beatles "reunite" for a TV special known as *The Beatles Anthology*. The "Threetles" overdubbed two John Lennon piano demos recorded in the 1970s, 'Free As A Bird 'and 'Real Love'. While not receiving universal praise, both tunes were commercial successes, especially for their iconic music videos.

George Harrison sadly passed away on November 29th 2001 as a result of lung cancer. Thankfully, as of writing, both Ringo and Paul are alive and well (despite rumours of Paul being killed in a car crash in 1966 and being replaced by a lookalike named William Shears Campbell) and they both still make music and perform live to this day. The Beatles are still considered to be the biggest band ever, selling countless records (around 800 million), and they pioneered the way music is today.

Chapter One
From The Beginning: Beatles Film and TV Apeaances

If you don't promote yourself on television or on film, how are you going to get your sound heard by millions of people? The Beatles understood this very well, and worked hard to promote their music to a larger audience. Thanks to these appearances, they became a worldwide phenomenon - all without the help of social media, which didn't exist back then. They also made numerous radio and press appearances, which I have not listed in this book, as I am primarily focusing on visual mediums.

Especially in The Beatles 'home country of the United Kingdom, during the 1970s, storage and cost saving measures meant that many valuable clips from this era were wiped out and recycled. If only they'd known how valuable they would prove to be in later years.

So here we go, in chronological broadcast and release date order...

Liverpool City Police Recruitment Film (1958)

Written and Produced By - G.Twist, L.L.M.
Release Date - 1958
Running Time - 41 Minutes

A rare recruitment film for Liverpool's police department; it may not sound like much, but according to Paul McCartney's brother, Mike McGear (McCartney), the future Beatles - John, George and Paul, make a very brief appearance in the crowd when the film documents the annual police parade, and, according to Peter Hodgson, who discovered the video in 2017, *"They are seen, stood on top of their outside toilet roof, watching the annual police horse and dog display. I love watching old films about Liverpool on YouTube and I made the connection with Forthlin Road (the McCartneys' home) when I saw the Mather Avenue Police Show footage. Then I worked out which house was the McCartneys' and thought, 'Bingo!' I nearly fell off my chair when I saw it."* [1]

Whether it is really them is up to you to decide - it's very hard to see the actual faces! The film is available on YouTube, and their appearance is 34 minutes and 33 seconds into the 41 minute video. [13]

People and Places (1962)

First Broadcast - October 17th 1962

The Beatles 'official television debut. This was a regional programme made by Granada Television in Manchester for the North of England, filmed at Studio Four at Granada Television Centre in Quay Street. In their first appearance, they perform two songs live in the studio - 'Some Other Guy '(a rock & roll standard) and their official first single 'Love Me Do'.
The footage doesn't exist anymore, beyond a handful of still photographs and some off-air audio recordings, which can be heard online.

People and Places (1962)

First Broadcast - October 29th 1962

A reappearance on this programme for Granada Television, performing live 'Love Me Do 'and 'A Taste of Honey'. The stage setup was different from the usual Beatles appearances, as during 'Love Me Do 'John sang seated, while Paul, George and Ringo all stood behind him, almost like a backing group. During the performance of 'A Taste Of Honey', all the band stood up, and played their instruments live, but they wore waistcoats, discarding their suit jackets.
This performance was actually pre-recorded, as they had an engagement at their residency in Hamburg, Germany.
Like their debut appearance, it only exists nowadays as stills and off-air audio recordings online.

Discs A Go-Go (1962)

First Broadcast - December 3rd 1962

The Beatles make a very early television appearance for a weekly Welsh pop music show called *Discs A Go-Go* for TWW (Television Wales and West). Recorded in a studio in Bristol on the 3rd December and broadcast on the same day, they were seen lip-syncing to their first official single 'Love Me Do'. The clip is now assumed lost, like so many shows from that era.

Tuesday Rendezvous (1962)

First Broadcast - December 4th 1962

The Beatles appeared in this children's programme to promote their debut single 'Love Me Do/PS I Love You'. Filmed in Studio Four at Wembley Studios, lip-syncing in front of an audience, this was the first time The Beatles ever appeared on television in the London area. Other people on the bill that day included guitarist Bert Weedon, folk singer Wally Whyton and glove puppets Fred Barker and Ollie Beak. Another tape assumed lost.

People and Places (1962)

First Broadcast - December 17th 1962

Reappearance for a regional TV programme for Granada Television on the 17th December 1962 performing live 'Love Me Do 'and 'Twist and Shout'. The programme only survives today as off-air audio and stills taken by fans, which can be seen online via YouTube.

Roundup (1963)

First Broadcast - January 8th 1963

The Beatles 'first appearance on Scottish Television (STV) for a children's TV series called *Roundup* hosted by Paul Young and Morag Hood, miming to their forthcoming single 'Please Please Me', which would be released three days after the broadcast. Another priceless Beatles artefact presumed lost to posterity.

People and Places (1963)

First Broadcast - January 16th 1963

The Beatles lip-synced their new single 'Please Please Me', as well as the B-side 'Ask Me Why 'for their fourth appearance in this regional TV programme for Granada Television in Studio Four, Quay Street, Manchester. Nowadays, this only survives as off-air audio and still photos, which have since surfaced on the internet on sites like YouTube.

Thank Your Lucky Stars (1963)

First Broadcast - January 19th 1963

Thank Your Lucky Stars was an incredibly popular UK pop music show for ITV affiliate ABC Television, presented by DJ Brian Matthew. All The Beatles 'appearances were in front of a live audience, but they were mimed performances, except for their two appearances in the 1964 and 1965 specials. As time went on, The Beatles became less enthusiastic about doing lip-synced shows, as they seemed to be "going through the motions". Compare their appearance in 1963 to their November 1964 set, and you will see what I mean.

For their first appearance - surprisingly, bottom of the bill - they "performed" only one song, their second single 'Please Please Me', which was released the previous week, and was their first No.1 in the UK Singles Chart. Also appearing on the bill were Petula Clark, Acker Bilk, Mark Wynter, Chis Barber's Jazz Band, The Brook Brothers and David Macbeth, and the guest DJ was Sam Costa.

This appearance is currently missing in the archives.

Beatlefacts

*   This engagement was organised by Dick James, who went on to make a fortune as The Beatles 'publisher.

Thank Your Lucky Stars (1963)

First Broadcast - February 23rd 1963

Recorded on Sunday 17th February 1963 at Teddington Studio Centre in Middlesex, like their debut appearance, they are performing a mimed version of their second single 'Please Please Me'. This time, they were third on the bill, which also included Billy Fury, Jet Harris and Tony Meehan, Carol Deene, Duffy Power, Billie Davis and the Clyde Valley Stompers, and the guest DJ compere was the rather unsavoury figure that was Jimmy Saville, who was later discredited after his death for his unacceptable behaviour.

Like their first appearance, it is currently assumed lost in the archives.

ABC At Large (1963)

First Broadcast - March 2nd 1963

Straight off the heels of a tour, opening for UK pop singer, Helen Shapiro, The Beatles recorded an appearance for *ABC At Large* for ITV affiliate ABC at Didsbury Studio Centre in Manchester. They were interviewed by host "Diddy" David Hamilton alongside their manager Brian Epstein, which was then followed by a clip of them miming to 'Please Please Me 'recycled from an episode of *Thank Your Lucky Stars*. Gerry Marsden (Gerry and The Pacemakers) also appeared on the show, which also included interviews with fans.
    Another victim of the infamous archival culls.

Tuesday Rendezvous (1963)

First Broadcast - April 9th 1963

A reappearance for the Associated Redifussion children's series, recorded at Wembley studios live between 5pm-5:55pm. They mimed to their single 'From Me To You', as well as a truncated version of 'Please Please Me 'while the closing credits rolled. The programme is assumed missing.

The 625 Show (1963)

First Broadcast - April 16th 1963

Their first non-regional TV appearance, and their debut for the BBC. *The 625 Show* was a programme giving young up-and-coming talent the opportunity to showcase three songs in front of a live audience. Recorded at Lime Grove Studios in Shepherd's Bush in London on the 13th April, it was a long day for the boys, with them arriving for a band call at 10:30am, and final rehearsals taking place between 4:30-6pm before the recording at 7:30pm.
    The Beatles performed (assuming live, as it was a showcase) 'From Me To You', 'Thank You Girl 'and closed the show with 'Please Please Me', where they were joined by the other guests on stage. Also appearing on the show, introduced by compere Jimmy Young, were singers Rolf and Tino, Bobbi Carrol, Hank Locklin, guitarist Wout Steenhuis, a four-piece classical ensemble, pianist Johny Pearson and conductor Edwin Braben.
    No recording of this set has surfaced as of writing.

Beatlefacts

* Following their appearance on this show, The Beatles went to a party in London hosted by Shadows guitarist Bruce Welch, where they met legendary UK pop singer Cliff Richard for the first time. [22]

Scene at 6:30 (1963)

First Broadcast - April 16th 1963

Another regional TV programme broadcast in the North of England in the early evening, filmed at Granada Television Centre, Manchester. The Beatles mimed to 'From Me To You', and unfortunately, the programme clashed with their first national TV appearance on *The 625 Show*, which was broadcast at the same time.

The footage is presumed missing.

Thank Your Lucky Stars (1963)

First Broadcast - April 20th 1963

Recorded on Sunday 14th April 1963, this was John, Paul, George and Ringo's third appearance on this iconic show for ABC Television, this time miming to their single 'From Me To You'. Also appearing were The Dave Clark Five, The Vernons Girls, Bert Weedon, Del Shannon, Johnny Tillotson and Mike Berry, and the guest DJ compere was Kent Walton.

The archival status of this appearance is unknown.

Pops And Lenny (1963)

First Broadcast - May 16th 1963

A children's television series hosted by Terry Hall and his glove puppet, Lenny The Lion. Making their second appearance on national BBC Television, The Beatles were on the show performing live 'From Me To You 'and an amended version of 'Please Please Me'. The band also sang the old standard 'After You've Gone 'with Terry Hall and the other guests on the show, Patsy Ann Noble, The Raindrops and The Bert Hayes Octet.

The video has been lost, but the audio survives via off-air fan recordings, which can be found on YouTube.

Thank Your Lucky Stars (1963)

First Broadcast - May 18th 1963

Recorded on the 12th May 1963, this was another booking on the famous and legendary series for ABC Television. In this, their fourth appearance and topping the bill, they perform 'From Me To You 'and 'I Saw Her Standing There', lip-syncing, as before. Also on the bill were Petula Clark, The Countrymen, Shane Wallis, Al Saxon, Peter Jay & The Jaywalkers, Heidi Bruhl and The Guv'nors, and the guest DJ compere was Jimmy Young.

As for their first three appearances, the archival status of this show is currently unknown.

Lucky Stars (Summer Spin) (1963)

First Broadcast - June 29th 1963

Recorded on the 23rd June, this was a spin-off of the ABC Television series *Thank Your Lucky Stars*. As usual with this show, these were mimed performances. For this first special, they played 'From Me To You 'and 'I Saw Her Standing There'. This was a headline TV appearance, which was recorded at Alpha TV Studios in Birmingham, and was especially dedicated to Mersey Beat Groups, presented by Pete Murray.

This show was notorious for the final 10 minutes clashing with John Lennon's appearance on BBC's *Juke Box Jury*.

No copies are known to survive.

Juke Box Jury (1963)

First Broadcast - June 29th 1963

John Lennon recorded an appearance on the BBC's *Juke Box Jury* on the 22nd June 1963, which was broadcast one week later on June 29th. *Juke Box Jury* was a weekly programme, featuring a panel of four celebrities reviewing newly-released records and voting them either a "hit" or a "miss". John's appearance was rather controversial, as he rated every record as a "miss"! A notable scathing review was for 'Devil In Disguise 'by Elvis Presley. The video of this appearance no longer exists, but luckily, most of the audio has survived. All four Beatles would appear together on this programme later in the year on December 7th. [23]

Scene at 6:30 (1963)

First Broadcast - August 14th 1963

The Fab Four's second appearance on this regional news programme for Granada Television, this time performing 'Twist And Shout'. This was filmed at the Granada TV Centre in Manchester, and after filming was finished, they drove to Llandudno, to complete a six-night residency at the Odeon Cinema. Interestingly, they wore black polo necks and jeans, which was a change from their normal suits.

Unlike previous and subsequent appearances, the footage of this show was spared from the archive culls, and film of them performing 'Twist and Shout' can be seen in the 1995 documentary *Beatles Anthology*. Looking at the footage, they appear to be singing live.

Scene at 6:30 (1963)

First Broadcast - August 19th 1963

A historical TV appearance for The Beatles. This was the debut of their hit single 'She Loves You', which would be released four days later, and which became The Beatles 'all-time best selling UK single based on information compiled by the Official Charts Company.

The clip is currently assumed missing in the TV archives. As no footage exists, it is not known whether this was a live or lip-synced performance.

Day By Day (1963)

First Broadcast - August 22nd 1963

A regional news magazine show for Southern Television. In their debut appearance for the show, they lip-synced to their hit single 'She Loves You', which came out the following day. The performance was broadcast between 5:55-6:40pm.

On the same day, photographer Robert Freeman took a photo of them, which was to become the iconic front cover of their second album *With The Beatles*. They were accompanied by Freeman to the Southampton studios, and after filming, returned to Bournemouth, where they performed that evening at the Gaumont Cinema.

The archival status of the programme is unknown.

Lucky Stars (Summer Spin) (1963)

First Broadcast - August 24th 1963

Recorded after their concert at Llandudno in North Wales on 18th August, their second appearance on *Thank Your Lucky Stars Summer Spin* was recorded at the Alpha (ATV) Studios in Birmingham, and was presented by DJ Pete Murray. They mimed to 'She Loves You '(which had just been released the previous day) and its B-side 'I'll Get You'. After recording this appearance, they drove to the Princess Theatre in Torquay for a concert - another example of how their schedule was always incredibly hectic in those days.

The tape is assumed missing.

Big Night Out (1963)

First Broadcast - September 7th 1963

Recorded on 1st September 1963, the Fab Four appeared on this talk show for ABC Television hosted by various celebs of the era, including comedian brothers Mike and Bernie Winters. It was recorded at Didsbury Studio Centre in Manchester, and broadcast the following week. They lip-synced to the songs 'From Me To You', 'She Loves You 'and 'Twist And Shout'. It was filmed in front of a studio audience of 600, and broadcast from 7:40-8:30pm across most of the ITV network. Other artists appearing on the bill that day included Billy Dainty, Patsy Ann Noble and Lionel Blair.

The footage is still in the archives, and can be viewed online. [17]

Ready, Steady, Go! (1963)

First Broadcast - October 4th 1963

The Beatles appeared three times for lip-synced performances on this iconic television series for Rediffusion TV, hosted by Keith Fordyce and Cathy McGowan. Their first appearance was particularly memorable, as Paul judged a dance competition, won by a young lady called Melanie Coe, who would, unknowingly at the time, help inspire the Beatles song 'She's Leaving Home ' in 1967, as she ran away from her parents' home and her story was in the local paper that Paul was reading at the time. We don't know if he made the connection at the time he wrote the song. Their first appearance on *RSG* saw them being interviewed by the lovely singer Dusty Springfield, and also had them sharing the bill with Helen Shapiro (who they opened for earlier that year on her tour), and they joined in when she sang 'Look Who It Is'. This performance is "internet meme" famous, because when Helen sings the line "Fancy meeting you suddenly", John Lennon turns around and pulls a silly face to the camera - something he often did when the camera focused on him.

This legendary performance is currently still in the archives, and has since resurfaced online. [19]

The Mersey Sound (1963)

Directed By - Don Haworth
First Broadcast - October 9th 1963
Running Time - 30 Minutes

A BBC documentary directed by Don Haworth that showcased three bands from the Liverpool area - The Undertakers, Group One, and a band that's a little more known these days - The Beatles. Haworth first met the boys on the 21st July 1963, as he wanted to capture the spirit of Mersey Beat, and he signed a contract with Brian Epstein on the 6th August.

The Beatles 'segment on the show was shot, without an audience, at 9:30am on the 27th August 1963 at the Little Theatre in Southport (The Beatles were in the town for a series of six nights at the Odeon Cinema), and they performed versions of the songs 'Twist and Shout 'and 'She Loves You ' while wearing their iconic grey collarless suits, changing into black collarless suits for 'Love Me Do'. The Undertakers were a band probably best known for the song '(Do The) Mashed Potatoes', but thanks to bad business practices they faded to obscurity; while Group One were a skiffle band (a bit like The Quarrymen, the Proto-Beatles) who actually opened for The Beatles back in the day.

Haworth later edited in footage of fans from a concert at the Odeon the previous night, to give the impression there was an audience present. In the final cut, the EMI recordings of the songs were dubbed onto the footage replacing the live audio.

The documentary is still in the archives, and footage would later be recycled in *The Compleat Beatles* and *The Beatles Anthology*.

Val Parnell's Sunday Night At The London Palladium (1963)

First Broadcast - October 13th 1963
Running Time - 60 Minutes

Tonight At The London Palladium was a British variety series filmed at the famous London Palladium theatre in the West End, which lasted from 1955-2017. It was hosted by a myriad of famous light entertainment acts of the time, but when The Beatles appeared in 1963, it was arranged by actor, managing director and theatrical impresario Val Parnell (1892-1972), a man known for giving Mary Poppins herself, Julie Andrews, her big break at age 12. The presenter of the night was none other than the late British television legend, Sir Bruce Forsyth.

It was this performance, recorded and shown on the 13th October 1963, that led journalists to coin the now famous term "Beatlemania" to describe their hysteric fanbase of screaming prepubescent girls. Getting on the show was a big coup, as there was a lot of competition to appear on it from artists of the day, and it gave massive exposure. They were top of the bill, closing the evening. Starting their live set with 'From Me To You 'and 'I'll Get You', which was introduced by Paul, interspersed with Lennon's trademark joking around, this was followed by 'She Loves You 'announced collectively by John, Paul and George, and because the screams got so loud, Paul found it difficult to announce their final number 'Twist and Shout 'so John yelled *"SHUT UP!"*. Paul then asked them all to clap their hands and stamp their feet.

The show made the front page of many newspapers the following day, and on that day of the 13th October 1963 - Beatlemania was born!

Despite this being a historic Beatles concert, the show only survives as off-air audio recordings and still photographs, which can be found online.

Thank Your Lucky Stars (1963)

First Broadcast - October 26th 1963

The Beatles' fifth appearance on ABC Television's historic series, recorded at the Alpha Television Studios in Birmingham, England on 20th October. Songs performed (lip-syncing, as was the norm for their appearances on this show) were 'All My Loving', 'Money (That's What I Want) 'and 'She Loves You'.

The programme only partially survives today, with only the performance of 'Money (That's What I Want) 'surviving - the 'All My Loving 'segment only exists as a fragment, and the 'She Loves You 'performance is completely missing.

Beatlefacts

* When they were in the Alpha Television Studios recording this appearance, approximately 3000 fans blocked the streets outside and attempted to storm in.

Drop In (1963)

First Broadcast - November 3rd 1963

Recorded after their tour of Sweden on the 30th October 1963 and broadcast on November 3rd, The Beatles returned to Stockholm to record an appearance on a Sveriges Television music show called *Drop In*. Performing in front of a studio audience at the Arenateatern Theatre, in the Grona Lund Amusement Park, they shared the bill with two other acts: Gals & Pals and singer Lill-Babs.

Initially, they wanted to only perform 'She Loves You 'and 'Twist and Shout', but the producer of the show, Klaus Burling, was so impressed with them that he gave them one more song to perform, so they opted to play 'I Saw Her Standing There 'followed by 'Long Tall Sally'. All songs were sung live.

This appearance survives in its entirety, and segments appear in the 1995 *Beatles Anthology* documentary.

Beatlefacts

* The Beatles had lunch in the afternoon at a restaurant in Solliden, joined by roadies Mal Evans and Neil Aspinall, producer Klas Burling, presenter Kersti Adams-Ray and photographers. John and Paul are rumoured to have played a piano in the room.
* Before filming began at 7pm, Paul and Ringo went shopping at Stockholm's largest store, NK. [24]

Know The North (1963)

First Broadcast - November 6th 1963

A regional news programme for the Lancashire area made by Granada Television. This one is notable for showing a clip of pre-fame Beatles performing at The Cavern Club in Liverpool on the 22nd August 1962, just after Ringo had joined the band, and it was their 126th lunchtime performance at this celebrated venue. They are shown performing the 'Kansas City/Hey! Hey! Hey! Hey! 'medley which would later be used in the *Beatles For Sale* album and a cover of the rock & roll standard 'Some Other Guy'. After that song, you can hear a frustrated fan yell *"We want Pete!"*, as there was a lot of initial backlash against having Ringo in the band following Pete Best's departure.

Back in 1962, Granada Television was receiving an increasing number of letters from early Beatles fans, and a crew decided to investigate what would eventually become Beatlemania. The producers initially saw them perform at Cambridge Hall in Southport on July 26th 1962, and producer Dick Fontaine visited The Cavern Club on the 1st August to check the lighting conditions before the film crew attended on this date.

Because the footage was considered to be of substandard quality, it wasn't shown in public until The Beatles became famous.

While the Cavern footage is still in the archives, the rest of the show isn't. It can be seen in many documentary films such as *The Beatles Anthology* and is available online.

Beatlefacts

* The audio and video sometimes don't match, and it has been speculated that the audio came from a different date, as, while both John and Paul sing in the film footage, only John's voice is audible. This theory is probably correct, as sound technician Gordon Butler returned to the Cavern on the 5th September to make a second recording, this time using three microphones rather than the initial one.

In Town (1963)

First Broadcast - November 7th 1963

The Beatles were interviewed by Frank Hall before one of only two live appearances on Irish soil - the first being at the Adelphi Cinema in Dublin, with the latter show the following day, at the Ritz Cinema in Belfast. The interview was recorded on their arrival at Dublin airport, and still exists in the archives, and has since resurfaced online.

Each show was seen by a 2,304 capacity crowd. There was no sound check or rehearsal beforehand. The Beatles performed their standard set, which included: 'I Saw Her Standing There', 'From Me To You', 'All My Loving', 'You Really Got Me', 'Roll Over Beethoven', 'Boys', 'Till There Was You', 'She Loves You', 'Money (That's What I Want) 'and 'Twist And Shout'.

Beatlefacts

*   Harry Lush, then manager of the Adelphi Cinema, said *"The Beatles were all so nice, courteous, and answered all the questions. They had respect for their seniors, and called you sir. I look back on the day The Beatles came to Dublin as one of the shiniest days in my career".* [24]
*   In the evening, the boys stayed in the Gresham Hotel in fear of being mobbed by hysterical teenage girls outside.

The Royal Variety Performance (1963)

First Broadcast - November 10th 1963

Legendary Royal Command Performance at the Prince of Wales Theatre in London in the presence of The Queen Mother and Princess Margaret. The Beatles were seventh in a huge 19-act bill, but they were, by far, the most anticipated of all the acts to appear. Singing live, starting with 'From Me To You 'before the curtains had opened, they then followed on with 'She Loves You', with Paul dropping a gag about Sophie Tucker being their 'favourite American group', which was then followed by a performance of 'Till There Was You 'from the 1957 film *The Music Man*. The most memorable part of the show would easily be their performance of 'Twist and Shout', which was preceded by the following words from John Winston Lennon:
"For our last number I'd like to ask your help. The people in the cheaper seats clap your hands, and the rest of you, if you'd just rattle your jewellery!" - classic Lennon humour, and a wonderful refuge in audacity!
This one was spared from the archive culls, and can be viewed in the 1995 documentary *Beatles Anthology*.

Beatlefacts

*   During Lennon's famous quote mentioned above, there's an urban legend that he was allegedly about to drop a very naughty word before the word jewellery, but was talked out of it by Paul and Brian Epstein.

Day By Day (1963)

First Broadcast - November 12th 1963

The Beatles make a return appearance on this regional news magazine show for Southern Television. In this programme, they are interviewed backstage at the Guildhall Theatre in Portsmouth. Sadly, the show was cancelled, as Paul was suffering from stomach flu, and he got more uneasy as the interview with Jeremy James went on - the show was rescheduled for the 3rd December 1963. The interview was broadcast at 6:05pm, followed by another interview they had recorded at their Southsea Hotel, the Royal Beach. Interestingly, footage from the interview was recycled for comedic purposes in the 1994 UK comedian Harry Enfield special *Smashie and Nicey - The End Of An Era* on BBC2.

The footage is currently still in the archives, and has since resurfaced online. [16]

Move Over, Dad (1963)

First Broadcast - November 16th 1963

Made by Westward Television for ITV, this show for the teenage audience is billed as being *"a gay new show with the accent on the beat of the young"*. In this programme, the Fab Four are briefly interviewed by the show's presenter, Stuart Hutchinson, recorded on the 13th November before a performance at the ABC Cinema in George St. Plymouth in Devon. It was broadcast from 5:15pm.

The archival status of this appearance is currently unknown.

Late Scene Extra (1963)

First Broadcast - November 27th 1963

Scene at 6:30 was Granada Television's popular local news programme. It had a late night edition entitled *Late Scene Extra*. The *TV Times* described it as *"with a no-punches-pulled, hard-hitting, bang-up-to-date, look at today's big talking points. And what's new and original in music."*

Recorded during an exhausting autumn tour, the band spent an afternoon on the 25th November 1963 filming two lip-synced performances of 'I Want To Hold Your Hand 'and 'This Boy'. The backdrop of the set contained fictional headlines from the newspaper *The Daily Echo*. On the same set, they were interviewed by presenter Gay Byrne and joined by the wonderful late stand-up comic (and fellow Liverpudlian) Sir Ken Dodd O.B.E. featuring Ken and the boys larking about. The clips of them performing would be used on the 27th November edition of *Late Scene Extra* and the 20th December edition of *Scene at 6:30*.

These clips survived the archive purge of the 1970s, and can be found online.

Juke Box Jury (1963)

First Broadcast - December 7th 1963
Running Time - 30 Minutes

On the 7th December, our boys appeared on this classic BBC Television series, hosted by David Jacobs, where celebrities judged various pop songs released at the time. It was taped at the Empire Theatre in their home town of Liverpool, before they performed two shows at the nearby Odeon Cinema. The audience consisted of members of The Beatles Northern Area Fan Club, and was watched by an estimated 23 million people on TV. They voted three of the tracks a hit, including Elvis Presley's 'Kiss Me Quick '(this time, even John voted it a hit). Unfortunately, they voted a miss for Paul Anka's 'Did You Have A Happy Birthday', 'The Nitty Gritty Song 'by Shirley Ellis, Billy Fury's 'Do You Really Love Me', Bobby Vinton's 'There! I've Said It Again 'and 'Love Hit Me 'by The Orchids. It was revealed then that the Orchids were actually in the audience (ouch!).

The programme only exists today as audio and still photographs, which can be seen online.

Beatlefacts

*   Because they ran overtime, there was no time to discuss The Merseybeats' 'I Think Of You', 'Broken Home 'by Shirley Jackson, 'Where Have You Been All My Life 'by Gene Vincent and 'Long Time Ago 'by The Batchelors, but the boys judged all of them to be hits.

Thank Your Lucky Stars (1963)

First Broadcast - December 15th 1963

The Beatles 'sixth appearance on ABC Television's famous series. Unlike their previous appearances, which had been hosted by Brian Matthew, the host for this edition was friend and fellow Liverpudlian, the late Cilla Black, who was also managed by Brian Epstein. The songs lip-synced were 'I Want To Hold Your Hand', 'Twist And Shout 'and 'She Loves You'. Unlike preceding appearances, this performance is still in the archives, and has resurfaced on YouTube, meaning it can be seen by a new generation of fans.

The Jack Paar Program (1964)

First Broadcast - January 3rd 1964

There is a misconception that The Beatles 'first American television appearance was on *The Ed Sullivan Show* but this isn't correct - the Americans' very first look at the Fab Four was on *The Jack Paar Program*, where they performed 'She Loves You', which was taken from a live performance at The Winter Gardens Theatre in Bournemouth, UK. Paar, having seen their performance, wasn't particularly impressed with their music, replaying the footage mostly for a cheap laugh. He was later quoted as saying *"I never knew that these boys would change the history of the world's music, which they did. I thought it was funny, and I had 'em filmed and brought it to American months before Sullivan"*. After the clip, Paar quips *"It's nice to know that England has finally risen to our cultural level"*. [25]

Val Parnell's Sunday Night At The London Palladium (1964)

First Broadcast - January 12th 1964
Running Time - 60 Minutes

The Beatles returned to play at the Palladium again for the *Sunday Night At The London Palladium* variety series on January 12th 1964. This time, their fee was raised from £250 to £1000 (around £21,000 in 2021 money). They took part in an amusing card-carrying sketch with compere Bruce Forsyth, and performed a five-song live set consisting of 'I Want to Hold Your Hand', 'This Boy', 'All My Loving', 'Money (That's What I Want) 'and 'Twist And Shout'. The Beatles also took part in the traditional waved finale to the show, set to the song 'Startime'.

Like their first appearance, this only survives today as off-air audio recordings and still photographs, which can be found online.

The Ed Sullivan Show (1964)

"Beatles, eh? Yes, I seem to remember their off-key caterwauling on the old Sullivan Show. What was Ed thinking?" Mr Burns - *The Simpsons*

Arguably their most iconic appearances on television would have to be their legendary performances on *The Ed Sullivan Show*. This was an American variety show that ran from 1948-1971 with its host, Richard Nixon lookalike Ed Sullivan, whose catchphrase was *"we have a really big show tonight"*, which often gets exaggerated as *"willaybigsheewwww!"* by comedians.

It all started in 1963, when Sullivan and his cronies happened to be passing through Heathrow Airport, and witnessed how their fans greeted the Fab Four after their return from Stockholm in Sweden. Sullivan was impressed, believing that this combo of Liverpudlians could be the next Elvis, and he contacted Brian Epstein to pay them top dollar for a single show, but Brian had a better idea - The Beatles would appear three times on the show as top of the bill, with the band opening and closing the show (even if it was for a small fee!). But would Epstein's crazy idea work?

On three consecutive Sundays in February 1964, The Beatles appeared on *The Ed Sullivan Show*, just as 'I Want To Hold Your Hand 'reached No.1 in the *Billboard* chart, with their first appearance on February 9th drawing estimated figures of 73 million viewers! They opened with live renditions of 'All My Loving','Till There Was You 'and 'She Loves You', which featured the names of John, Paul, George and Ringo superimposed on close-up shots, and also the caption 'SORRY GIRLS, HE'S MARRIED 'on John. They returned at the end of the programme performing live 'I Saw Her Standing There 'and 'I Want To Hold Your Hand'.

This appearance is readily available, and can be seen online, and has featured in countless documentaries including 1995's *The Beatles Anthology*.

The Ed Sullivan Show (1964)

First Broadcast - February 16th 1964

One week after arguably their most famous TV appearance, they made a second appearance on the show. This performance was filmed at the Deauville Hotel in Miami in front an audience of approximately 2600 screaming girls (and guys), but tickets for the event had oversold, as CBS had given out 3500 passes, and the police had to calm down the naturally very upset people who were denied entry. Bizarrely, despite their legendary first appearance, they weren't headliners, and the top of the bill was American singer and actress Mitzi Gaynor, known for films such as 1954's *There 's No Business Like Show Business*.

A crush of people almost prevented them from even making it onto the stage, and a wedge of policemen were needed - the band went on immediately after, grabbing their instruments!

They performed six songs live, which were 'She Loves You', 'This Boy', 'All My Loving', 'I Saw Her Standing There', 'From Me To You', and 'I Want To Hold Your Hand'. An extremely impressive 70 million people watched the show, and afterwards, hotel owner Maurice Lansberg gave a party for the performers, which included food such as lobster, beef, chicken and fish - food that The Beatles would later shun, as all four of them would end up becoming either vegetarian or vegan. It was also during this time that they met the super-famous boxer, Cassius Clay (later known as Muhammad Ali) - an immodest, but very charismatic gentleman, who floated like a butterfly but stung like a bee. They took various publicity shots together.

Like their debut appearance, this is readily available and has since resurfaced online and on DVD.

Grandstand (1964)

First Broadcast - February 22nd 1964
Running Time - 470 Minutes

A pioneering BBC sports programme, which lasted from 1958-2007, and The Beatles made an appearance in 1964, despite them having nothing to do with sports! Filmed right after their first triumphant trip to America, we see The Beatles disembarking from the famous Boeing 747 plane, in a famous snapshot encapsulating Beatlemania, waving to thousands of screaming girls who had waited hours at the airport to get a glimpse of them. This is then followed by an interview, talking about their time in the US, meeting Cassius Clay (AKA Muhammad Ali), and Ringo saying one of his famous malapropisms *"tomorrow never knows"*, which would later inspire the title of the 1966 song of the same name on the *Revolver* album.

This historical appearance was spared from the 1970s archival purges, and can be viewed online.

The Ed Sullivan Show (1964)

First Broadcast - February 23rd 1964

John, Paul, George and Ringo's third appearance on *The Ed Sullivan Show*. This time they performed live 'Twist and Shout 'and 'Please Please Me 'for their opening set, and closing the show they performed 'I Want To Hold Your

Hand'. Also on the bill were Gloria Bleezarde, Morecambe & Wise, Acker Bilk, Gordon and Sheila MacRae, Dave Berry, Monty Gunty, Cab Colloway and helium-voiced marionette pig puppets, Pinky and Perky. Like previous appearances for Ed Sullivan, this one remains in the archives.

Big Night Out (1964)

First Broadcast - February 29th 1964

Straight off the heels of their first tour of America, the ever-so-busy Beatles snuck in an appearance for this famous ITV series, amidst all the chaos that was Beatlemania. Filmed at Teddington Film Studios in London, they mimed to six songs, which included 'All My Loving', 'I Wanna Be Your Man', ''Till There Was You', 'Please Mister Postman', 'Money (That's What I Want)' and 'I Want To Hold Your Hand'. As well as being interviewed, they also took part in comedy sketches with the hosts, comedians Mike and Bernie Winters; one sketch involved the Fab Four returning from America, sailing down the river Thames, being driven to the studio in a vintage car, and arriving through a door labelled 'Customs'. Also appearing on the bill were Billy Dainty, Jackie Trent and dancer/choreographer Lionel Blair.

This appearance is still in the television archives, and has since resurfaced online. [18]

The Variety Club Of Great Britain Awards For 1963 (1964)

First Broadcast - March 19th 1964
Running Time - 30 Minutes

A regular luncheon that took place at the famous Dorchester Hotel in Park Lane, central London. In 1964, future Prime Minister Harold Wilson (who would later be referenced in their 1966 song 'Taxman') presented them with the awards for Show Business Personalities of 1963, and this moment was later captured on film by several TV and newsreel companies of the time. The BBC screened a 30 minute show of the footage from 10:30pm the following day, where John famously said *"thanks for the purple hearts!"* (a cheeky reference to a slang term for amphetamines).

The footage is still in the archives, and can be seen online.

Ready, Steady, Go! (1964)

First Broadcast - March 20th 1964

The Beatles make a return appearance on this famous and iconic UK music programme for ITV. They were lip-syncing to 'It Won't Be Long', 'You Can't Do That 'and 'Can't Buy Me Love', and were also presented with a special award from the US magazine *Billboard* in recognition of our Fab Four having three top-3 singles in the charts simultaneously. They also took part in a mock fashion parade, and were interviewed by host Cathy McGowan, who has been in a long-term relationship with famous British West End singer Michael Ball since 1992.

This appearance is currently in the television archives, and can be viewed online via YouTube.

The Carl-Alan Awards (1964)

First Broadcast - March 23rd 1964

The Carl-Alan Awards was a regular event that took place at the Empire Ballroom in Leicester Square, London. The Duke Of Edinburgh himself, Prince Phillip (the Queen's late husband), presented The Beatles with two awards for their musical achievements in 1963. As well as being broadcast by the BBC live as it happened, this event was also filmed by several newsreel companies, and can be viewed online via YouTube. [20]

Top Of The Pops (1964)

First Broadcast - March 25th 1964

A famous (or nowadays infamous) music programme made by the BBC that lasted from 1964-2006, and was presented by a myriad of people including Pete Murray, Tony Blackburn, Kenny Everett, Steve Wright, Zoe Ball and many more. The show was infamous for having the artists lip-sync their performances, which led to many of them having fun with it, purposely miming their vocals and instruments poorly.

The Beatles made several pre-recorded appearances on this show, starting with an episode broadcast on 25th March 1964, lip-syncing to 'Can't Buy Me Love 'and 'You Can't Do That'. It was filmed at BBC's Television Centre in West London, which is nowadays the famous venue the Shepherd's Bush Empire, and their performance of 'Can't Buy Me Love 'was shown again on the

April 8th edition. This edition was hosted by the very discredited DJ Jimmy Saville, and also on the bill were The Applejacks, Peter and Gordon, and Billy J. Kramer.

As the BBC no longer shows footage which includes Jimmy Saville, the footage of the show survives today as a silent 8mm off-air recording made by a fan, and can be viewed online.

Beatlefacts

* This was the first time George Harrison was seen playing his Rickenbacker 12-string guitar, the second such model ever made, which sold for $657,000 at an auction in New York in 2014. Also sold at the auction was a handwritten placard with doodles signed by John and Yoko, which fetched $187,000, and a Hofner Bass rented by Paul in the mid-1960s, which sold for $125,000.

Star Parade (1964)

First Broadcast - April 4th 1964

An unusual engagement for ITV franchise Tyne Tees, based in the North East of England. The popular TV programme of the time, *Star Parade* invited our fabulous foursome for something of a Q&A session with the fans, the best questions being filtered and moderated by the show's presenter, Adrian Cains. The Beatles 'segment of them answering the questions was filmed at Twickenham Film Studios, right in the middle of filming their debut motion picture *A Hard Day's Night*, but the actual (and very obviously staged) footage of the Beatle fangirls asking the questions was filmed up north in Newcastle! This looked very obvious when transmitted, making the whole programme seem very unnatural. It was later concluded with a brief interview with The Beatles by Adrian Cains.

The programme is still in the TV archives, and can be seen online.

Two of A Kind (1964)

"Hello Bongo!" Eric Morecambe greeting Ringo Starr

First Broadcast - April 18th 1964

33

Eric Morecambe O.B.E. and Ernie Wise O.B.E. (AKA Morecambe and Wise) were a legendary British comedy duo, who were just really, really funny. They were pretty much mainstays of UK television from the 1950s to the 1980s and they continue to remain popular to this day (even if their airtime is mainly reduced to retrospective programmes around Christmas time). In 1961, they were the stars of the very popular TV sketch show for ATV (ITV) called *Two Of A Kind*, which ran until 1968. In 1964, The Beatles had a guest spot on the show.

Their appearance was filmed at ATV's Elstree studios on December 2nd 1963. They played three live songs to a small studio audience - 'This Boy', 'All My Loving 'and 'I Want To Hold Your Hand'. They were then joined by Eric and Ernie for some hilarious banter, followed by The Beatles and Eric and Ernie collaborating with a cover of the 1912 standard 'Moonlight Bay', while Eric yells *"Twist And Shout"*, and *"I Like It, I Like it"* (as in 'I Like it ' by Gerry And The Pacemakers). Hilarious stuff - you had to be there!

The programme is still in the archives, and an extract appears in the amazing 1995 Beatles documentary *The Beatles Anthology*.

Beatlefacts

* Most websites and books misidentify this appearance as being on *The Morecambe And Wise Show* - that was the show Eric and Ernie did for the BBC, which didn't start until 1968. Even the *Anthology* documentary gets this fact wrong!

Six Ten (1964)

First Broadcast - April 30th 1964

The Beatles were interviewed at the Callander Hotel in Perthshire, Scotland, on this local news programme for BBC Scotland during their spring 1964 tour. The interview was conducted by Evelyn Elliot.

This appears to have been erased from the television archives.

Roundup (1964)

First Broadcast - May 5th 1964

The Fab Four returned in this programme for Scottish Television (STV), this time being interviewed backstage by Morag Hood and Paul Young at the Royal Theatre in Glasgow. They took part in the show's 'Personality Parade ' section. Unlike their previous appearance, this footage has survived the programme culls and has since resurfaced online.

Big Beat '64 (1964)

Directed By - Mark Stuart
Release Date - May 10th 1964
Running Time - 90 Minutes

An alternate name for rock & roll music was big beat. The Beatles played at a series of events called Operation Big Beat, the US Beatles album *The Beatles Second Album* states *"Electrifying Big Beat Performances"*, and big beat was also the name of a magazine at the time that regularly featured The Beatles... but what was *Big Beat '64*?

Big Beat '64 was a recording of the 1964 *New Musical Express* (*NME*) Poll Winners concert, which took place at the Empire Pool (now The Wembley Arena) in London, and was a showcase of pretty much every big name of that year, such as The Hollies, The Searchers, Manfred Mann, Billy J. Kramer, The Tremeloes, Cliff Richard, The Rolling Stones and of course The Beatles performing live 'She Loves You', 'You Can't Do That', 'Twist And Shout', 'Long Tall Sally 'and 'Can't Buy Me Love'.

It is extremely unlikely that this special will ever get broadcast on television or be released on home video nowadays, as the host of the event was none other than the previously mentioned infamous DJ Jimmy Saville, who also hosted many episodes of *Top Of The Pops*, and was later discredited for his heinous acts.

Beatlefacts

* The first time The Beatles and The Rolling Stones shared the bill together!
* This features an appearance by the American DJ, Murray The K, who gives a big build-up to The Beatles.
* John Lennon sang the right words in the wrong order to 'She Loves You'.

Lucky Stars (Summer Spin) (1964)

First Broadcast - July 11th 1964

As mentioned previously, this was the summer edition of *Thank Your Lucky Stars*, a programme where The Beatles had appeared on a frequent basis in the early stages of their fame. This edition was recorded at ABC's Teddington Studio Centre in Middlesex, rather than the usual studio in Aston, Birmingham, due to a strike by studio technicians. As it was made during the heady heights of Beatlemania, they arrived at the studio by boat on the Thames, just after attending the Liverpool premiere of *A Hard Day's Night* at the Odeon Cinema, and only getting a few hours 'sleep the night before! Rehearsals began at 1:45pm and it was broadcast live from 5:30-6:35pm. They mimed to four songs:' A Hard Day's Night', 'Long Tall Sally', 'Things We Said Today 'and 'You Can't Do That'.

The archival status is unknown.

Blackpool Night Out (1964)

First Broadcast - July 19th 1964

Summer spin-off of the variety series *Big Night Out* presented by comedians Mike and Bernie Winters from the ABC Theatre in Blackpool. In this programme, for ABC Television UK, they performed live 'A Hard Day's Night', 'Things We Said Today', 'You Can't Do That', 'If I Fell '(which was notable as John and Paul had the giggles during this performance, which had to be restarted), and 'Long Tall Sally', as well as appearing in one of the sketches, where they dressed up as characters. Also appearing were Chita Rivera, Frank Berry, Jimmy Edwards and Lionel Blair.

While the off-air audio for this appearance has survived, the video elements are currently missing.

Shindig! (1964)

First Broadcast - October 7th 1964

On the 3rd October 1964, The Beatles recorded a spot for the US pop show *Shindig!* at the Granville Studios in London, to an audience of Beatles Fan Club members, performing live 'Kansas City/Hey! Hey! Hey! Hey', 'I'm A Loser 'and 'Boys'. There were several acts on the day including Sandie Shaw, PJ Proby, The Karl Denver Trio, Tommy Quickly, Sounds Incorporated, and Lyn Cornell. The Beatles even joined the Karl Denver Trio on the show's finale. This performance has survived the culls, probably because American stations at the time had less apathy towards preserving their archives than their British counterparts.

Beatlefacts

* This was never broadcast in the UK.

Grampian Week (1964)

First Broadcast - October 10th 1964

The Beatles were interviewed by June Shields for this programme for Scottish ITV affiliate, Grampian Television. This was filmed before a performance at the Caird Hall in Dundee. It was only broadcast in the north and north east of Scotland.

The interview still exists in the archives, and can be seen online.

Scene at 6:30 (1964)

First Broadcast - October 16th 1964

Recorded before an engagement at the ABC Cinema in Ardwick, Manchester, The Beatles appeared on the regional television programme *Scene At 6:30* for Granada Television. As well as being interviewed, they mimed to 'I Should Have Known Better 'from the *A Hard Day's Night* LP. The interview and lip-synced performance (which was recorded on the 14th October) were broadcast on Friday 16th October at 6:30 pm in the north west of England.

This appearance is still in the archives, and can be seen online, meaning it can be appreciated by a new generation of fans. [15]

Thank Your Lucky Stars (1964)

First Broadcast - November 21st 1964

After nearly a year's gap, our fabulous foursome made a reappearance for this historic show for ABC Television. Recorded at Teddington Studios on the 14th November, they performed lip-synced versions of their hits 'I Feel Fine', 'She's A Woman', 'I'm A Loser', and 'Rock & Roll Music', albeit without an audience. After the recording, John and Ringo had a bop at the Flamingo Club in Soho, London, where they had gone to see Georgie Fame and The Blue Flames, while Paul and George went to their respective homes. This appearance is spared from the archival culls, existing in its entirety, and has since resurfaced online. [14]

37

Ready, Steady, Go! (1964)

First Broadcast - November 27th 1964

The Beatles 'third and final appearance on this beloved ITV music programme. It was filmed at Wembley Studios in London on the 23rd November
1964, and they lip-synced to the songs 'I Feel Fine', 'She's A Woman',
'Baby's In Black 'and the 'Kansas City/Hey-Hey-Hey-Hey! 'medley. They
were also interviewed by presenter Keith Fordyce. The show currently remains in the archives.

Pop Gear AKA Go Go Mania (1965)

Directed By - Frederic Goode
Release Date - March 1965
Running Time - 68 Minutes

The Beatles perform live 'She Loves You 'and 'Twist and Shout 'via footage
of the newsreel short 'The Beatles Come To Town 'in this theatrical revue of
rock & roll acts of the British Invasion of 1964. Like *Big Beat '64*, we will
probably never see this released on home video as it's hosted once again by
the infamous Jimmy Saville. Thankfully, his segments were erased out of the
Spanish dub and replaced with Palito Ortega and Graciela Borges.

Thank Your Lucky Stars (1965)

First Broadcast - April 3rd 1965

The Beatles 'final appearance on this seminal music programme for ABC Television. Filmed at the Alpha Television Studios in Aston, Birmingham, for
their last appearance they did three songs (lip-synced, as per usual with this
show):' Eight Days A Week', 'Yes it Is 'and 'Ticket To Ride'. As well as the
lip-sync performances, they were also interviewed by the show's host, Brian
Matthew.
  The archival status is currently unknown.

The Eamonn Andrews Show (1965)

First Broadcast - April 11th 1965

Produced for ITV, this was filmed and broadcast following on from their third appearance at the *NME* Poll Winners All Star Concert. This engagement on *The Eamonn Andrews Show* was recorded at ABC's Teddington Studios in London, and they appeared in three parts of the show. John joined Eamonn at the presenter's desk, while George and Ringo sat on a sofa, and Paul was in a swivel chair. They talked about the filming of their second movie *Help!*, Beatlemania and the possibility of solo careers once they finally called it quits.

The second part of the show included mimed performances of 'Ticket To Ride 'and 'Yes It Is 'and the final segment had them taking part in a discussion forum joined by journalist Katharine Whitehorn and critic Wolf Mankowitz, who wasn't a fan of The Beatles!

This appearance is presumed lost.

Top Of The Pops (1965)

First Broadcast - April 15th 1965

The Beatles 'return appearance on the historic BBC Television series. Filmed at Riverside Studios in London, they performed two songs,' Ticket To Ride ' and 'Yes It is', and it was the final time they performed a mimed appearance for the show. This programme was notable for having them don their famous fawn-coloured jackets, which they would later wear in their legendary Shea Stadium performance in August 1965. While the show in its entirety didn't survive, a fragment of them performing 'Ticket To Ride 'has been spared, thanks to appearing in an episode of *Doctor Who*. Speaking of *Doctor Who*, I think it's appropriate that the next appearance I talk about is...

Doctor Who (1965)

"You squashed my favourite Beatles!" The Doctor

Directed By - Richard Martin
Written By - Terry Nation
Running Time - 25 Minutes
First Broadcast - May 22nd 1965

Ever since 1963, a BBC TV series about the stories of a time lord (or sometimes a time lady) from the planet Gallifrey, called The Doctor, has been delighting millions of people worldwide, and is still an immensely popular show today. In the show's early days, when The Doctor was played by actor William

Hartnell, The Beatles actually made an appearance, of sorts, in a 1965 serial called 'The Chase'.

The story begins when The Doctor has installed a Space and Time Visualiser into his TARDIS time machine, where they can watch events from history, past, present and future. The Doctor's companion from the future, Vicki (Maureen O'Brien) chooses to watch a clip of The Beatles, as she had heard about them, but didn't realise they played "classical" music - so we get a clip of The Beatles miming to 'Ticket To Ride '(lifted from an episode of *Top Of The Pops*, which is now missing, like many *Doctor Who* episodes).

The reason I've included this is because, originally, The Beatles were actually going to film a proper cameo, playing older versions of themselves from 1996, performing at the 'Festival of Ghana'. Their manager, Brian Epstein, vetoed the idea, which is a shame.

The episode is readily available on DVD uncut in most regions, but due to clearance issues, The Beatles 'portion isn't on the US Region 1 release.

Blackpool Night Out (1965)

Directed By - Pat Johns
Written By - Brad Ashton and John Morley
First Broadcast - August 1st 1965

Made for ITV company ABC Television, like *Big Night Out* this was recorded at the ABC Theatre in the British seaside town of Blackpool, and the boys performed live 'I Feel Fine', 'I'm Down', 'Act Naturally', 'Ticket To Ride ' and, for the first time on British television, 'Yesterday'. After John jokingly says to Paul, who had just sung 'Yesterday', *"Thank you Ringo, that was wonderful"* the show ends with them performing 'Help!', which was apt, as it was the movie and album they were promoting at the time.

Like the regular edition of *Big Night Out*, it was compered by comedians Mike and Bernie Winters, and other performers on the show included Pearl Carr and Teddy Johnson, Johnny Hart and Lionel Blair. While some clips survived, the full show is lost, but the full audio survives, thanks to an off-air recording by Beatle fans, and can be heard online.

The Ed Sullivan Show (1965)

First Broadcast - September 12th 1965

The Beatles' final appearance on the ground-breaking American television variety series, which earned Sullivan a 60% share of the night-time audience. They performed live 'I Feel Fine', 'I'm Down', and 'Act Naturally' following on from the first three acts in the show, then they came on during the end of the programme with 'Ticket To Ride', 'Yesterday' and 'Help!'.

When they appeared again in 1966, 1967 and 1970, they didn't appear in the flesh, and opted to use pre-recorded music videos instead, as they were getting increasingly tired of the whole Beatlemania thing.

The programme is currently still in the archives, and can be seen on DVD.

Hollywood Discotheque (1965)

First Broadcast - November 8th 1965

The Beatles supposedly made an appearance of sorts on this seemingly lost American music show hosted by Bob Hudson, Charlie O'Donnell and Johnny Hayes. They appear in episode 8 alongside Freddie Cannon, Dick and Dee Dee, Ronnie Dove, Jackie Lee, The Moon Rakers, The Remarkables and The Safaris, all appearing as themselves. Information on their appearance is very scarce and hard to find, with no mention of any music performed. As their current single in the US at the time was 'Day Tripper/We Can Work It Out', one assumes they would have been promoting this. As the harmonium wasn't an easy instrument to transport, they probably mimed! [21]

The New Musical Express Poll Winners All Star Concert (1966)

First Broadcast - May 15th 1966

The Beatles' final live appearance at the regular *New Musical Express* Poll Winners All Star Concert was on the 1st May 1966, and is also notable for being their last gig on UK soil (until the legendary rooftop gig of 1969, that is!). This concert is famous for having both The Beatles AND The Rolling Stones on the same bill - totally epic... not to mention The Who, Dusty Springfield, The Small Faces, The Spencer Davis Group, Roy Orbison, The Seekers, Cliff Richard, The Shadows, Sounds Incorporated, Dave Dee Dozy Beaky Mick and Titch, The Fortunes, Herman's Hermits, The Walker Brothers, The Overlanders, Alan Price Set, Crispian St. Peters and The Yardbirds.

They performed in front of an audience of approximately 10,000 people, and the songs played live were 'I Feel Fine', 'Nowhere Man', 'Day Tripper', 'If I Needed Someone' and 'I'm Down'.

For an all-star concert of 1960s greats, it doesn't get better than this - get me a time travelling machine, and get me a ticket!

This programme is still in the archives, and can be seen online.

Beatlefacts

* ABC TV was filming the concert, but the cameras were turned off while The Beatles performed, because Brian Epstein didn't reach an agreement over fees; but they were filmed receiving their poll awards.

Top Of The Pops (1966)

First Broadcast - June 16th 1966

The Beatles 'final appearance on the famous (or infamous) BBC music programme. Unlike their earlier performances, which were pre-recorded, or promo clips that were issued to be played on the show, this time they performed live in the studio, albeit lip-syncing, performing their new single 'Paperback Writer 'and its B-side, 'Rain', and were introduced by the host, Pete Murray. The band arrived at BBC Television Centre at 2:30pm for a rehearsal for the cameras, and then later posed for publicity photos and conducted some press interviews, followed by subsequent rehearsals at 4:15pm and 6:30pm. The live broadcast took place at 7:30pm, and was shown on BBC One, and they were the final act to appear.

A silent 8mm off-air fan recording of this appearance was discovered in April 2019, and can be seen online.

Reporting '66 (1966)

First Broadcast - December 28th 1966
Running Time - 25 Minutes

After their abandonment of touring, the tabloids posted exaggerated stories about The Beatles splitting up (which wouldn't be a reality until spring 1970), and to settle the case once and for all, the boys contacted ITN's (Independent Television News) John Edwards; this resulted in a special for the weekly news programme *Reporting '66* entitled 'Beatles Breaking Up Special', which was renamed to the rather less "clickbait' "End Of Beatlemania'. Broadcast on various ITV regions on the 28th and 29th December, this news special showed them being interviewed separately outside EMI's Abbey Road Studios getting ready to record the album that would end up being *Sgt. Pepper's Lonely*

Hearts Club Band. At this time, they all had moustaches, and George had a beard.

John arrived first, confirming they all still had good relations, and although unlikely to tour again, would continue to write songs. Paul arrived next, with roadie Mal Evans, explaining the difficulties of performing well on tours. George didn't answer any questions apart from denying they were splitting up. Ringo was the last to arrive, with roadie Neil Aspinall, and was happy to take questions. He did say he would consider making another film without the boys, denied he was bored with The Beatles, wished everyone a Merry Christmas and signed autographs for waiting fans.

The remainder of the programme consisted of stock footage of their final tour of America, interspersed with interviews from Beatles fans, as well as comments from people like Richard Lester, who directed the first two Beatles theatrical films.

The programme still exists in the archives, and sections can be seen in the 1995 documentary *The Beatles Anthology.*

Our World (1967)

Directed By - Derek Burnell and Ernst-Ludwig Freisewinkel
First Broadcast - June 25th 1967
Running Time - 150 Minutes

A very historic programme: this was the first live international satellite television programme, broadcast all the way back on the 25th June 1967. This two and a half hour show had the biggest TV audience of the time, with an estimated 400-700 MILLION people around the globe watching. The brainchild of BBC producer Aubrey Singer, the project took ten months to bring together and was broadcast in many countries around the world, though the Eastern Bloc countries bailed out at the last minute, protesting against the Western world's response to the Six-Day War.

A showcase of what our wonderful, but broken, world had to offer, the highlight of the show (of course) was The Beatles 'appearance. As this was during the height of the Vietnam War, they were asked to write a song with a positive message about love and peace and all that good stuff - so at 8:54pm GMT, The Beatles, for the first time, performed their "summer of love" anthem aptly titled 'All You Need Is Love'. To create a rousing chorus, several Beatle friends joined them in the studio including Mick Jagger and Keith Richards from The Rolling Stones, Eric Clapton, Paul's girlfriend at the time, Jane Asher, Paul's brother Mike McGear, George's wife at the time, Pattie Boyd, Marianne Faithful (who was Mick Jagger's partner at the time), Keith Moon from The Who and Graham Nash from The Hollies. Despite being broadcast in black and white, it was eventually colourised for the 1995 *Beatles Anthology* documentary, using colour pictures taken on the day as a reference.

A beautiful song with a timeless message that never gets old, and it is currently in the archives. The footage is readily available online, and has since appeared in many documentaries, including 1995's aforementioned *The Beatles Anthology*.

Music! (1968)

Directed By - Michael Tuchner
Produced By - James Archibald
Release Date - 1968
Running Time - 45 Minutes

Shown as a second feature to the classic Gene Wilder black comedy masterpiece *The Producers* (which was coincidentally George Harrison's favourite movie!), this short film is about music of all kinds, and features six minutes of The Beatles recording the song 'Hey Jude 'at EMI's Abbey Road Studios. The movie is very obscure, and information on it is scarce, but luckily, the footage has since been leaked online, and can be seen on YouTube.

Chapter Two
A Hard Day's Night (1964)

Directed By - Richard Lester
Produced By - Walter Shenson
Written By - Alun Owen
Release Date - July 6th 1964
Running Time - 87 Minutes

Summary

Arguably the most famous of all the Beatle movies. Originally, this was envisioned as being nothing more than just a quick throwaway project, at a time when the band were considered nothing more than just a passing fad. *"At one time or another everyone has imagined themselves starring in either a rock film or a James Bond movie,"* recalled John Lennon in a 1980 interview. *'We weren't any different, except suddenly we got the opportunity to do it. But what'd we know about making movies? Absolutely nothing, except that we instinctively knew if something was crap. And there were a lot of crap rock movies about. We'd made it clear to Brian that we weren't interested in being stuck in one of those typical 'nobody understands our music' plots where the local dignitaries are trying to ban something as terrible as the Saturday night hop. The kind of thing where we'd just pop up a couple of times between the action... how could we have faced each other if we had allowed ourselves to be involved in that kind of movie?"* [12]

In the summer of 1963, United Artists signed a deal for three motion pictures with Beatles manager Brian Epstein, but as their EMI contract didn't cover movie soundtracks, they figured that this could be very lucrative. Commissioned on a modest £189,000 budget and filmed in glorious black and white, everything had to be ready by the middle of 1964. Producer Walter Shenson would hire Richard Lester to direct (he would later direct the Superman movies) and this was his debut full length motion picture. Alun Owen was hired to write the screenplay and at the end of October 1963 was forming the script by shadowing them on their tour, to observe their wacky personalities and their sense of humour. He then commissioned a script, which would end up being a fictionalised account of the "day in the life" of our awesome foursome with Paul's (fictional) sleazy grandfather, John McCartney (played

45

by Wilfred Brambell, better known as Steptoe from BBC TV series *Steptoe and Son*), in tow.

The film's indoor scenes were shot at the famous Twickenham Film Studios in London, and the location shots were done in real locations to convey the impression of a kind of realism, as the film was, after all, a pseudo-documentary. None of The Beatles had any acting experience, so screenwriter Alun Owen constructed the film's dialogue in a way that reduced their acting contributions to a series of hilarious one-liners, akin to their press interviews of the time.

Despite the film having a wafer-thin plot, the movie is a really entertaining look at what the Beatles got up to on a day-to-day basis while, despite all the hard work of being rock stars on the road, they had a lot of fun along the way. You may get the impression that the whole film was improvised, but in reality, every line had to be tightly scripted. Filming for *A Hard Day's Night* took the relatively short time of 8 weeks, with the editing process taking from May-June 1964, literally weeks before the film's premiere. The editing techniques were ahead of their time, and preceded the way music videos are made today, especially when a Beatle song is being used in a scene.

The script was approved by The Beatles on the 29th February, and filming began two days later, ending on the 24th April. The only missing piece of the puzzle was a title - proposed names included 'Beatlemania 'and the more generically titled 'The Beatles Film'. George suggested 'It's A Daft, Daft, Daft, Daft World '(a reference to the comedy classic, *It's A Mad, Mad, Mad, Mad, World*) and Paul rather humorously chipped in with the rather morbid 'Oh, What A Lovely Wart! '(a nod to the musical *Oh, What A Lovely War*). Other suggested titles included 'What Little Old Man? '(as it was one of the first sentences uttered in the film), 'On The Move', 'Travelling On', 'Moving On ' and 'Let's Go'.

The final title came about one day after a long day of filming - *"We went to do a job, and we'd worked all day and we happened to work all night,"* said Ringo in a 1964 interview for DJ Dave Hull. *"I came up still thinking it was day, I suppose, and I said, 'It's been a hard day...' and I looked around and saw it was dark so I said, '...night!' So we came to A Hard Day's Night"* [2], though the phrase was originally seen in John Lennon's book *In His Own Write* in the story 'Sad Michael'. Everyone liked Ringo's malapropism, so *A Hard Day's Night* it was, unless you were German or Swedish, as the film was called *Yeah Yeah Yeah*; *All For One* if you were Italian; *Four Boys in The Wind* if you were French; *Yeah! Yeah! Here We Come* if you were Finnish and *The Kings Of Yeah Yeah Yeah* if you were Brazilian.

The movie got a great reception with the Fab Four's first excursion into acting being very well received. Each member was given a very likeable personality, with their own cuddly sense of humour and innuendoes (such as John snorting a bottle of Coke) - even if John considered their onscreen characters

46

as being phoney and not true to life. Many reviewers compared their performances to that of The Marx Brothers, as well as The Goons, by whom The Beatles were heavily influenced.

The film is notable for including actor Victor Spinetti, who would appear in the first three Beatles films. In this first film, he plays a TV director in all the studio sequences.

The film premiered on the 6th July 1964 at the London Pavilion at Piccadilly Circus, with Royal Beatles fan, Princess Margaret, being in attendance, as well as 20,000 screaming fans and 200 policeman (in a row). It also had a "northern" premiere in the Beatles 'home town of Liverpool, with over 200,000 people lining The Beatles 'ten mile route from the airport to the city centre, and they would be later honoured with a civic reception at the Town Hall. It had its American premiere at the Beacon Theatre in New York on the 12th August 1964, and it later opened in 500 cinemas throughout the country the very next day.

It earned $11 million at the box office and the film's scriptwriter, Alun Owen, was nominated for an Academy Award for his work, but lost out to the authors of *Father Goose*.

On the 12th July 1964, the soundtrack album was released, and it was the third album in the canonical Beatles albums. It was the first Beatles album to consist entirely of Lennon/McCartney compositions, and was universally acclaimed by critics. The American release of the album also included instrumental cover versions from George Martin, with the orchestra that was used in the film's soundtrack. Recording of the album took place between January 29th and June 2nd 1964, and was recorded at EMI Studios in London (now Abbey Road Studios). An exception was 'Can't Buy Me Love', which was recorded at EMI's Pathe Marconi Studios in Paris, France, during their 18-day residency at the Olympia Theatre. It was during this time when The Beatles re-recorded 'She Loves You 'and 'I Want To Hold Your Hand 'in German, as The Beatles 'label in Germany at the time, Odeon, insisted that they wouldn't sell enough records unless they actually sang in the German language.

While lacking in terms of story, *A Hard Day's Night* is a brilliant time capsule of the early days of Beatlemania, as well as having a flawless soundtrack - it's a classic worth checking out.

Music Performed (Mimed)

1. A Hard Day's Night

These first sequences for the film took place on Sunday 5th April and Sunday 12th April 1964 at Marylebone Station, London, as the station was closed to the public on Sundays. During this sequence, The Beatles can be seen across

Melcombe Place and into the station, using the telephones and photo booth, Paul wearing a disguise on a bench, and the boys then running down the platform, and jumping onto the train. Another sequence was used at the beginning of the film under the title cards, while the title track plays in the background, where John, George and Ringo ran towards the camera, with George falling over and the others laughing. The song is played again in the film's closing credits.

2. I Should Have Known Better

Filmed on a stage set to resemble the train guard's van, on Wednesday 11th March 1964. The shot was made to look like the train was moving, and the small, cramped environment added to the feeling of intimacy. We see The Beatles starting out playing cards, then playing their instruments, miming to the track, accompanied by two schoolgirls – one of whom was Patti Boyd, who would later marry George on the 21st January 1966. This song is played again in the final "TV performance" sequence at the end of the film.

3. I Wanna Be Your Man
4. Don't Bother Me

Shot on Friday 17th April 1964 at Les Ambassadeurs nightclub in London in the club's Garrison suite – The Beatles are dancing with the crowd to 'I Wanna Be Your Man 'and 'Don't Bother Me'. Watch out for some groovy moves from Ringo!

5. If I Fell

While the crew are setting up the boys' gear before their "studio appearance", John sings this track to Ringo to cheer him up. Interestingly, on the 8th April 1988, John's lyrics for this track written on back of a Valentine's Day card were sold at Sotheby's in London for £7800 (over £161,000 in 2021 money).

6. Can't Buy Me Love

Initial filming began on Friday 13th March 1964, with subsequent filming talking place on the 22nd and 23rd April at Gatwick Airport in Surrey. After lunch, the boys were filmed fooling around on a nearby helicopter launch pad (the cameraman was on board the helicopter) and the track played while the boys were ecstatically enjoying their freedom. Richard Lester, the director, felt they should have more footage in this sequence, so they filmed on Thursday 23rd April at Thornbury playing fields in Isleworth near London Airport, and a fake helicopter pad was constructed, so filming could be done at ground level. John had to leave to attend a literary luncheon at the Dorchester Hotel, and this is why only Paul, George and Ringo appear at the very end of the sequence.

7. And I Love Her

Another performance on the studio set with Paul centre stage at the front and George playing a Jose Ramirez classical guitar, hugging it, having finished his solo spot. Atmospheric, with moody lighting. The song appears again in the finale sequence at the Scala Theatre, London, which was filmed on Tuesday 31st March.

8. I'm Happy Just To Dance With You

A great upbeat track with George on vocals. Filmed on a "studio" set with posters of actual beetles, this was the first time there was a filmic representation of George on vocals. The song was covered by Anne Murray in 1980.

9. Ringo's Theme/This Boy (George Martin)

This is an instrumental cover version of 'This Boy 'arranged by the "fifth Beatle", George Martin. One of the highlights of the film was Ringo's long solo sequence, which probably led to him having a cinematic career of his own. Filmed initially on Tuesday 10th March 1964, the first sequence is at the Turks Head pub in Twickenham, Middlesex, where he complains about sandwiches, smashes a beer bottle, and throws a dart at a dartboard, narrowly missing a parrot! The second sequence was filmed on Thursday 9th April 1964 by the River Thames in Kew, Surrey, on the embankment near Kew bridge, where we see him throwing stones in the river and befriending a young lad. The track plays over the entire sequence.

10. Tell Me Why
11. She Loves You

Filmed on Tuesday 31st March at the Scala Theatre in London along with reprises of 'And I Love Her 'and 'I Should Have Known Better', this was the film's showcase finale in front of 350 screaming fans (and a future member of Genesis - 13-year-old Phil Collins, who found himself on the cutting room floor!).

Beatlefacts

* The word 'Beatles 'is never said in the entire movie.
* The very first movie to make a profit before it even came out, thanks to strong advance orders of the soundtrack album.
* The movie premiered on the eve of Ringo Starr's 24th birthday.
* In one scene, a female reporter asks John Lennon if he has any particular hobbies, and he writes down 'TITS'!
* To give the movie a U Rating in the UK (meaning suitable for all ages) by the BBFC, the phrase "get knotted" had to be cut out - ironically, the film's many innuendos, including John snorting a Coke bottle, went past their heads.
* The song 'I'll Cry Instead 'was considered to be used beyond the soundtrack album, but was cut out. It did however get used in the 1982 reissue by Universal Pictures, in a slideshow prologue made in tribute to John Lennon, and consisted of photos from the time of the film shoot. This was done without director Richard Lester's approval, and has since been cut out of future releases.
* The film is known for popularising a new word into the English language - grotty - an abbreviation of the word 'grotesque'. Screenwriter Alun Owen claims that he heard the word as a Liverpool slang term, but The Beatles had never heard of it, and believed that Owen made it up.
* The song 'I Call Your Name '(from the 'Long Tall Sally 'EP) was also considered for the film, but was cut out for unknown reasons.
* The roadie characters, Norm and Shake, are loosely inspired by The Beatles' real life roadies and Beatle buddies, Neil Aspinall and Mal Evans.
* While The Beatles were in attendance at the premiere, none of them stayed for the whole show.
* The scene where Paul McCartney's grandpa John is forging autographs to deceive fans is actually true to life. During the time The Beatles were together as a group, several people from the Beatle entourage would ghost-sign for them on their behalf if they weren't available, most notably roadies Neil Aspinall and Mal Evans, as well as press officer Derek Taylor, the Fan Club secretaries and even family members such as Aunt Mimi Smith and Louise Harrison, George's Mum. Unlike Grandpa John, this was all done with good intentions.
* Mal Evans actually makes a small cameo in this film. He is the person carrying the cello, when Lennon is talking to Millie (Anna Quayle) back-

stage. He would also make an appearance in *Help!* playing a channel swimmer, as well as *Magical Mystery Tour* playing a magician and a bus passenger.

* Because of the success of this film, demand for the Rickenbacker 360/12 12 string guitar skyrocketed thanks to George Harrison using it in the film.

* Some of the recordings of the songs actually play 4% slower in the film, possibly to match the lip-syncing.

Chapter Three
Help! (1965)

Directed By - Richard Lester
Produced By - Walter Shenson
Written By - Marc Behm and Charles Wood
Release Date - July 29th 1965
Running Time - 92 Minutes

Summary

They're back - this time in **TECHNICOLOUR!**

After the massive success of their first foray into celluloid, *A Hard Day's Night*, The Beatles were very much on the gravy train in pretty much any form of media, and this encouraged United Artists to produce the obligatory follow-up film, and expand them from being not just mere pop stars but legitimate actors too. Richard Lester was back in the director's chair, while Walter Shenson returned as producer; Victor Spinetti also returned, this time as the "baddie", Professor Foot. The Fab Four wrote new music material without reading the script and, as previously, a title was needed. The rather uninspired 'Beatles 2' was the first suggestion, but then it evolved into 'Eight Arms To Hold You', but that didn't really roll off the tongue, and didn't make a particularly good song title...

... so Richard Lester suggested *Help!* (even though the title was being considered for another film).

Because of the success of *A Hard Day's Night*, the budget was raised to £500,000, and it was shot around an 11 week schedule. Unlike the previous film, this film had something of a more elaborate plot, written by Marc Behm, whose credits included *Charade*, *How To Get It* and *The Knack*. The film's story is about a cult (based on the Thuggee) who worship a goddess called Kaili. The followers of Kaili want a sacred ring that has attached itself to one of Ringo's fingers, but if he can't remove it, he will become sacrificed to Kaili's will. The Beatles used this film as an excuse to travel abroad, so scenes were shot in the Bahamas and Austria. Despite the exotic locations, the boys seemed less enthralled with the whole filming process.

The movie premiered on the 29th July 1965 in London and, as to be expected with The Beatles, public hysteria ensued, resulting in police officials shutting down Piccadilly Circus for public traffic, with at least 10,000 people amassed. The area became so crowded that John's Rolls Royce was held up for 20 minutes! Those in attendance at the film's premiere included Princess Margaret and Lord Snowden, with the premiere being sponsored by the Variety Club of Great Britain in aid of the Docklands Settlement and the Variety Club's Heart Fund - £6000 was raised for both charities (around £117,000 in 2021 money).

Critical reception was healthy but not outstanding. John Lennon remembered in 1980, *"Well, it was 1965. The movie was out of our control. With 'A Hard Day's Night' we pretty much had a lot of input, and it was semi-realistic. But with 'Help!', Dick (Lester) didn't tell us what it was about... though I realise, looking back, how advanced it was. It was a precursor for the 'Batman' 'POW!WOW!' on TV - that kind of stuff."* [12]

It was still a big commercial success earning $12.1million, and it even won first prize at the International Film Festival in Rio de Janeiro in Brazil. When it was exported to American shores, some of the British terminology had to be changed - *"The thing is, for America, we had to cut out the word 'toilet',"* remembered Paul in 1965. *'We had to call it a bathroom for America."* John added *"That's true. We actually cut out a few words because they wouldn't take it over there."* [12]

The soundtrack album was released on the 6th August 1965 and it is, of course, the LP containing probably the most famous song in The Beatles' back catalogue -' Yesterday '- a song so good it was covered over 2,200 times! The US version however included incidental music from the film by Ken Thorne, which coincidentally contains one of the first uses of the Indian Sitar on a pop record. As for their previous albums, recording took place at the EMI Studios in London, between February 15th and June 17th 1965. Quite a few songs would end up being cut, or being moved to later projects. 'If You Got Trouble 'sung by Ringo was cut because the band were not happy with the song (but it does appear on 1996's *Anthology 2* compilation), and Ringo sang 'Act Naturally 'instead. Another song 'That Means A Lot 'was also recorded, and was given to P.J. Proby - like the previous song, this resurfaced on the *Anthology 2* compilation. The song 'Wait 'from the *Rubber Soul* album was originally made during the *Help!* sessions, but remained unfinished, and of course didn't appear until the release of *Rubber Soul* later in November.

Music Performed (Mimed)

1. Help!

The title track is a John song, reflecting that the whole Beatlemania thing was getting a little too much, giving the song a very apt name. The track plays over the opening titles, and the boys are seen performing the song in a TV studio (ironically in black and white) and in the context of the film, the antagonist Clang (Leo McKern) is seen throwing darts at the TV, while watching our Fab Four perform. The Beatles 'portion of the scene was filmed on April 22nd 1965 at Twickenham Film Studios in London, and the footage (sans the colour scenes with Clang) was distributed by NEMS Enterprises to TV companies to promote the single for shows like *Top Of The Pops*. The single would later be released on July 19th 1965, reaching the rather unsurprising position of No.1.

2.   You're Going To Lose That Girl

Shot on April 30th 1965, this segment of the film takes place in a recording studio, not too dissimilar to that of the real EMI Studios, but, like the previous music scene, this was filmed at Twickenham. There is a really cool, almost moody silhouette-like approach to the lighting, making the smoke effects on Ringo's cigarette very effective.

3.   You've Got To Hide Your Love Away

John's very good attempt at trying to be Bob Dylan. In the context of the film, the boys play this in John's quarters of the Fab Four's shared house at Ailsa Avenue in London. The flute solo in the film is played by George's in-house gardener (though in the actual song itself, it's played by English film composer and music conductor, John Scott). While this is being sung, the antagonist, Clang, is hiding underneath a manhole cover outside the flat.

4.   Ticket To Ride

This portion of the film was shot on their final day of filming in the cold mountains of Austria on the 30th March 1965. The Beatles are really wrapped up warm, wearing duffel coats and red and white striped scarves; John is seen wearing a beret, and George even has a top hat. It's rumoured that The Beatles were high on something not-quite-legal while filming this portion! In the evening after filming had concluded, John and Ringo were interviewed on Radio Luxembourg by Chris Denning.

5.   I Need You

A number sung by George; this part of the film was shot on the second day of location filming on Salisbury Plain on the 4th May 1965, and the band are surrounded by military tanks and equipment. This came about because troops from the Third Division Royal Artillery were carrying out some training exercises, and agreed for their equipment and tanks to appear during the shooting.

6. The Night Before

While staying at a local hotel on a cold Salisbury Plain - the Antrobus Arms in Amesbury - they filmed a number sung (mimed) by Paul, as well as the aforementioned 'I Need You'. Just as the song ends, a bomb explodes in the film, which was shot in the shadow of Stonehenge.

7. Another Girl

This segment of the film was shot on the 27th February 1965 in the Bahamas in a place called Balmoral Island, which is now known as Discovery Island. Paul uses a girl in a bikini to convey playing a guitar, and George mimes Paul's guitar parts as if he was the one playing them. To cause more confusion, each of the band changes instruments, as George is seen playing Paul's bass parts, looking very confused, Ringo is seen playing acoustic guitar and John is seen playing drums. This would later be spoofed in 1978 in the TV movie *The Rutles - All You Need Is Cash* in the 'Ouch! 'part of the film.

8. She's A Woman

A Paul number, which was the B-side to their single 'I Feel Fine'. A small portion of the song's chorus can be heard in a scene in which the band are replaying it on a tape while they are recording 'I Need You 'in a field surrounded by tanks (filmed once again at Salisbury Plain).

9. A Hard Day's Night/Can't Buy Me Love/I Should Have Known Better (Instrumental arranged by Ken Thorne)

10. I'm Happy Just To Dance With You (Instrumental arranged by Ken Thorne)

11. You Can't Do That (Instrumental arranged by Ken Thorne)

12. From Me To You (Instrumental arranged by Ken Thorne)

Cover versions of older Beatles songs (with the majority of them from their previous film *A Hard Day's Night*) were composed as incidental music by Ken Thorne (1924-2014). Thorne would later write music for *How I Won The*

War, which starred John Lennon, and he is probably best known for composing the incidental music for *Superman II* and *Superman III* (both directed by Richard Lester, coincidentally).

Beatlefacts

* Another working title for the film was 'Tomorrow Never Knows'. This was one of Ringo's malapropisms that would later end up being the title of a Beatles song.
* The tagline of the film is *"Please don't reveal the beginning of this movie to your friends (they'd never believe it, anyway)"* which spoofs the tagline from the Alfred Hitchcock classic *Psycho*: *"Please do not reveal the ending of this movie to your friends (it's the only one we have)"*.
* Peter Sellers turned down a role in the film, as he didn't want to be second fiddle to J, P, G, and R.
* This film was the first time we see John Lennon wearing his trademark granny glasses (AKA metal British NHS style frames) during a scene where The Beatles are in disguise in an airport during a trip to the Bahamas.
* Kalli is actually a real Hindu goddess, the Hindu equivalent of the grim reaper. Kalli is also the goddess worshipped by the occult in the film *Indiana Jones and The Temple of Doom*.
* Wendy Richard (Miss Brahms from *Are You Being Served*) and Frankie Howerd (*Carry On*) were supposed to have roles in the film, but ended up on the cutting room floor. Howerd would later appear as Mr. Mustard in the infamous 1978 *Sgt. Pepper's Lonely Hearts Club Band* film.
* As for *A Hard Day's Night*, John bailed out during a scene on the beach as he had an appointment, and once again a double had to replace him.
* The album and film poster's iconic cover has the band spell out a word in flag semaphore. They do not spell out HELP, but actually spell out NUJV.

Chapter Four
The Beatles Cartoons (1965-1967)

Directed By - Various
Written By - Dennis Marks, Jack Mendelssohn, Heywood King, Bruce Howard
Release Date - September 25th 1965-October 21st 1967
Running Time - 16-20 Minutes Each

List of Episodes

SEASON ONE

1. A Hard Day's Night/I Want To Hold Your Hand (First broadcast, September 25th 1965)
2. Do You Want To Know A Secret/If I Fell (First broadcast, October 2nd 1965)
3. Please Mister Postman/Devil In Her Heart (First broadcast, October 9th 1965)
4. Not A Second Time/Slow Down (First broadcast, October 16th 1965)
5. Baby's In Black/Misery (First broadcast, October 23rd 1965)
6. You Really Got A Hold On Me/Chains (First broadcast, October 30th 1965)
7. I'll Get You/Honey Don't (First broadcast, November 6th 1965)
8. Any Time At All/Twist & Shout (First broadcast, November 13th 1965)
9. Little Child/I'll Be Back (First broadcast, November 20th 1965)
10. Long Tall Sally/I'll Cry Instead (First broadcast, November 27th 1965)
11. I'll Follow The Sun/When I Get Home (First broadcast, December 4th 1965)
12. Everybody's Trying To Be My Baby/I Should Have Known Better (First broadcast, December 11th 1965)
13. I'm A Loser/I Wanna Be Your Man (First broadcast, December 18th 1965)
14. Don't Bother Me/No Reply (First broadcast, December 25th 1965)
15. I'm Happy Just To Dance With You/Mister Moonlight (First broadcast, January 1st 1966)

16. Can't Buy Me Love/It Won't Be Long (First broadcast, January 8th 1966)

17. Anna/I Don't Want To Spoil The Party (First broadcast, January 15th 1966)

18. Matchbox/Thank You Girl (First broadcast, January 22nd 1966)

19. From Me To You/Boys (First broadcast, January 29th 1966)

20. Dizzy Miss Lizzy/I Saw Her Standing There (First broadcast, February 5th 1966)

21. What You're Doing/Money (First broadcast, February 12th 1966)

22. Komm Gib Mir Deine Hand/She Loves You (First broadcast, February 19th 1966)

23. Bad Boy/Tell Me Why (First broadcast, February 26th 1966)

24. I Feel Fine/Hold Me Tight (First broadcast, March 5th 1966)

25. Please Please Me/There's A Place (First broadcast, March 12th 1966)

26. Roll Over Beethoven/Rock & Roll Music (First broadcast, March 19th 1966)

SEASON TWO

27. Eight Days A Week/I'm Looking Through You (First broadcast, September 10th 1966)

28. Help!/We Can Work It Out (First broadcast, September 17th 1966)

29. I'm Down/Run For Your Life (First broadcast, September 24th 1966)

30. Drive My Car/Tell Me What You See (First broadcast, October 1st 1966)

31. I Call Your Name/The Word (First broadcast, October 8th 1966)

32. All My Loving/Day Tripper (First broadcast, October 15th 1966)

33. Nowhere Man/Paperback Writer (First broadcast, October 22nd 1966)

SEASON THREE

34. Penny Lane/Strawberry Fields Forever (First broadcast, September 16th 1967)

35. And Your Bird Can Sing/Got To Get You Into My Life (First broadcast, September 23rd 1967)

36. Good Day Sunshine/Ticket To Ride (First broadcast, September 30th 1967)

37. Taxman/Eleanor Rigby (First broadcast, October 7th 1967)

38. Tomorrow Never Knows/I've Just Seen A Face (First broadcast, October 14th 1967)

39. Wait/I'm Only Sleeping (First broadcast, October 21st 1967)

By September 1965, Beatlemania was at its peak, and they had just completed their second US concert tour, which had included their legendary show at Shea Stadium in New York. That month saw the debut of an animated version of our Fab Four created by Al Brodax for the US company King Features Presentations. Each episode took around a month to make, and contained two Beatles hit songs, around 8-10 minutes in length. Brodax pitched the initial concept for the show in late 1963 - he was already a known figure, having been an executive producer for over 200 *Popeye* cartoons from 1960-62. After a $3million investment, Brodax commissioned a group of artists to come up with cartoon versions of the Fab Four, but he was not happy with the results. While the show was announced in November 1964, the development stage was a turbulent one, as funding for the show was tough, but eventually it was pitched to ABC Television in America, and it premiered in September the following year.

In this series, John is the leader of the group with Paul as second in command. George meanwhile has a dry sense of humour, while Ringo is played as something of a buffoon. Unfortunately, their voices were provided by some very unconvincing not-so-soundalikes with Paul Frees (best known as the voice of Boris Badenov in *Rocky & Bullwinkle*) voicing John and George, while Lance Percival (of *Carry On* fame, who would later voice Old Fred the Sea Captain in *Yellow Submarine*) voiced Paul and Ringo. To say they didn't really sound like them would be an understatement. Brian Epstein was furious with the way they sounded, and it is believed that he banned the series from being shown in Britain.

To get a fundamental idea of how to animate the Fab Four, the animators watched footage of the band performing live to become familiar with their characteristics. Unfortunately, the low budget animation suffers from reusing footage frequently. Like many Saturday morning cartoons of the time, the animation for the show was outsourced to many countries, such as Great Britain (whose animation companies at the time mainly stuck with advertisements), The Netherlands, Canada and Australia. The most observant of fans could tell which animation company animated which episode - for example, if Ringo's nose size was inconsistent, it was an episode animated by the Australian animation team. Also, for the keen-eyed Beatle fans, you will notice sometimes that the wrong Beatle might be singing a particular song; you might catch John singing 'I'm Happy Just To Dance With You 'instead of George or Paul singing 'Mr. Moonlight 'instead of John.

The show would eventually run for 3 seasons and 39 episodes, and was rerun throughout the 1980s. Every episode was loosely based around the lyrics of a Beatle song that was featured in a particular episode, and there were two sing-a-long segments, where the words of a Beatle song appeared on the bottom of the screen. Each episode took place in various countries around the world, giving it a truly international flavour, and each location was used at least twice (or in some cases, even four times) and often in the same weekly episode. The episodes were also known for their rather simplistic and repetitive storylines, but remember, this show was designed for young Beatle fans living in the 1960s.

The first episode racked up a 52% audience share. *"It took about four weeks to animate each film and I enjoyed it immensely,"* recalled Chris Cuddington, a man who animated for the show. *"The characters were easy to draw, and the stories were simple and uncomplicated."* [3] Because of the success of the Beatles cartoon, animated adaptations of Herman's Hermits and Freddie And The Dreamers were considered, but they never fully materialised - but similar shows such as one based on The Jackson Five (*Jackson 5ive*) and The Osmonds have emerged in its wake.

The series was a massive success, but as stated, it never saw a release in the UK until 1980. While The Beatles initially hated it, each of the members warmed to the show, thanks to its "so-bad-it's-good" nature, and it had something of a cult following. The cartoon has never seen an official home video release (though Apple did secure the rights to the series in the early 1990s, possibly with the intention of making sure it never gets commercially released). There is even a campaign for the show to have an official DVD or Blu-Ray release, but nothing, as of writing, has materialised. Interestingly, it wasn't shown on native British shores until 1980 on an early morning slot on ITV Granada, and it was repeated again in 1988, as part of ITV's Night Network magazine show slot.

Beatlefacts

* In the cartoon's universe, the story of how The Beatles met was drastically different from how it was in the real universe. According to the cartoon Beatles, in the episode 'Paperback Writer', Ringo was originally a theatre "Starr", Paul was a scientist, who was knighted for his work, George was a spy akin to James Bond, and John was a World War I fighter pilot, which doesn't make sense, as the real John was born in 1940. One fact that they prophetically got right was Paul being knighted, which really happened on the 11th March 1997, but for his contribution to popular music. Ringo was later knighted on the 20th March 2018.

Chapter Five
Magical Mystery Tour (1967)

Directed By - The Beatles (and an uncredited Bernard Knowles)
Produced By - The Beatles
Written By - The Beatles (and an uncredited Mal Evans)
First Broadcast - December 26th 1967
Running Time - 52 Minutes

Summary

This is certainly their most bizarre and weird film, but for some reason it has something of a "proto-Pythonesque" feel to it, and for that matter, despite being nothing more than a home movie on a budget (something that John Lennon said in an interview), it has its own charm.

Obviously the first thing a successful movie needs is a good plot, and in the pre-production stage, they were struggling to find one. While the movie was in its formative stage, John said in an interview *"We haven't got a script yet. But we've got a bloke going round the lavatories of Britain, cribbing all the notes off the walls."* [12]

The plot for the finished film, as it is, is basically Ringo and his Auntie Jessie (played by Jessie Robins), with whom he is constantly bickering, purchasing a ticket to the titular Magical Mystery Tour Bus - they get on the bus and... things happen under the will of four or five magicians (the fifth one being none other than their roadie, Mal Evans).

On the journey, we see a variety of loosely connected sketches; an impromptu race, where the Magical Mystery Bus races with cars and bikes and they all enter an army recruitment office; Aunt Bessie falling in love with the bus conductor, Mr. Bloodvessel (played by Derek Royle); plus they go into a cinema inside a tiny tent; a sequence where Aunt Bessie dreams of being in a restaurant, where a waiter named Pirandello (played by John) shovels spaghetti onto the table (which in turn was inspired by a dream Lennon had); and in the end they all finish up in a strip club, as was typical of a northern working man's day out (and we get to see the legendary Bonzo Dog Doo-Dah Band make an appearance.)

As in the previous two Beatle films, we see the return of Victor Spinetti, this time playing an army drill sergeant, who talks in gibberish, and insults a stuffed cow - weird! Regarding the film's mismatch, patchwork "storyline",

61

Paul McCartney recalled for David Frost in 1967 *"When we were making it, I think all of us thought, 'This has got a very thin plot. We hope this idea of doing a thing without a plot works, because the one thing we're gonna be able to say is, it hasn't got a plot.' But yeah. We thought, 'You don't need a plot. You don't always need one.' Because, like, the things you did today probably didn't have much of a plot."* [11]

The movie eventually came about during a difficult time in the life of our four heroes. While 1967 was, in many ways, their greatest year, their manager Brian Epstein had passed away on the 27th August. Five days later, on the 1st September, the Beatles had a crisis meeting at Paul's house in St. John's Wood, London, to discuss their uncertain future. A few months earlier, Paul had the basic concept for *MMT* formalised in April, on a flight from Los Angeles to London from the Monterey Pop Festival - his initial concept was for The Beatles to hire a bus, while a camera crew followed them around the British countryside with magical things happening along the way, inspired by popular coach trips from Liverpool to see the Blackpool illuminations. So, as a bit of light relief after this terrible tragedy of losing Epstein, the *Magical Mystery Tour* movie was green-lit. As they were not on the road anymore - and even before Brian's tragic death - they had been thinking of alternative ways to promote their music.

The script was written in a very unconventional way, with Paul drawing a circle on paper and dividing it into a series of sketches loosely connected with some sort of "plot" - though around 70% of the film was in fact improvised on the fly. Filming was mainly done in a two week period from 11th-25th September 1967, with locations including a decommissioned military airfield in Kent, and the majority of the actual trip itself was shot around the West Country.

In a 1995 interview, George Harrison remembered the filming process of *MMT*: *"I remember quite a bit of it, really... in the big hangar down in Kent. We were driving around this air field in the Mini Cooper. 'Your Mother Should Know'...that was quite interesting, I quite enjoyed that. But you see, there was always good songs, there's a couple of good songs and there was a few funny scenes. I mean, the scene that, to me, stands out is the one of John shovelling the spaghetti on the fat woman's plate. I mean, that was the best bit of the movie for me."* [12]

The film took eleven weeks to edit, cutting it down from 10 hours of shot footage to a meagre 52 minutes, with many scenes being cut out of the finished film. This included a sequence where the band Traffic performed the song 'Here We Go Round The Mulberry Bush'. Also, Jimi Hendrix was scheduled to make an appearance, but had to pull out at the last minute, as he was appearing at the Monterey Pop Festival (which ironically was under the suggestion of Paul).

For your hardcore Beatle nuts, watch out for cameo appearances of several people from the Beatle entourage such as their road manager, Neil Aspinall, Fan Club secretary Freda Kelly, and John's first son, Julian Lennon.

Unlike the previous films, which were cinema releases, *MMT* was in fact a TV movie, with its UK premiere on Boxing Day 1967 on BBC1 to an estimated audience of between 14-15 million people; to put it politely, reception was not kind. For a movie that relied heavily on colour, it was ironically shown in black and white (making the multi-coloured 'Flying 'sequence pointless), and even when it was shown in colour on BBC2 on January 5th 1968, reception was still apathetic. It was The Beatles 'first major failure. Personal assistant Peter Brown put the blame on McCartney, and in an interview for *The David Frost Programme*, Paul had to make a public apology. Regarding whether the film was a success or not, he responded with *"Uhh, it's both. You know, it's a Success Failure."* [11]

He also added: *"Was the film really all that bad compared to the rest of Christmas TV? You could hardly call the Queen's speech a gasser. We could put on a moptop show, but we really don't like that sort of entertainment anymore. We could have sung carols and done a first-class Christmassy show starring The Beatles with lots of phoney tinsel like everyone else. It would have been the easiest thing in the world, but we wanted to do something different. So maybe we boobed... maybe we didn't. We don't say it was a good film. It was our first attempt. If we goofed, then we goofed. It was a challenge and it didn't come off. We'll know better next time."* [12]

Because of the critical bashing, US TV networks refused to show the film, but it was shown in the Netherlands on the 10th February 1968, and was sold to Japanese TV in April of that year. It even got a very limited theatrical release in America for a few special screenings in May 1968, mainly in Los Angeles and San Francisco. It was later shown at the Savoy Theatre in Boston, where it actually received positive reviews. The movie got a full-scale theatrical release in the USA in 1974, and was even considered to be a support film for the wonderful 1975 comedy classic *Monty Python And the Holy Grail*. Despite this, reception has been a little kinder over time, with people praising its "out-there" humour as being ahead of its time, and fans of the film include none other than Stephen Spielberg - now that's a compliment! Many modern day Beatle fans speculate that the initial backlash of the movie was unjust and perhaps a little biased, and was mainly an excuse to finally pan The Beatles after they'd been riding high for so many years.

The film's legacy lives on, as since 1983 Liverpool has been marketing its own Magical Mystery Tours, with the bus travelling around Beatle landmarks, and has seen many releases on VHS, DVD and, in 2012, Blu-Ray. *Magical Mystery Tour* is a fun time capsule of popular culture circa 1967.

The soundtrack EP was released on the 8th December 1967, and it contains some of their finest moments as a band. The original EP was expanded into an LP for its American release on Capitol Records, with additional tracks including the double A-side single 'Strawberry Fields Forever/Penny Lane ' (infamous for being kept off the No.1 spot by Englebert Humperdinck), 'Hello Goodbye', 'Baby You're A Rich Man '(with backing vocals provided by Mick Jagger from The Rolling Stones), climaxing with the ultimate 'Summer Of Love 'anthem 'All You Need Is Love'. Recording for the film's soundtrack took place between April 25th and 3rd May with a second session lasting from August 22nd to November 7th 1967. The latter sessions were not recorded at the regular EMI Studios, but instead at Chappell Recording Studios in central London, as they were unable to book EMI at short notice.

Music Performed (Mimed)

1. Magical Mystery Tour

The famous title track of this bizarre TV movie. In the context of the film, the song plays during the opening titles, featuring some psychedelic animated text, and portions of film clips from the movie. In the original, un-remastered copies of the film, John's *'roll up, roll up for the Magical Mystery Tour"* spoken introduction is different to that of the EP/LP version, and in all movie versions, there is also a spoken word segment in the middle eight from John, which doesn't appear in the EP/LP version. The song gets briefly reprised during the film's closing credits.

2. The Fool On The Hill

A fantastic Paul composition. The 'Fool On The Hill 'daydream segment, with Paul ad-libbing, was filmed (possibly illegally, as it was anti-union to have just one cameraman) in the mountains of Nice, France on October 31st 1967. The cinematography, courtesy of Aubrey Dewar for this portion, is brilliant, creating a beautiful sense of atmosphere, easily one of the film's highlights. It was the only musical segment to use professional photography, and filmed at an exterior location.

3. She Loves You (Fairground Organ Cover)

A cheesy fairground cover version of a Beatles classic, done in the style of something you would hear in a fairground or circus. This is played during the scene where they all take part in an impromptu car race, each of the passengers taking on a different mode of transportation. Very strange!

4. Flying (Instrumental)

A moody instrumental number, and one of the few Beatle compositions to have writing credits for all four Beatles. The boys themselves don't appear in this segment, and in the film this instrumental piece is accompanied by stock footage of Iceland taken from an aeroplane, and unused clips from the 1964 Stanley Kubrick film *Dr. Strangelove: or How I Learned to Stop Worrying and Love The Bomb*.

5. All My Loving (Orchestral Cover Version)

An "over-the-top" cinematic orchestral rendition of the 1964 Beatles hit of the same name. This is played when Mr. Bloodvessel (Ivor Cutler) confesses his love for Ringo's Aunt Jessie (Jessie Robins). This is accompanied by a fantasy sequence, where Bloodvessel and Jessie are strolling along in the British seaside. This all comes out of left field, and the sub plot is forgotten about immediately afterwards!

6. I Am The Walrus

A John number - probably the most famous song in the film, and arguably the best. This part of the movie was filmed on the 23rd September 1967 at West Malling Air Station in Maidstone in Kent. As well as the Fab Four wearing an array of costumes (including those creepy halloween fancy dress animal masks that feature on the EP/LP cover), they are accompanied by people dressed as policemen, Little George The Photographer (played by dwarf George Claydon, who would later end up being an Oompa Loompa in Willy Wonka & The Chocolate Factory) and a group of people daisy-chained together by a very large sheet, all wearing white turban-esque hats.

7. Jessie's Dream (Instrumental)

One tune from the film's soundtrack that has never seen a commercial release was a surreal avant-garde piece called 'Jessie's Dream', which was used in the fantasy sequence where Ringo's Auntie Jessie is dreaming about sitting at a table with Mr. Bloodvessel, while John Lennon shovels copious amounts of spaghetti onto the table in front of her. The tune was recorded around October 1967 at John Lennon's house and, like 'Flying', it was one of the few compositions credited to all four Beatles. It has since surfaced in the bootleg circuit. The fantasy sequence was filmed on the 20th September 1967 at the interiors of West Malling Air Station in Kent.

8. Blue Jay Way

A great and very "trippy" George number. This segment was filmed on the 3rd November 1967 at Sunny Heights in Weybridge, which was Ringo's residence at the time. Each member is seen pretending to play a white cello, and additional shots included George running down some steps in the garden, and some clips of children playing, with the cello accompanied by lit fireworks behind it.

9. Death Cab For Cutie (performed by The Bonzo Dog Doo-Dah Band)

This song is not actually by The Beatles, but a famous comedic rock band called The Bonzo Dog Doo-Dah Band, who got their break after appearing in the Monty Python prototype show *Do Not Adjust Your Set* - one of the members was the late Neil Innes, who would later affectionately spoof The Beatles as The Rutles in the 1970s. This song was played during the scene where John, George and the rest of the Mystery Tour gang of misfits watch a striptease show, and it was filmed on the 18th September 1967 at the Raymond Revuebar strip club in London's Soho area. The stripper in question was a lady named Jan Carson, and this was her only film appearance. As it was shown before the watershed, the nudity was covered up with a black censor bar.

10. Your Mother Should Know

A very catchy oldies "throwback" song with Paul on vocals. This portion was shot on the last day's filming at West Malling Air Station in Maidstone, Kent, on September 24th 1967. This segment was made to look like the band were performing in a huge ballroom, and all four members look very dapper in their vanilla white suits coming down a large staircase in time to the track. They are accompanied by a parade of 160 dancers from the Peggy Spencer's Formation Dancing Team, in very nice vintage regalia and 24 RAF female cadets as extras, and the whole piece looks like it could be from a classic 1950s Busby Berkeley musical.

11. Hello Goodbye

The double A-side to 'I Am The Walrus', the *"Heba, heba hello-ah"* part of the song gets briefly played during the film's closing credits.

Beatlefacts

* Aunt Jessie (Jessie Robins) is in fact a drummer, just like her fictional nephew, Ringo.

* Davy Jones from The Monkees watched it during its first broadcast. His family found it too *"out there"*, but Jones however enjoyed the film's surreal qualities.

* The film took a while to get onto DVD. The first release was in 1997, and was low key. It then returned as a "grey market" release with poor-quality video in 2003. In 2012, it was finally given a proper release on both DVD and Blu-Ray.

* The song the Bonzo Dog Doo-Dah Band sing at the strip club scene 'Death Cab For Cutie 'would inspire a famous band to use it as their name. The song was also featured in the 1967 comedy sketch series *Do Not Adjust Your Set -* a forerunner to *Monty Python's Flying Circus*.

* An incidental piece of music, an accordion piece by Shirley Evans called 'Shirley's Wild According 'was eventually cut out of the film. Paul and Ringo were on percussion and the piece was arranged by Mike Leander.

Chapter Six
Yellow Submarine (1968)

"Once upon a time, or maybe twice - there was an unearthly paradise called Pepperland . . . ."

Directed By - George Dunning
Produced By - Al Brodax
Written By - Lee Minoff and Roger McGough (uncredited)
Release Date - July 17th 1968
Running Time - 90 Minutes

Summary

AKA The greatest film The Beatles never made!

In 1963, Paul McCartney was on holiday in Greece, and was enjoying some dessert, known locally as a submarine. It contained various colours including yellow. Three years later, he had the idea of a tune about a submarine, and, remembering his holiday – Voila! 'Yellow Submarine' was born (with the assistance of John, who had a similar idea a year earlier during an experience with an illegal recreational substance). With Ringo on vocals, 'Yellow Submarine' became a unique tune in the Beatles canon because of its innocent charm, and it was featured on their fantastic seventh studio album *Revolver* in 1966. It was also released as a single (a double A-side with 'Eleanor Rigby') which, as per usual, reached No.1 with a bullet.

Also in 1966, Al Brodax, who produced the infamous Beatles cartoons for King Features, had approached Brian Epstein about the possibility of doing an animated feature film based on The Beatles, something he had been trying to do since 1965. Despite the band being very hesitant, as they hated the 1965 cartoons (at the time), the Fabs and Epstein agreed to the film going ahead as a contractual obligation, as this would fulfil their three film deal with United Artists. Commissioned on a $1 million budget and an 11 month timeframe, Lee Minoff (who had previously worked on *2001 - A Space Odyssey*) was chosen to write the script, and he wrote an original story based on the 'Yellow Submarine' song (suggested by Ringo), while George Dunning took the director's chair.

Paul McCartney remembers the making of this cinematic masterpiece in a 1996 interview:

"Al Brodax talked to us about the possibility of doing a feature and we met at my house in London. Erich Segal came along as well. At the start, all four of us hoped for something a little bit groovier... sort of more classic 'Pinocchio' or 'Snow White'. Right away, they (Brodax and Segal) made it clear that they weren't keen to do just a straight Disney thing... and said, 'We think you're further out now.' So from being rather childish, which the (Saturday morning) cartoon series most definitely was, they wanted to go completely psychedelic!" [12]

Many initial script treatments were rejected, and The Beatles were consulted on the film's direction, which leaned towards the psychedelic phase of their careers. A two minute test animation was made using George Harrison's sitar music in the background, and animator Charlie Jenkins provided some sequences using a polarisation technique, which was followed by characters in backgrounds using some music from the *Sgt. Pepper* album.

Brodax and Minoff teamed up with Erich Segal and Jack Mendelsohn to write a screenplay which takes place once upon a time - or maybe twice, in a magical world known as Pepperland.

Pepperland was a utopian paradise, until the evil music-hating Blue Meanies came along and launched a merciless attack on the innocent folk. With help from Old Fred the Sea Captain and Jeremy Hillary Boob PHD AKA The Nowhere Man, a weird looking monster with a high intellect, The Beatles arrive to save the day and with the power of Beatle music - well... you have to watch the film to find out what happens next! As stated previously, unlike the former Beatles cartoons, which were firmly stuck in the Beatlemania era, this film was more centred on the famed "druggy" psychedelic era of *Sgt. Pepper's*, which complemented the film's tone and storyline.

Heinz Edelmann, a German graphic artist, created the colourful cast of characters that would be joining the Fab Four on this psychedelic journey, complemented by a team of 40 animators and 140 technical artists, resulting in over 500,000 animation cels. Rotoscoping was also used to create the film's unique animation style - rotoscoping is a technique which was created by Walt Disney in the 1930s to film a live-action sequence, and then trace over and paint it to make it look like it's animated - this would later be used in Ralph Bakshi's animated adaptation of *Lord Of The Rings*.

Because of their dissatisfaction with their initial animated adaptation on TV, The Beatles had little involvement in the finished product, resulting in their voices being replaced by professional actors, with John Clive voicing John Lennon, Geoffrey Hughes as Paul McCartney and Paul Angelis voicing

Ringo Starr and George Harrison. As well as voicing the Chief Blue Meanie, joining the cast was comedian Dick Emery playing Jeremy Boob, Lord Mayor and Max The Meanie, and Lance Percival (who had previously voiced Paul and Ringo in the original Beatles cartoons) voicing Old Fred. *"I'm not sure why we never did our own voices, but the actors probably did it better anyway,"* remembers George in a 1994 interview. *"You know, 'cuz you needed to be more cartoon-like and our voices were pretty cartoon-like anyway, but you know, the exaggeration that you've got with the other actors voices - I think it suits it."* [12]

Despite featuring some corny jokes, usually relying on puns and wordplay, the animated characterisations of The Beatles are really fun, and the new tunes (which they considered as ephemeral) are excellent.

The movie received universal acclaim, and is considered a milestone of psychedelic far-out animation, at a time when animation was going through something of a dark age. Despite their initial fears, The Beatles loved the film, and even agreed to make a short live action cameo appearance at the end of the movie, which was filmed at Twickenham Film Studios in London. *"I loved 'Yellow Submarine'. I thought it was innovative with great animation,"* remembered Ringo Starr in a 1994 interview. *"It's still great and I'm glad we were involved with it."* [12]

The movie's premiere at the London Pavilion on the 17th July 1968 was attended by all four Beatles (and Yoko), which resulted in traffic coming to a standstill, like it was 1964 all over again! Also in attendance at the premiere were Mick Jagger from The Rolling Stones, Donovan, Sandie Shaw, P.J. Proby, supermodel Twiggy, Simon Dee, radio DJ Tony Blackburn and Alan Price.

This is a fantastic movie, and is strongly recommended for any Beatle fans young and old.

Music Played

1.   Yellow Submarine

The movie's title track, which was originally featured on the 1966 album *Revolver* (more details on this song in the summary section). This track plays over the opening credits, right after the mayor of Pepperland gets hit on the head with apples by The Apple Bonkers (the apples being a shout out to The Beatles 'own Apple Corps. company).

2. Eleanor Rigby

Like the title track, this song has its origins in the 1966 *Revolver* album, and it was also the B-side to 'Yellow Submarine 'when it was released as a single. In the context of the film, this is played for a surrealistic introduction to the movie's incarnation of Liverpool, with animation that combines cel animation and stock photography, giving it a bit of a vibe similar to that of Terry Gilliam's animations in the Monty Python series.

3. Love You To

Another song from the *Revolver* album. An instrumental fragment of this tune is played when the animated incarnation of George Harrison is introduced, who happens to be in a room in Ringo Starr's mansion, with a photorealistic animated sky background. It's all in the mind y'know!

4. A Day In The Life

Originally from 1967's *Sgt. Pepper's Lonely Heart's Club Band*, a short section of this song (the orchestral climax section) is played when The Beatles and Fred pilot the Yellow Submarine for the first time, accompanied by zooming stock photos moving at very fast speed.

5. All Together Now

An original song with both John and Paul on vocals. Paul came up with the initial idea, and wrote the song's verses and chorus, while John contributed to the bridge section. A fun, sing-a-long children's song. The song reappears at the very end of the film, introduced by the real life Beatles, and with the lyrics put on screen, and the words 'All Together Now 'being translated into multiple languages.

6. When I'm Sixty-Four

Another song from *Sgt. Pepper's* - a nostalgia song, and funnily enough, one of the very first Lennon/McCartney compositions, written all the way back in The Quarrymen days. In the film, the band accidentally mess about with the space-time continuum while on the Yellow Submarine, which turns The Beatles and Fred into children, and eventually into senior citizens with oversized beards. We also get a caption that says 'sixty four years is 33,661,440 minutes and one minute is a long time', and then during the song's final minute we get a demonstration of this, with a new number appearing on screen every second.

7. Only A Northern Song

Another original song, this one sung and written by George. This tune is, funnily enough, a "diss" track, aimed at the Fab Four's publishing company, Northern Songs, who Harrison was expressing dissatisfaction towards. In the film, this song plays through the sequence where the band enter the Sea of Science. There is a scene featuring Warhol-esque pictures of the band accompanied with footage of an oscillator depicting sound waves of the track. Be warned, there is a lot of flashing imagery in this section.

8. Nowhere Man

Originally a song from the 1965 Beatles album *Rubber Soul*. In the film, the Nowhere Man is a creature named Jeremy Hillary Boob PHD, who our Fab Four would later befriend, but initially, they didn't take an interest in him because of his ultra-intelligence and eccentric personality. Boob is naturally upset by their taunting, but Ringo is more sympathetic, and offers to take him on board.

9. Lucy In The Sky With Diamonds

Another classic from the *Sgt. Pepper* album - despite tabloid rumours, this is NOT a song about LSD. In the film, we get to see a parade of "trippy" visuals, which aptly accompany the "druggy" nature of the song.

10. Think For Yourself (A Capella)

Initially a song from 1965's *Rubber Soul* LP, a brief repeated vocal-only portion of the line *"And you've got time to rectify"* is played to wake up the mayor of Pepperland after he got bashed by the Apple Bonkers.

11. Sgt. Pepper's Lonely Hearts Club Band

12. With A Little Help From My Friends

The first two tracks from probably the most famous of all Beatles albums. In the film, Sgt. Pepper's are, in fact, a real band, who reside in the land of Pepperland, who have been imprisoned in a giant sphere by the Blue Meanies, as the Blue Meanies really, really HATE music! To rally Pepperland into rebellion, The Beatles masquerade as Sgt. Pepper's Lonely Hearts Club Band, by singing the album's iconic title track, followed naturally by 'With A Little Help From My Friends'. This leads to a bit of a continuity error, as Billy Shears is played by John, even though on the album, Billy Shears is in fact

Ringo (you can even hear Ringo singing). In the movie's version of 'Pepper's', the *"It's wonderful to be here . . ."* bridge is actually spoken by John (played by John Clive).

13. All You Need Is Love

The summer of love anthem was a rather appropriate fit for this far-out psychedelic movie. In the film, John sings this song at the Dreadful Flying Glove, and peacefully attacks it, by having the words of the song's chorus literally come out of his mouth, and then retreating. The colours are finally restored to Pepperland!

14. Baby You're A Rich Man

The B-side to 'All Your Need Is Love', a small instrumental fragment of this song appears in a brief scene, where the hole Ringo found in the Sea Of Holes is used to free the real Sgt. Pepper's band from their bubble, which was set up by The Blue Meanies.

15. Hey Bulldog!

A really underrated and rocking song in The Beatles' canon, which only recently is getting the love it deserves. This was an original track, made especially for the film, and is a John composition. In the film, this song plays when The Beatles and Sgt. Pepper's Lonely Heart's Club Band mess with the mind of a four-headed blue dog. During the spoken word section, the actors didn't overdub John's voice and in this instance John Lennon is talking in his real voice.

16. It's All Too Much

The final original song for the movie, which was initially a *Sgt. Pepper* era outtake. Another underrated Beatle tune, written and sung by George, and in many ways it's a predecessor to acts like The Stone Roses and The Happy Mondays, and others in the British 'Madchester 'movement. In the film, this plays near the end, when The Blue Meanies finally accept defeat, and the whole of Pepperland celebrates with a sensory-overloading psychedelic freak-out party - Jeremy Boob and The Chief Blue Meanie even fall in love! The film's version differs from the one used in the soundtrack album, as it contains the line *"Nice to have the time to take this opportunity/Time for me to look at you and you to look at me"*, which isn't in the version used on the album, but it does appear in an eight-minute extended mono recording which has never been commercially released, but can be found on Beatles bootleg recordings.

Beatlefacts

* Allegedly one of the favourite movies of none other than Her Majesty (is a pretty nice girl) Queen Elizabeth II.

* While a big hit in America, the UK's response to the film was more critical, because of the press 'cynicism surrounding The Beatles' recent activities in India and their costly Apple Boutiques. It was shown in relatively few cinemas, and had decent but not earth-shattering box office returns.

* This film was an influence on the Japanese 1974 film *Space Battleship Yamato*, which in turn indirectly inspired films such as *Battlestar Galactica* and most notably the *Star Wars* franchise. Yep, no Beatles, no *Star Wars*!

* The co-founder of the famed Pixar movie studios, John Lasseter (*Toy Story, Cars* etc.) has credited *Yellow Submarine* with bringing more interest in animation as a serious art form, and he even wrote the liner notes in the 2012 DVD/Blu-Ray reissue.

* When the Yellow Submarine's motor breaks down, George comments that he knows something about motors - George's real life brother was, in fact, a mechanic.

* The actor who initially voiced George (Peter Batten) was a deserter from the British Army, and was consequently arrested. Paul Angelis, who voiced Ringo and the Chief Blue Meanie, had to fill his shoes and complete the rest of George's dialogue.

* The 'Hey Bulldog! 'song segment was originally missing in the US version of the film, due to rights issues - it was later restored in the 1999 rerelease.

* Paul Angelis, who voices Ringo, had a brother called Michael Angelis, who narrated the children's TV Series *Thomas The Tank Engine & Friends*; Michael Angelis replaced Ringo Starr as narrator for the show in 1991, who left due to concert commitments.

* One of the writers of the screenplay was an uncredited Roger McGough - a famous Liverpool poet, who was in the group The Scaffold with Paul McCartney's brother, Mike McGear.

Chapter Seven
Let It Be (1970)

Directed By - Michael Lindsay-Hogg
Produced By - Neil Aspinall
Release Date - May 20th 1970
Running Time - 81 Minutes

Summary

The premiere of the *Yellow Submarine* film was the final time all four Beatles attended a movie screening - by the time this film came out, none of them were there!

By late 1968, it was the beginning of the end, with the mood of the band becoming increasingly apathetic, and it shows. You would see a beloved rock band dissolve before your very eyes... unless you were Paul, who was pretty much the only member who wanted to keep going, although he was suggesting that they should return to the way things used to be. The rest of the band (especially John and George) were less than enthusiastic, but they halfheartedly went along with the idea of performing a one hour set consisting of eight songs in front of an audience for a live or taped television broadcast. The only question was where? Many ideas were discussed, such as a disused flour mill, a ship, a stage in the middle of the Sahara Desert, a huge Roman coliseum in the middle of North Africa, the planet Mars (maybe not the last one!), but they were all rejected. Denis O'Dell, who was appointed to produce this special, suggested that they should get started by rehearsing for The Beatles 'triumphant return to stage... even if they didn't have a finalised location to perform in!

Denis O'Dell was also the producer of the film *The Magic Christian* with Peter Sellers, coincidentally also starring Ringo, which was going to be filmed during February of 1969, and the band accepted his advice to rehearse at Twickenham Film Studios, agreeing to be filmed there for a possible TV documentary. In the director's chair was Michael Lindsay-Hogg, but as soon as the boys assembled at Twickenham, things were not looking good. *"The days were long and it could get boring, and Twickenham just really wasn't conducive to any great atmosphere. It was just a big barn,"* remembered Ringo in a

1995 interview. *"We were taking a long time and there were many heated discussions."* [12]

(Not so lovely) warts and all, everything was captured on film, such as Paul and George bickering, John and his future wife Yoko never more than two centimetres apart, and Ringo, poor Ringo, looking bored stiff. On the 10th January, George was getting increasingly fed up with it all, so he temporarily left the band... and he returned a few days later, but this time, the thought was, why not scrap the idea of a return to the stage, and just do an album? Within a matter of days, the concept of a live show to be broadcast on TV was axed, and they moved from Twickenham Film Studios to the new Apple Recording Studios with the intention of making a documentary of the creation of a new album. The title? *Get Back.*

Keeping the group together during this turbulent period, under Harrison's suggestion, was the fantastic funk and soul musician Billy Preston (who was also signed to their Apple Records, and had been a friend to The Beatles since the Hamburg days). When he was in the room, the attitude changed for the better, and the Beatles were on their best behaviour. By the end of January, somebody came up with the idea of doing an unannounced live performance at the rooftop of the Apple building - they could do this as a bit of free lunchtime entertainment for people working in the central London area, and despite some last minute reservations, all agreed to do this. On Thursday, 30th January 1969, The Beatles gave their final live performance, and it was epic - a fitting finale to the film, which was given the more wistful title of *Let It Be* (obviously named after the song of the same name) - and in the words of John at the end of the performance *"I'd like to say thank you on behalf of the group, and ourselves, and I hope we passed the audition."* They certainly did!

The film was in development hell for around a year because of the decaying state of the group, and it finally came out in May 1970, with the band even winning an Oscar for Best Original Song Score, but by then The Beatles were essentially "over". While not the most cheerful of Beatle movies, *Let It Be* serves as a great time capsule of the Fab Four's final phase before their eventual disbandment, but still, it's worth it for the roof top gig at the end! *"My cut of the movie would have been different,"* recalled Ringo in a 1994 interview. *"And I'm sure John's cut at the time would have been different - and Paul's cut. I thought there was a lot more interesting stuff than Michael Lindsay-Hogg put in."* [12]

After going through many revisions, the soundtrack album was released on the 18th May 1970, and was assembled and remixed by notorious American producer, Phil Spector, who added orchestral overdubs, interspersed the songs with studio chatter, and put choir overdubs on four of the tracks. The tune 'Don't Let Me Down '('Get Back''s B-side) was omitted from the track listing, and was replaced with a 1968 take of the song 'Across The Universe'. The Phil Spector additions in particular didn't impress Paul, and in 2003, Paul made his own revised version of the soundtrack entitled *Let It Be . . . Naked*. This version omitted the studio chatter, and removed most of the additions made by Spector, as well as removing the filler tracks, 'Dig It 'and a cover of the Liverpool folk song 'Maggie Mae'. The revised album did relatively well commercially, reaching No.5 in the US *Billboard* chart and No.7 in the UK albums chart, with the album selling over one million copies in America alone.

Because it doesn't show The Beatles in a good light, the film is also notorious for not having an official home video release since the 1980s, becoming a very popular item on the bootleg circuit. In 2021, an updated version called *The Beatles - Get Back* came out, directed by none other than Peter Jackson of *Lord Of The Rings* fame, whose purpose was to make a "happier" version of the film. In this remake, we are told that the mood of bitterness was actually somewhat exaggerated, and that the original version mainly focused on the unhappy times. Having seen a trailer for the 2021 film, it's great to see them all smiling and having a laugh - so it wasn't all doom and gloom at all!

Music Performed (Live)

1. **Paul's Piano Piece (inspired by Barber's 'Adagio For Strings')**
2. **Don't Let Me Down**
3. **Maxwell's Silver Hammer**
4. **Two Of Us**
5. **I've Got A Feeling**
6. **Oh! Darling**
7. **Just Fun**
8. **One After 909**
9. **Jazz Piano Song**
10. **Across The Universe**
11. **Dig A Pony**
12. **Suzy Parker**
13. **I Me Mine**

The initial part of the film was filmed at the start of January 1969 at Twicken-ham Film Studios, which was also where they filmed indoor shots for their first two feature films *A Hard Day's Night* and *Help!*, as well as the promo clip for 'Hey Jude 'and the brief live action segment in *Yellow Submarine*. Also in tow are roadie Mal Evans and John's wife-to-be Yoko Ono, who is at John's side at all times. All the songs were works in progress at the time, so it's interesting to see how these songs evolved. This phase of the 'Get Back/Let It Be 'sessions lasted from the 2nd-15th January 1969. Michael Lindsay-Hogg was in the director's chair, Tony Richmond was director of photography, and Glyn Johns, who was invited by Paul, was to oversee all the sound aspects. Even though he wasn't given a title as such, John Lennon was in fact the sound producer.

14. **For You Blue**
15. **Bésame Mucho**
16. **Octopus 'Garden**
17. **You've Really Got A Hold On Me**
18. **The Long and Winding Road**
19. **Rip It Up**
20. **Shake, Rattle And Roll**
21. **Kansas City**
22. **Miss Ann**
23. **Lawdy Miss Clawdy**
24. **Dig It**
25. **Let it Be**

It was evident that the atmosphere of Twickenham Film Studios wasn't working well, so recording moved back to Apple Recording Studios in Saville Row. To help soothe tensions, the funk/soul maestro Billy Preston (who they had known since Hamburg) joined them at the suggestion of George. This phase of the 'Get Back/Let It Be 'sessions started on the 22nd January 1969 and concluded on the 29th January 1969. As the initial title suggests, the boys decided to "get back" to basics with this album, forsaking all the pioneering techniques they had used in their more recent work, and playing every track live, even with the mistakes!

26. **Get Back**

The Beatles 'legendary final gig, which took place on the roof top of Apple HQ on January 30th 1969. As well as 'Get Back', we also hear 'Don't Let Me Down', 'I've Got A Feeling', 'One After 909', and 'Dig A Pony'. There were also a few songs which were cut from the film version of the concert. These included alternate takes of 'Get Back', 'I Want You (She's So Heavy) '(which would later be featured on the *Abbey Road* album), alternate versions of 'Don't Let Me Down 'and 'Dig A Pony', as well as covers of the traditional songs 'Danny Boy',' A Pretty Girl Is Like A Melody 'and the British national anthem 'God Save The Queen', while the band were fooling around between takes. Accompanying The Beatles at this show was Billy Preston playing electric piano. They brought part of London to a standstill, until the police brought the show to an enforced conclusion. The audio for this gig was recorded onto two eight-track recorders by studio engineer Alan Parsons, who would later form his own group, the prog-rock outfit The Alan Parsons Project.

Beatlefacts

* The movie received a U Rating (suitable for all ages) from the BBFC (British Board Of Film Classification) despite the song 'I Got A Feeling 'containing the line *"Everybody had a wet dream"* and some cussing.
* A VHS video release was planned in 1992, and was digitally remastered especially for this release, but was cancelled at the last minute. It was planned to be released again in 1997, only to be shelved once more.
* Peter Sellers visited The Beatles during this period, as shown in bootleg versions of the film.

Chapter Eight
The Promo Clips

As we all know, The Beatles pretty much pioneered everything from music to fashion to science - maybe not the latter, but you get what I'm saying, they pioneered everything!

They were also the innovators behind the music video, and here is how it came about (though saying that, music videos have been around in some form since the dawn of the talkies in the late 1920s!).

Back in 1964, they were filming *A Hard Day's Night* and the director, Richard Lester, had filmed The Beatles performing 'You Can't Do That 'at the Scala Theatre in London. This sequence was cut from the film, but while Lester was working on the film *The Knack...And How To Get It* in late 1964, he was approached by Ed Sullivan to forward the clip to his show. Lester didn't have time to edit the clip, with the editing duties being handed over to John Victor Smith, and the way he edited the footage was compelling, and was influential on the way music videos are edited today.

This clip would prove to be a life-saver in the long-run, as they figured out if they could make a spiffy promo clip instead of physically appearing on a show, they could save money and time; plus they were getting increasingly fed up with the frequency of these appearances, and the whole Beatlemania thing, which was getting out of hand. This was considered very unusual for the time period, and in many ways could be considered an apology for not appearing in the flesh. Press agent Tony Barrow stated *"The boys would normally have appeared on television themselves to plug their new single, but they have been busy preparing an entirely new stage act, featuring all new numbers from their forthcoming album for their tour"*. [8]

Day Tripper/We Can Work It Out/Ticket To Ride/I Feel Fine/Help! (1965)

Directed By - Joe McGrath
Release Date - December 2nd 1965

As stated previously, this was made as The Beatles were increasingly fed up with having to appear on TV shows like *Top Of The Pops*. The promo clips for these classic songs were filmed at Twickenham Film Studios in London on the 23rd November 1965. On that day, they filmed promo clips for their double A-side single 'Day Tripper/We Can Work It Out', as well as performing previous hit singles 'I Feel Fine', 'Ticket To Ride 'and 'Help!'. All these clips were lip-synced to the studio versions (John has fun with this on the 'Ticket To Ride 'clip).

"They were the first independently produced pop films to be made and distributed specifically for the international market, anticipating the beginning of contemporary pop video," says film scholar, Bob Neaverson. *"Moreover, while their ultimate raison d'être closely mirrors that of the group's move into feature films, so does their form. Unlike the performance-oriented construction of contemporary pop shows, several of McGrath's promos partially disposed of this notion, the most notable example being the 'I Feel Fine ' clip, which features the group miming into a punch-bag while Ringo rides an exercise bicycle."* [8]

The clips for 'Day Tripper 'and 'We Can Work It Out 'had their premiere on *Top Of The Pops* on the 2nd December 1965, with extracts from the other promo clips filmed in that session appearing on the 25th December edition. The 'Day Tripper 'and 'We Can Work It Out 'promo clips had their American television debut on the show *Hullaballoo* but the 'I Feel Fine 'segment didn't get a US screening until 1993, when Apple Music provided MTV with copies of these clips to promote a CD re-release of the compilation *The Beatles 1962-1966*.

Paperback Writer/Rain (1966)

Directed By - Michael-Lindsay Hogg
Release Date - May 30th 1966

The promo clips for 'Paperback Writer 'and 'Rain 'were shot on 35mm colour film at Chiswick House in West London, which dates back to the 18th century, and they were shot in and around the conservatory in the grounds of the house. The Beatles were filmed outside the gates and under a cedar tree as well as performing with some children, who played with the branches. A notable fact about these clips is that The Beatles 'performances show them slowly phasing out their cheery mum-friendly "mop-top" image and opting for a more cool and detached appearance.

After the film shoot, John and his first wife, Cynthia, attended a party with Rolling Stone Mick Jagger and his then-girlfriend Chrissie Shrimpton (sister of the famous model, Jean Shrimpton). The 'Paperback Writer 'clip debuted on BBC 1's *Top Of The Pops* on the 2nd June, while 'Rain 'was shown a week later on the 9th June. Despite being made in colour, ironically they were shown in black and white.

Michael-Lindsay Hogg was an experienced TV director, whose credits included the weekly music television series *Ready, Steady, Go!* in which The Beatles appeared several times. Presumably because of their numerous appearances on the show, Hogg was hired to direct these films.

Beatlefacts

* If you notice in these clips, poor Paul chipped a tooth. This was because he fell while driving a moped – ouch!
* .euqinhcet taht esu ot drocer tsrif eht - sdrawkcab dias saw *"Sdeah reiht edih dna nur yeht"* enil eht, 'niaR 'nI

Strawberry Fields Forever (1967)

Directed By - Peter Goldmann
Release Date - February 17th 1967

"Psychoanalysis set to music," to quote John - 'Strawberry Fields Forever' was part of a double A-side single with Paul McCartney's chipper 'Penny Lane'. Both songs are nostalgic reflections of John and Paul's childhood in Liverpool. The actual Strawberry Fields (or Strawberry Field, notice no "s") is the name of a Salvation Army Children's Home near John's childhood house in Woolton. The track was, like every other Beatle single, a massive hit, but is infamous for being kept off the top spot thanks to middle-of-the-road crooner Englebert Humperdink's 'Release Me'.

Shot on the 30th January 1967 at Knole Park, which is in Sevenoaks in Kent, it was filmed in 35mm colour by Don Long Productions, a London based film crew. Swede Peter Goldmann, who directed this, was hired on the suggestion of longtime Beatle friend Klaus Voorman. Interestingly, there is a Knole Park in Liverpool that's just a short distance away from the actual Strawberry Field(s) that inspired the song. There was going to be a sequence where Macca was supposed to drop down from a dead oak tree, but because of poor lighting, that idea had to be scrapped, and in the finished film, the clip was reversed to make it look like he leapt onto the tree. It was also during this shoot that Lennon bought the circus poster that helped inspire the *Sgt. Pepper* track 'Being For The Benefit Of Mr. Kite!'.

"Originally, my enthusiasm for presenting English groups on TV in Sweden was fired by Dick Lester's fine film of the Beatles in 'A Hard Day's Night'," reminisces the film's director, Peter Goldmann. *"I thought that was*

fantastic and wanted to try to present this music in an original and interesting manner on TV." [8]

As well as being one of my very favourite Beatle tunes, the clip is really awesome, not to mention very trippy. I love the rather random sequence where The Beatles paint a piano for no particular reason.

Penny Lane (1967)

Directed By - Peter Goldmann
Release Date - February 17th 1967

While John's 'Strawberry Fields Forever' was a trippy and dark tribute to a childhood landmark, Paul's track was the antithesis, and was a very upbeat, chipper tune, more celebratory in tone. Shot in the actual Penny Lane in Liverpool, it was also filmed around Angel Lane in Salford, East London. The clips on Angel Lane featured the band riding around on horseback, and were filmed on the 5th February. More filming was done on Knole Park, where the 'Strawberry Fields' promo video was filmed, and featured the boys in red tunics, sitting at a table and drinking tea, rather like the Mad Hatter's Tea Party. They are presented with their instruments by two attendants (one of them being played by their roadie and buddy, Mal Evans).

A great tune with a great video.

A Day In The Life (1967)

Directed By - The Beatles
Release Date - May 26th 1967

Ahh - the epic grand finale track from The Beatles 'grandiose masterpiece of an album *Sgt. Pepper's Lonely Hearts Club Band*! What can I say about it that hasn't already been said before? Inspired by stories John read in newspapers of the time, and Paul recalling his youth, riding on the bus, having a ciggie and going to class, climaxing with John saying *"I'd Love To Turn You On"* followed by an orchestrated orgasm and then... Duuuuunnnnnnnn!!!!!... and then a dog whistle and some weird gibberish!

It doesn't get much better than this! A record so good, it was banned by the BBC!

The video, on the other hand, is basically The Beatles and their Beatle buddies, Donovan, Mal Evans, Mick Jagger and Keith Richards from The Rolling Stones, Patti Boyd (George's wife at the time) and an orchestra, in the studio, interspersed with some psychedelic effects, random footage, and the orchestra themselves in funny fancy dress disguises (much to their annoyance)... about as crazy and left-field as the tune itself. Awesome!

Hello Goodbye (1967)

Directed By - Paul McCartney
Release Date - November 24th 1967

The cheerful flip side to the classic double A-side with John's more psychedelic 'I Am The Walrus '(Goo-goo-g-joob!). The song was actually inspired by a response to a question from Beatle aide Alistair Taylor. Paul asked Taylor to say the opposite of whatever he said.

The video was directed by none other than Macca himself and was filmed at the Saville Theatre in London. It begins with them in their *Sgt. Pepper* uniforms, and as a nostalgia throwback, we cut to them in their classic 1963-era matching collarless suits. During the "*Heba, heba hello-ah*" bit, female hula dancers join them on stage. Macca's intention behind the video was to undermine the BBC's regulations against musicians lip-syncing on TV, though the BBC noted that they were obviously not playing the song live.

Two alternate versions of the video exist - one features them in more conventional clothes, while the other features them performing behind a glitter pastel backdrop.

Beatlefacts

* According to film editor Roy Benson, who edited The Beatles TV movie *Magical Mystery Tour*, the Fab Four wanted to use outtakes from *MMT* for the 'Hello Goodbye 'promo clip, which included footage shot at the luncheon at the Atlantic Hotel and footage shot in Nice in France. The footage to this day remains unseen.

Lady Madonna (1968)

Directed By - Tony Bramwell
Release Date - March 14th 1968

After the crazy psychedelia of 1967, 1968's first Beatles single 'Lady Madonna 'was more "poppy" and conventional, with a bit of a Fats Domino vibe to it. The music video for this song was shot on the 11th February 1968 at EMI Studios, and documents them recording 'Hey Bulldog! 'from the *Yellow Submarine* soundtrack, while having some fun studio larks at the same time. Not much to report from a music video perspective, but the song is great nonetheless, plus it's the final time all four Beatles are clean-shaven.

Filming for this clip was shot by Denis O'Dell, a big player in Apple Records, who recalls the editing process by saying *"We tried to edit the footage so that it echoed the rhythm of 'Lady Madonna '(which wasn't too difficult since the songs have roughly similar tempos)"* [8]

The clip premiered on the March 14th 1968 edition of BBC1's *Top Of The Pops* and was shown again on the following day's edition of *All Systems Freeman*. Despite the BBC's rules at the time restricting lip-synced performances, they were able to show this, as they were not seen miming 'Lady Madonna ' and were actually playing 'Hey Bulldog!'.

Hey Jude/Revolution (1968)

Directed By - Michael Lindsay-Hogg
Release Date - August 26th 1968

Everybody knows the classic 'Hey Jude', so there is no need to cover the tune for the thousandth time, and 'Revolution '- that is one epic track! Michael-Lindsay Hogg (who directed 'Paperback Writer/Rain 'and would later direct the *Let It Be* movie) was hired to direct the promotional clips for these two songs. For 'Hey Jude', they settled on having it with a live, albeit controlled, audience (so no screaming teenage girls!). The 'Revolution 'video, however, had no audience, and actually uses a different take to that of the single release, with Paul and George adding *"shoo-bee-doo-wap"* backing vocals. 'Hey Jude 'premiered on *Frost On Sunday* on the ITV network, while 'Revolution ' debuted on *Top Of The Pops* on the 19th September 1968.

Beatlefacts:
* 'Hey Jude 'is the bestselling Beatles single of all time, selling over 6 million copies in the first three months after the single's initial release date.
* Initially, film editor Rory Benson was asked to design and storyboard a promotional clip for 'Hey Jude', which contained 38 elaborate scenes. This was vetoed by The Beatles, as the shoot would take 3 days.
* To get past the BBC's "no lip syncing" policy, The Beatles filmed a special introduction for the clips when it premiered on *The David Frost Show*, to give the false impression that they were actually playing live.

The Ballad of John and Yoko (1969)

Directed By - Unknown
Release Date - April 14th 1969

John and Yoko - 1969's favourite celebrity couple. John wrote this song while he and Ocean Child were on their honeymoon in "Gay Paris". It talks about their wedding and their famous bed-in activities for Peace at the Amsterdam Hilton. The song received some minor controversy for the lines *"Christ, you know it ain't easy"* and *"they're gonna crucify me!"*, which upset some people in the Bible Belt regions of America.

The video is basically clips of J&Y lounging about in a limousine, The Beatles jamming during the 'Get Back 'sessions, J&Y hanging about in Paris and Amsterdam and J&Y being interviewed. If you're a fan of J&Y, you'll enjoy this one!

Beatlefacts:

* The Ballad Of John & Yoko 'is technically not a Beatles song, as the only Beatles playing on that tune are John and Paul, with Paul on drumming duties.

Something (1969)

Directed By - Neil Aspinall
Release Date - 1969

George Harrison's 'Something 'was one of the highlights of their grand finale album *Abbey Road*, and like 'Yesterday', it has seen its fair share of cover versions from the likes of Frank Sinatra, James Brown, Shirley Bassey, Ike & Tina Turner, Isaac Hayes, Martha Reeves and even the guy that prevented 'Strawberry Fields Forever 'from reaching No.1, Englebert Humperdink!

Directed by their long time friend, Neil Aspinall, the promo clip for this tune was shot in late October 1969, but by this stage, The Beatles were crumbling away, and the film consisted of clips of each Beatle walking around John Lennon's house, accompanied by their respective wife of the time. The usually very handsome Paul McCartney looked a little worse for wear, as he was going through depression, because of the realisation that The Beatles were on their way out. Thanks to clever editing, Aspinall avoided showing the fact that no two Beatles were seen together; as we all know, the end was nigh. It's an incredibly beautiful song, even if Ol 'Blue Eyes thought it was written by Lennon & McCartney!

Back In The U.S.S.R. (1976)

Directed By - Unknown
Release Date - 1976

Made to promote the Beatles compilation *Rock 'n 'Roll Music* in 1976, this promo clip showed The Beatles in 1964, despite the song being recorded in 1968. Footage shown included their arrivals in America, Australia, Liverpool and the Netherlands. A fun, nostalgic look at the heyday of Beatlemania, showing their impact on large gatherings of hysterical screaming teenage girls, and even some hysterical screaming teenage guys!

Baby It's You (1994)

Directed By - Unknown
Release Date - 1994

Made to promote the Beatles CD *Live At The BBC* in 1994, this was a BBC Live recording of the Shirelles song 'Baby It's You', as covered by The Beatles on their 1963 debut album *Please Please Me*, which was also released as a single, reaching the surprisingly healthy position of No.7 in the UK singles chart. Nothing too amazing, music video-wise, mainly showing The Beatles travelling around Britain in a Volkswagen circa 1963, and their photoshoot which was used for the cover of the *Live At The BBC* album sleeve.

Free As a Bird (1995)

Directed By - Joe Pytka
Release Date - December 4th 1995

AKA Easter eggs - The music video.
For those who were not aware, The Beatles actually "reformed" in the early 1990s as part of *The Beatles Anthology* project, and produced two new recordings using old demo tapes of John Lennon jamming on his grand piano in the Dakota Building in New York in the late 1970s. The first song from this was 'Free As A Bird', originally made in 1977, but remixed in 1994, and it came out in December 1995. While not getting rave reviews by critics, it was a big commercial success going top 10 worldwide, and it even won a Grammy in 1997 for Best Pop Performance By A Duo Or Group With Vocal.

The highlight of the song is in fact the music video, and if you are a die-hard Beatle nut who knows almost everything about The Beatles, you will love it! It is told through the first person point of view of a bird in flight (which is actually never seen in the video), containing 80-100 allusions to the Beatles story. Directed by Joe Pytka, who had previously worked with the likes of Michael Jackson, it was shot on location in Liverpool, and we get to see iconic Beatle locations such as the Penny Lane roundabout and Strawberry Field(s), and thanks to some clever digital editing, the contemporary footage was interspersed with historical Beatles footage from the 1960s.

Because of the song's atmospheric nature, one notable exclusion from the video is footage of screaming hysterical teenage girls, or The Beatles trying to escape from a mob of said-fans.

The video won the Grammy for Best Short Form Music Video in 1996.

Real Love (1996)

Directed By - Kevin Godley (of 10cc and Godley and Crème fame)
Release Date - March 4th 1996

The second of the two Beatles "reunion" singles created for *The Beatles Anthology* project. Basically a compilation of archive clips of The Beatles, interspersed with new footage of the "Threetles" recording the song circa 1995. The video played upon the theme of resurrection, by having many iconic Beatle related objects such as the *Sgt. Pepper* costumes, and notably having instruments such as John Lennon's white grand piano flying above Liverpool, and Paul McCartney's Hofner bass ascending into the sky (with diamonds).

Come Together (2000)

Directed By - Christophe Branche and Alexander Gainer
Release Date - November 13th 2000

Produced by the company Melon Dezign. This CGI animated video was made using a cel-animation technique (think the Nintendo video game 'The Legend of Zelda - The Wind Waker') for The Beatles '1969 classic 'Come Together'. It was done to promote and celebrate the release of The Beatles 'bestselling compilation album *1*.

Within You Without You/Tomorrow Never Knows (2006)

Directed By - Simon Helton
Release Date - November 20th 2006

A mashup of two classic Beatles songs created for the Cirque De Solei show 'Love 'made in 2006. A promo video was made, which interspersed footage of previous Beatles music videos.

Chapter Nine
Beatle Documentaries and Specials

Over the years, as you would expect with such a successful group, there have been countless documentaries about The Beatles. They vary in terms of length, informality and general quality: some were produced with direct involvement from members of The Beatles, while others were unauthorised, with some being of "bargain basement" quality. These cheap documentaries (usually budget DVD releases) contain many factual errors, and interviews from people with passing involvement in The Beatles 'story, not to mention no actual music from The Beatles themselves. Arguably the best documentary would have to be 1995's multi-part *The Beatles Anthology*, which is of course authorised by the band themselves, and has more or less all the essential information you'll need if you want to learn the story of the Fab Four.

As well as the documentaries, in this chapter I will also be including notable TV specials that have been made about The Beatles. Some of these are very informative, and very much worth checking out.

With a few notable exceptions, this book will only contain documentaries that are either authorised by the band, or feature non-archival interviews from either John, Paul, George or Ringo - otherwise we could be here all day!

It's The Beatles (1963)

First Broadcast - December 7th 1963

A recording for BBC TV of their performance at the Empire Theatre in their hometown of Liverpool, with the screaming somewhat less audible, so you can actually hear them! Songs performed on the night included 'From Me To You', 'I Saw Her Standing There', 'All My Loving', 'Roll Over Beethoven', 'Boys', 'Till There Was You', 'She Loves You', "This Boy', 'I Want To Hold Your Hand', 'Money 'and 'Twist and Shout'. Thankfully, this one got spared from the BBC archives grim reaper!

The Beatles Come to Town (1963)

Release Date - December 22nd 1963
Running Time - 8 Minutes

Short Pathe newsreel clip that was shown in cinemas, which documents a performance of our Fab Four gigging at the ABC Cinema in Manchester on the 20th November 1963, performing 'She Loves You 'and 'Twist and Shout 'to a crowd of screaming teenagers, as well as some great backstage footage too. Narrated by someone with a very charming R.P. accent (Received Pronunciation AKA the Queen's English) - a great time capsule of the era.

Beatlefacts

* United Artists, who distributed The Beatles' films, acquired this short subject film in 1964, and it was a support feature with the film *For Those Who Thank You*, shown before the Beatles' debut film *A Hard Day's Night* in the US.

Yeah! Yeah! Yeah! The Beatles in New York (1964)

Directed By - David Maysles
First Broadcast - February 12th 1964
Running Time - 40 Minutes

A short documentary by Granada Television about The Beatles 'initial trip on American soil, which was broadcast on UK television. Footage of this documentary would later be recycled in the US CBS documentary film *What's Happening! The Beatles In The U.S.A.*, which was broadcast the following November.
This programme is still in the archives.

Around The Beatles (1964)

Directed By - Rita Gillespie
First Broadcast - May 6th 1964
Running Time - 52 Minutes

This was a television variety special produced by Jack Good for ITV/Rediffusion, videotaped at Wembley Park Studios (now Fountain Studios) in London on the 28th April 1964, and broadcast on the 6th May. It was shown in America on ABC on the 15th November.

This special opens with an image of the Globe Theatre in London with Ringo unfurling a flag which reads 'Around The Beatles'. The studio is arranged like a theatre in the round (which explains the name of the special). The show officially opens with a reenactment of 'Pyramus and Thisbe '(Act 5, Scene 1) from William Shakespeare's *A Midsummer Night's Dream* with Macca playing Pyramus, John as Thisbe, George as Moonshine and Ringo as Lion, as well as actor Trevor Peacock as Quince. Other acts to appear in this special included Long John Baldry, P.J. Proby, The Vernons Girls, Cilla Black, Sounds Incorporated and Millie Small.

The special has never seen a home video release outside of bootlegs, but segments do appear in *The Beatles Anthology* documentary film, as well as sections appearing on Laserdisc as *Ready Steady Go! Special Edition - The Beatles Live*.

Beatlefacts

*   All the music for the show had been pre-recorded and The Beatles mimed during the show.
*   Long John Baldry, who appears in this special, would later become a voice actor for cartoons - most notably his memetic role as Dr. Robotnik in *The Adventures of Sonic The Hedgehog*, based on the very popular Sonic The Hedgehog video games.

The Beatles In Nederland (1964)

First Broadcast - June 8th 1964
Running Time - 40 Minutes

Focusing on The Fab Four's trip to the Netherlands in 1964, Ringo, who was ill with tonsillitis, was replaced by a man named Jimmie Nichol. We also get to see footage of them (sans Ringo) perform at the Cafe Restaurant Treslong in Hillegom, as well as a clip of the band answering a Q&A session, with John Lennon referring to himself as John Leopard! There were loads of technical hitches, as their actual vocals could be heard during their lip-sync performances, and the stage ended up being surrounded by girls wanting to hug and kiss them, so their roadies, Neil Aspinall and Mal Evans, and press agent Derek Taylor had to come in and save the day - with little success!

92

Beatles At The Stadium (1964)

Directed By - Unknown
Release Date - June 25th 1964

The Beatles 'first ever theatrical "film" preceding *A Hard Day 's Night* by one month - yes, I am not making this up! Released only in Australia, this was a recording of The Beatles 'three nights of performances at the Rushcutter's Bay Stadium in Sydney in Australia, which took place between the 18th and 20th June 1964. Opening literally five days after their third performance, exclusively at Wyngard and State Theatrettes in Sydney, the adverts for the film boasted: *'Hear them sing excerpts from their five greatest hits including 'She Loves You', 'Love Me Do', 'I Want To Hold Your Hand 'and more"*, which is false advertising, as 'Love Me Do 'wasn't on their set list during this particular tour.

This rare film has since however resurfaced on the bootleg circuit.

The Beatles Sing For Shell (1964)

Directed By - Denis deVallance and Ian Holmes
First Broadcast - July 1st 1964
Running Time - 60 Minutes

A recording of the sixth and final show of The Beatles 'tour in Melbourne in Australia on the 17th June 1964. The programme was named after the oil company, Shell (talk about selling out!), and we also get to see footage of their support act, Sounds Incorporated. Be warned, this programme contains John Lennon's ghastly impression of "cripples" when Paul asks the audience to clap their hands and stomp their feet. John might be a musical genius, but he sure did have a cruel sense of humour!

This programme is available on the bootleg circuit.

The Road To Beatlemania (1964)

First Broadcast - July 15th 1964

Broadcast on ITV and produced by ATV, very little is known about this documentary, and information about it is scarce. As it was broadcast around the time of *A Hard Day 's Night*'s premiere, I am presuming that the content of this programme would have had a strong focus on their debut feature film. The archival status of this film is unknown.

Follow The Beatles (1964)

Directed By - Richard Lester
First Broadcast - August 3rd 1964
Running Time - 25 Minutes

A behind-the-scenes look at The Beatles 'first major foray onto the big screen - *A Hard Day's Night*. Made for BBC television and narrated by Robert Robinson, we get to see a very interesting take on how the film was made, and learn that the Beatles were constantly grabbed and pushed around by fans and onlookers and even the police who were involved in the film, but the screenwriter, Allen Owen, was astonished at how calm they were about the situation and how they just went with it.

Unlike many programmes made for the BBC at the time, this one survived the infamous programme cull of the 1970s, which led to the destruction of many priceless TV shows.

Our Fair Beatles (1964)

First Broadcast - September 8th 1964

A look at The Beatles 'first tour of America, which aired on a station called WISH-TV, showing them performing at the Indianapolis State Fair Coliseum, answering questions, and meeting a local beauty queen. It is very rare, and copies are hard to come by.

The Beatles Live At The Washington Coliseum (1964)

First Broadcast - November 2nd 1964

A recording of The Beatles 'first concert on American soil at the Washington Coliseum - a massive boxing arena - to a large crowd of 8,092 fans. They performed 12 songs which included 'Roll Over Beethoven', 'From Me To You', 'I Saw Her Standing There', 'This Boy', 'All My Loving', 'I Wanna Be Your Man', 'Please Please Me', 'Till There Was You', 'She Loves You', 'I Want To Hold Your Hand', 'Twist and Shout 'and 'Long Tall Sally'. As the band were playing in the middle of the arena, The Beatles and their roadie, Mal Evans, had to move their equipment round after every few songs, so that the screaming girls could see them.

Many Beatle fans threw jelly beans at them, after a New York newspaper had reported The Beatles 'love of them... though in reality, their sweetie delicacy of choice was actually the much softer jelly babies. Because of jelly beans being so hard, it was a very frustrating experience. George Harrison recalled *"That night, we were absolutely pelted by the f***in 'things. They don't have soft jelly babies there; they have hard jelly beans. We don't mind them throwing streamers, but jelly beans are a bit dangerous, you see! Every now and again, one would hit a string on my guitar and plonk off a bad note as I was trying to play."* [9]

What's Happening! The Beatles In The U.S.A. AKA The Beatles: The First U.S. Visit (1964)

Directed By - Albert and David Maysles
First Broadcast - December 14th 1964
Running Time - 81 Minutes

Also known as *The Beatles: The First U.S. Visit*, this documentary is about The Beatles 'first trip to America in February 1964, documenting their travels to New York, Washington and Miami, and incorporates clips of them clowning around in front of the camera. The documentary was re-edited in 1990 to include footage of their performances on *The Ed Sullivan Show*, while removing some scenes with Brian Epstein. The film is still being shown at various movie festivals to this day, and is available on DVD.

The Music Of Lennon & McCartney (1965)

Directed By - Phillip Casson
First Broadcast - December 17th 1965
Running Time - 55 Minutes

Following on from The Beatles receiving their MBEs, this was a fun, but slightly corny, ITV Granada Television special celebrating the music of the greatest song writing team of all time (duh!) - John Lennon and Paul McCartney. Awkwardly hosted by John and Paul themselves, this special featured a very eclectic selection of Beatles covers from the likes of Peter and Gordon, Dick Rivers, Lulu, Fritz Spiegl, Billy J. Kramer, Cilla Black and even comedian Peter Sellers. The Beatles themselves perform two numbers - 'Day Tripper '(accompanied by go-go dancers) and they closed the show with 'We Can Work It Out'. Thankfully, this special has survived the infamous TV pro-

gramme culls that took place in Britain during the 1970s, and it was rebroadcast again in 1985 on Channel 4 as part of an evening of programmes celebrating 30 Years of Granada Television.

The Beatles at Shea Stadium (1966)

Directed By - Robert Precht
First Broadcast - March 1st 1966
Running Time - 48 Minutes

I think most Beatle fans will have heard of their legendary appearance at Shea
Stadium in New York, which took place on the 15th August 1965 to a massive
audience of 55,600 people. It was the centrepiece of the their 1965 tour, and
arguably the most famous of all the Beatles concerts (that or the rooftop gig
in 1969). In 1966, a TV documentary was made, following the whole event,
from their helicopter ride from Manhattan to Flushing Meadows, to their prep-
aration in the dressing room (which was actually the visiting baseball team's
locker), even including some clips of the opening acts, which included Brenda
Holloway, King Curtis, Sounds Incorporated and Killer Joe Piro & The Dis-
cotheque Dancers (Marvin Gaye was scheduled to support, but sadly didn't
show up - shame, and The Young Rascals and Cannibal & The Headhunters'
appearances were cut from the film). In attendance were Rolling Stones Mick
Jagger and Keith Richards, Ringo's future wife, Barbra Bach, Paul's future
wife, Linda Eastman, and even a young Whoopi Goldberg. Introduced by Ed
Sullivan, The Beatles came on stage, and the screams were REALLY loud,
and they performed a fantastic 30 minute set, even if they could not really hear
themselves. John in particular had an amazing time, notably when he used his
elbows during the organ solo in 'I'm Down! 'Songs played were 'Twist and
Shout', 'She's A Woman '(not included in the film), 'I Feel Fine', 'Dizzy
Miss Lizzy', 'Ticket To Ride', 'Everybody's Trying To Be My Baby '(not included in the film), 'Can't Buy Me Love', 'Baby's In Black', 'Act Naturally',
'A Hard Day's Night', 'Help! 'and as previously stated 'I'm Down'.

Despite VOX creating special amplifiers for the show, the sound system
was pretty ineffective and inadequate, and the audio came from the in-house
speakers making it sound "tinny". The audio for the gig had to go though a lot
of re-editing and post production, as some had to be either overdubbed or re-
recorded entirely at the CTS studio in London to cover up audio issues.

It's really worth a watch, to experience what it was like to see The Beatles
performing at the absolute peak of Beatlemania.

The Beatles Recital from Nippon Budokan Tokyo (1966)

First Broadcast - July 1st 1966
Running Time - 30 Minutes

A recording of The Beatles 'one-and-only tour in the land of the rising sun. There was a lot of controversy with them playing at the Budokan, as it was considered a sacred martial arts venue, and people saw it as sacrilegious. Despite massive security and reported death threats, the concert went ahead. Ironically, the venue is now one of Japan's premier music venues!

Die Beatles Und Ausschnitte Aus Dem Rahmenprogramm Inter Deutschlandtournee (1966)

Directed By - Helmut Rost
First Broadcast - July 5th 1966
Running Time - 45 Minutes

Despite the title of this documentary being very long, translated into English it's *The Beatles In Germany 1966 - Musical Documentary*. The Fab Four return a little older and a little wiser to the country that gave them their initial big break, and we get to see them perform in Munich, Essen and of course Hamburg (though in much nicer venues, and for MUCH shorter sets and a lot more moolah!). We also get some good footage of them doing one of their iconic amusing press conferences, as well as footage of their support acts, Cliff Bennett and the Rebel Rousers, Peter and Gordon, and The Rattles (not the be confused with the famous Beatles parody group, The Rutles!).

Damals In Hamburg - The Beatles (1967)

Directed By - Thomas Struck
First Broadcast - January 6th 1967
Running Time - 30 Minutes

A German documentary about The Beatles 'early years performing at the Star Club and the Top Ten Club in Hamburg, Germany. It contains interviews with the likes of Bettina Derlien, who was a bartender at the Star Club, as well as Hans-Walther Braun, who was a friend of The Beatles during the Hamburg days. Information on this documentary is scarce, and copies of the film have not resurfaced outside of rare private screenings in its native Germany.

All My Loving (1968)

Me with the legendary film director, Tony Palmer, who directed many projects The Beatles were involved with, and who was a friend of John Lennon.

Directed By - Tony Palmer
First Broadcast - April 19th 1968
Running Time - 55 Minutes

Directed by John Lennon's good friend, Tony Palmer, this controversial documentary about the 1960s music scene features interviews from all four Beatles, and also features Jimi Hendrix, Cream, Donovan, The Who, The Moody Blues, Pink Floyd, as well as Beatles inner circle members George Martin, Derek Taylor, Maharishi Mahesh Yogi and George's mum, Louise Harrison.

It was infamous for splicing the music clips with footage of the political up-
heaval of the time, and some shock imagery, which included a Buddhist monk
setting himself on fire, and some rather graphic Vietnam War footage.

Beatlefacts

*   The documentary is, of course, named after The Beatles song of the
same name from the 1963 album *With The Beatles*.
*   The Beatles footage from this documentary would be recycled in a later
Palmer documentary, 1977's *All You Need Is Love*.

Apple (1968)

Directed By - Tony Bramwell
Release Date - August 26th 1968
Running Time - 10 Minutes

This is a behind-the-scenes look at the offices of the Beatles 'Apple Company,
which had just recently formed at the time. As well as getting clips of Paul
recording 'Blackbird 'and an acoustic version of 'Helter Skelter 'from *The
White Album*, we get some clips of Paul and John in a boardroom meeting, as
well as appearances from their protégées, Mary Hopkin, James Taylor and,
more infamously, Magic Alex. We also get some footage of their Apple Boutique on Paddington Street as well.

The Beatles 'Mod Odyssey (1968)

Release Date - October 12th 1968
Running Time - 7 Minutes

A short "modyssey" about the making of the greatest film The Beatles never
made - *Yellow Submarine*. We get interviews from the animation staff, such
as George Dunning and Heinz Edelmann, as well as some clips of The Beatles
in the recording studio performing 'Hey Bulldog!', and footage of them promoting the film, as well as the animation staff working on the feature.

With A Little Help From My Friends (1969)

Release Date - December 14th 1969
Running Time - Unknown

An ITV tribute to the man who would easily be considered the fifth member of The Beatles - producer George Martin. Ringo Starr appeared in the flesh, performing the rather divisive 'Octopus 'Garden 'from the *Abbey Road* album, backed by some session musicians, as obviously, The Beatles were not on good terms at the time, and were on the verge of disbanding. Also appearing on the show were Dudley Moore, The Hollies, Blue Mink, Lulu, comedian Spike Milligan and the female dance troupe Pan's People - a collective responsible for many a happy teenage memory. George Martin himself appears conducting the 40-piece George Martin Orchestra.

Sadly, this programme is currently not in the TV archives.

A Salute To The Beatles: Once Upon A Time AKA David Frost Salutes The Beatles (1975)

Directed By - David Frost
First Broadcast - May 21st 1975
Running Time - 60 Minutes

Hosted by David Frost, this 1975 television special for ABC is a documentary that chronicles the life of the Fab Four, and is one of the few to be made during John Lennon's lifetime. It was one of the first TV projects to explore the history of The Beatles in great detail, and contained interviews with people like producer George Martin, press officer Derek Taylor and roadie Mal Evans, in a very rare interview before his tragic death in 1976, as well as commentaries from the likes of Chuck Berry, David Essex and Bobby Vinton.

The special has never seen a home video release, but has been circulating on the black market.

All You Need Is Love (1977)

Directed By - Tony Palmer
Written By - Derek Taylor
First Broadcast - May 14th 1977
Running Time - 60 Minutes

All You Need Is Love is a 17-part documentary series by legendary director and friend of The Beatles, Tony Palmer, tracing the development of 20th century popular music in all its forms (up to 1977 that is, as the series was broadcast that year, so no punk or hip-hop!). Episode 13 is entitled 'Mighty Good: The Beatles 'and, as you would expect, has a strong focus on the Fab Four. The documentary features interviews with Beatle people such as John Lennon and Paul McCartney (originally from a previous Palmer documentary *All My Loving*), Allan Williams (their first promoter), press officer Derek Taylor and, in a very rare interview, Queenie Epstein (Brian's Mum). It mainly focuses on the early years, ending with the death of Brian Epstein in 1967.

As well as The Beatles, we also learn about The Animals 'hit record 'House Of The Rising Sun', The Monterey Pop Festival, Jane Fonda's Birthday Party, and other acts on the Mersey Beat scene.

Beatlefacts

* As stated previously, John Lennon was a good friend of the film's director, Tony Palmer, hence the title of the series, *All You Need Is Love*.

The Compleat Beatles (1982)

Directed By - Patrick Montgomery
Release Date - May 28th 1982
Running Time - 120 Minutes

Before *Anthology* came long, this was the definitive documentary film on John, Paul, George and Ringo. Narrated by British actor Malcolm McDowell (best known for playing Alex from *A Clockwork Orange*), it contains many interviews with diverse people from the Beatle entourage such as George Martin, Billy Preston, Tony Sheridan and even their first manager, Allan Williams. It also contains some great live footage, and some rare photographs, making this a must watch.

Despite the documentary being successful and even being released theatrically, the movie has never seen a commercial home video release since the 1980s. It has however resurfaced on the bootleg circuit, making it more accessible to contemporary fans. For the man or woman on the go, who would find *Anthology* too long, this is the documentary for you!

Beatlefacts:

* The word 'compleat' is a nod to the intentional misspelling of 'Beetles' and a reference to the famous book on fishing, *The Compleat Angler*. Another fact that I've just "reeled" in (groan!).

An Orchestral Tribute To The Beatles (1983)

Directed By - Alan Birkinshaw
First Broadcast - 1983
Running Time - 62 Minutes

A special concert of Beatles songs being given a classical treatment at the wonderful Royal Albert Hall in London by the Royal Philharmonic Orchestra and Royal Choral Society, and conducted by Louis Clark. Paul McCartney was in the audience to raise funds for the RSPB (Royal Society of the Protection of Birds) and also appearing in this concert is the famous actress, Dame Joan Collins.

The Paul McCartney Special (1986)

Directed By - David G. Croft
First Broadcast - August 29th 1986
Running Time - 54 Minutes

Made for BBC TV in 1986, this retrospective of one of the greatest singer/songwriters of our times was filled with rare music and newsreel footage, and featured a new interview with the man himself conducted by Richard Skinner. It also contained an in-depth look on his life to date, such as his relationship with The Beatles, their break-up, his solo career, Wings and his most recent album at the time, *Press To Play*. It was later released on VHS, but is now unavailable.

It Was Twenty Years Ago Today (1987)

Directed By - John Sheppard
First Broadcast - June 1st 1987
Running Time - 105 Minutes

A Granada TV special to commemorate the 20th anniversary of The Beatles ' most iconic album *Sgt. Pepper 's Lonely Hearts Club Band* and the 1967 'summer of love'. The special contained original interviews with Paul McCartney and George Harrison, as well as producer George Martin and press officer Derek Taylor. It was accompanied by a book with the same name.

While the bulk of the film is about The Beatles 'iconic album, equal focus is on 1967 as a year. We also learn about the political and social events of the time, and other big artists of the era, such as Jimi Hendrix, Bob Dylan, The Rolling Stones, The Grateful Dead, Otis Redding and many more.

In the director's chair was John Sheppard, whose previous credits included the 1960s pop show *Ready, Steady, Go!* (which The Beatles had appeared on) and the current affairs programme *World In Action*.

The documentary received positive reviews from the critics.

Beatlefacts

* Footage from the stop-motion opening to this special was later recycled in the 1995 Beatles documentary *The Beatles Anthology*.

Imagine: John Lennon (1988)

Directed By - Yoko Ono
Written By - Sam Egan and Andrew Solt
Release Date - October 28th 1988
Running Time - 100 Minutes

Not to be confused with John's TV movie *John Lennon - Imagine*, this is a critically acclaimed documentary about, who else, the wonderful Mr. John Winston Ono Lennon, chronicling his life and his musical career both in The Beatles and as a solo artist. The film's screenwriter, Andrew Solt, was given access to the Lennon estate archives by Yoko herself, with the documentary's footage edited down from over 200 hours of private recordings and footage from the Lennon vaults.

While none of the three surviving Beatles make a physical appearance in the film, they reportedly approved of it.

The South Bank Show - The Making Of St. Pepper (1992)

Directed By - Alan Benson
First Broadcast - June 14th 1992
Running Time - 50 Minutes

Excellent documentary on the making of The Beatles 'arguably most iconic album, produced for London Weekend Television, broadcast as part of the long-running arts series *The South Bank Show* hosted by Melvyn Bragg. It contained new interviews with Paul, George and Ringo, as well as George Martin, who is shown playing back some of the *Sgt. Pepper* recording sessions directly off the original studio 4-track master tapes, something he would do again for *The Beatles Anthology* series three years later. Also interviewed are Peter Blake, who designed the album's iconic cover, Brian Wilson from The Beach Boys and Phil Collins.

This was made to coincide with the album's 25th anniversary, and was released on DVD and Blu-Ray in 2017 as part of the *Sgt. Pepper's Lonely Hearts Club Band*'s 50th Anniversary Box set. Really worth checking out!

Me with Mike McInnerney and Dudley Edwards at a special 'Spirit of '67' event. Mike is one of the authors of 'Sgt. Pepper at Fifty' and is an artist and designer (he designed record sleeves including The Who's 'Tommy') and Dudley has painted murals and customised cars for The Beatles (including the

iconic magic piano, that Paul still uses on stage), The Who and Jimi Hendrix. I was fortunate enough to be asked to do an exclusive remix of 'A Day In The Life', which was played at the event.

You Can't Do That! The Making of 'A Hard Day's Night '(1995)

Directed By - David Leaf
Release Date - 1995
Running Time - 62 Minutes

Made to coincide with the 30th anniversary of The Beatles 'classic debut on the silver screen, even if they missed the date by one year! Presented by Phil Collins (who was an extra in the film, but his bit was cut), this examination of the seminal film asks why was it such a big hit, what was its influence on other films, and how did it define the way the public viewed each member of The Beatles for years to come?

The Beatles Anthology (1995)

Directed By - Geoff Wonfor and Bob Smeaton
First Broadcast - November 23rd 1995 - December 31st 1995
Running Time - Originally Six Episodes, Each 60 Minutes

The definitive documentary on our Fab Four. *The Beatles Anthology* was a six part documentary series, chronicling the life and careers of our beloved band. Production for this project began all the way back in 1970, as their longtime buddy, Neil Aspinall, had compiled a decade's worth of concert, TV and interview footage from around the world, which he assembled into a documentary called *The Long And Winding Road*, which was completed in 1971, but was shelved. Neil recalled in 1996: *"In '69, in all the chaos, the traumas – things were falling apart, but they were still making 'Abbey Road – 'Paul called me saying, 'You should collect as much of the material that's out there, get it together before it disappears. 'So I started to do that, got in touch with all the TV stations around the world, checked what we had in our own library, like 'Let It Be ', 'Magical Mystery Tour ', the promo clips, what have you. Got newsreel footage in, lots and lots of stuff. We edited something together that was about one hour and three quarters long. But The Beatles had split up by then, so there was really no chance of anything happening with it. I sent them a copy of it each which they all quite liked, then I put it on the shelf from 1971 'til '89, about 20 years"* [8]

This was to change in 1980 as John Lennon was in a legal dispute against the producers of the Beatles musical *Beatlemania*, and was saying that he was planning to reunite The Beatles at long last, and use it as a finale to the film - sadly, this wasn't to be, with John's tragic murder on the 8th December.

The project remained in "development hell" until 1992, when it was revived as a six part TV series - this time with direct involvement from Paul, George Ringo, and John's widow, Yoko Ono. The project was renamed *Anthology* and was completed in 1995 (though a rough cut from 1993 has surfaced via bootlegs!). The hype machine was huge, and it was 1964 all over again, and from 1995-1996, The Beatles earned $130million from this project. Getting the documentary broadcast on television led to the biggest bidding war in TV history at the time, with the documentary being broadcast on ITV in the UK and ABC in the USA. While it had a very impressive 13 million people watching in the UK, 48 million watched in the United States.

The documentary was met with positive reception from critics, and as a finale we got... two new Beatle songs (kind of!)! While a true Beatle reunion would be off-limits, "The Threetles", as they would be nicknamed, contacted Yoko to see if they could overdub some old John Lennon demos as The Crickets did with Buddy Holly home recordings back in the 1960s, so she sent them the tunes 'Free As A Bird', 'Real Love', 'Now And Then 'and 'Grow Old With Me 'with the former two getting the Beatle treatment, and being produced by long-time friend Jeff Lynne (of ELO and Travelling Wilburys fame). While the "new" Beatle tunes did get somewhat of a mixed reception, both tracks were commercial successes with 'Bird 'reaching No.2 in the UK Chart, and 'Real Love 'reaching No.6, and they had some very creative promotional videos to go with them (as mentioned previously in this book!).

While Beatle diehards won't really learn anything they don't already know, I can't recommend this series enough, as it's incredibly well made and still holds up today, plus we get the bonus of hearing some "new" Beatle tunes. An extended version of the documentary came out on VHS in eight volumes in 1996, and eventually a 5-disc DVD box set topped DVD charts all around the world.

Arena - The Brian Epstein Story (1998)

Directed By - Anthony Wall
First Broadcast - December 25th 1998
Running Time - 280 Minutes

This two-part documentary for the BBC Arts series, *Arena*, is dedicated to probably the most famous music manager in history - Mr. Brian Epstein, the mastermind in making The Beatles the biggest band of all time. This BAFTA award winning retrospective talks about his turbulent life and career, starting with his ambitions of becoming a dress designer, then moving on to managing NEMS Record Department, to eventually putting his stamp onto the music scene in the UK back in 1963. It does however also talk about the dark side of his life, struggling with his homosexuality at a time when it was illegal, and his increasingly frantic and hedonistic lifestyle fuelled by gambling, sex and drugs, and his eventual extremely tragic death, which made front page news.

Paul McCartney and George Martin are interviewed in this documentary, as well as Brian's sister, Stella, Gerry Marsden, Marianne Faithful, Alistair Taylor, actor Jude Law and many more.

Wingspan (2001)

Directed By - Alistair Donald
First Broadcast - May 20th 2001
Running Time - 120 Minutes

A 2001 documentary that goes into the details of Paul's solo career post-Beatles, featuring a new non-archival interview with the man himself conducted by his daughter, Mary (who was then married to the documentary's director, Alistair Donald). Produced by Macca's company MPL Communications, and focusing mainly from the years 1970-1980, starting with the end of The Beatles, the bulk of the film focuses on his new band with his wife, the late Linda McCartney, Denny Laine, Denny Saiwell and Henry McCullough - Wings. We learn about their commercial breakthrough album *Band On The Run*, and their massive 1976 world tour, which was comparable to the days of Beatlemania. We also learn about their huge hit 'Mull Of Kintyre 'in 1977 (to this day, the best selling non charity single in UK history) and it ends with them disbanding in 1980.

The documentary got decent reviews, and was issued on VHS and DVD in the year it was broadcast (2001).

The U.S. vs. John Lennon (2006)

Directed By - David Leaf and John Scheinfeld
Written By - David Leaf and John Scheinfeld
Release Date - December 8th 2006
Running Time - 99 Minutes

A 2006 documentary film that primarily focuses on Lennon's political activities in the late 1960s and early 1970s. The documentary deals with his belief that the US Government during the Nixon regime were attempting to silence him and other notable figures, as they saw them as a threat. We also get to see Lennon and Yoko's peace campaigns and his views on the Vietnam War. As this film was released during the height of the second war in Iraq and the George W. Bush era, many people compared Lennon's activism to what was going on in America at the time, so the timing for releasing the documentary during the mid-2000s was apt.

The film received positive reviews from critics. It also received praise for portraying Yoko Ono in a more down-to-earth manner, rather than the clichéd stereotype of her being a pretentious eccentric outcast.

Beatlefacts

* Released 26 years to the day of John's assassination.

Imagine - The Beatles in 'Love '(2006)

Directed By - Steve Cole and David Mallet
First Broadcast - December 27th 2006
Running Time - 59 Minutes

An episode of the long running BBC Arts programme, *Imagine* (which also shares the name of a very famous Lennon solo track and two Lennon related specials!) - this is the making-of the famous Cirque De Solei Beatles show called 'LOVE', which premiered at the Las Vegas Mirage Hotel and Casino on the 30th June 2006. This programme has a big focus on the project's re-mixes and mashups of Beatles songs with George Martin and his son, Giles, demonstrating the process by which the remixes were created. Also inter-viewed are Paul McCartney, Ringo Starr and John and George's widows, Yoko Ono and Olivia Harrison.

The True History of the Travelling Wilburys (2007)

Directed By - Willy Smax
Release Date - June 12th 2007
Running Time - 25 Minutes

George Harrison, Bob Dylan, Jeff Lynne, Roy Orbison and Tom Petty in the same band? Yes it's true: in the spring of 1988, the most epic rock supergroup of all time was formed - The Travelling Wilburys - a collective of nearly 200 years of combined musical history that formed pure musical awesomeness.

Made as a DVD extra for the Travelling Wilburys collection for Rhino Records, this short documentary film talks about the band's genesis with the song 'Handle With Care', which originally was going to be a B-side for George Harrison, and eventually led to two very successful albums. Handle this documentary with care!

All Together Now (2008)

Directed By - Adrian Wills
Release Date - October 9th 2008
Running Time - 84 Minutes

Similar to 2006's *The Beatles in Love*, *All Together Now* is a look at the partnership between The Beatles and Cirque du Solei that resulted in the popular Las Vegas stage production 'LOVE'. As well as featuring new interviews from Paul, Ringo, George Martin, Yoko Ono and Olivia Harrison, it was the last documentary to feature a non-archival interview with former roadie, and Apple Records managing director, Neil Aspinall, who sadly passed away in March of that year.

Bestlesfact:
* All Together Now 'is of course a song from the 1968 Beatles animated film *Yellow Submarine*.
* Released on John Lennon's 68th birthday.

In Performance At The White House - Paul McCartney (2010)

Directed By - Linda Mendoza
First Broadcast - June 28th 2010
Running Time - 90 Minutes

In 2010, the President of the United States at the time, Barack Obama (the charming one), presented Macca with the Library of Congress Gershwin Prize for Popular Song at the White House, hosted by both Barack and the First Lady, Michelle Obama. Paul performed a special concert, where he was also joined by Stevie Wonder, Herbie Hancock, The Jonas Brothers, Corinne Bailey Rae, Faith Hill, Emmylou Harris, Jack White and more. When Macca performed 'Michelle 'he said *"This is probably the first time I'll get punched by the President!"*, but thankfully Obama was all smiles, and of course they all joined in with the *"na na na nanana na"* bit in 'Hey Jude'; and Obama himself doesn't have a bad singing voice!

Arena - Produced By George Martin (2011)

Directed By - Francis Hanly
First Broadcast - April 25th 2011
Running Time - 90 Minutes

Arena is a long-running arts programme for the BBC, which has been going since 1975 and continues to this day. The episode 'Produced By George Martin 'is a celebratory look at the late, great Fifth Beatle himself, with the help of his son Giles, his wife Judy, and contributions from an array of famous faces, including Michael Palin, Cilla Black, Howard Goodall, Bernard Cribbins, Jeff Beck and new interviews from Paul and Ringo. The documentary received positive reviews, and was issued on DVD and Blu-Ray worldwide on the 10th September 2012, featuring 50 minutes of unseen footage.

Beatlefacts

*   *Produced By George Martin* was also the name of a box set compilation released in 2001, featuring songs produced by George Martin.

George Harrison - Living In The Material World (2011)

Directed By - Martin Scorsese
Release Date - October 5th 2011
Running Time - 208 Minutes

Directed by the acclaimed Martin Scorsese, this documentary's focus is centred around George's life from his early Liverpool years, The Beatles days, his travels to India and being influenced by Hinduism and Krishna consciousness. It contains many previously unseen clips, as well as interviews with the likes of Paul and Ringo, Neil Aspinall, Yoko Ono, Eric Clapton, Tom Petty, George Martin, Eric Idle, Terry Gilliam, and George's former wife, Patti Boyd. It also includes interviews with his family, as well as his wife Olivia and his son, Dhani, who looks very much like his dad.

Set in two parts, this excellent documentary won two Primetime Emmy Awards for Outstanding Nonfiction Special and Outstanding Directing for Nonfiction Programming for Scorsese. It also received nominations for Outstanding Cinematography, Picture Editing, Sound Mixing and Sound Editing.

A tie-in book was released, published by Abrams, and was edited by Mark Holborn, which contained a forward from Martin Scorsese himself and an introduction from Paul Theroux, an author and literary critic.

A great film about a great man – highly recommended.

Arena - Magical Mystery Tour Revisited (2012)

Directed By - Francis Hanly
First Broadcast - October 6th 2012
Running Time - 150 Minutes

A two-part retrospective of their most critically divisive movie, which was part of the long-running BBC arts programme *Arena*. As well as featuring new interviews with Paul and Ringo, we also see interviews from the likes of Neil Innes, Terry Gilliam, Peter Fonda, Paul Merton and famous film director Martin Scorsese (who previously directed the excellent George Harrison documentary, *Living In The Material World*). One of the highlights of this documentary is that we get to see some very rare behind-the-scenes footage. Definitely worth a watch!

Good Ol 'Freda (2013)

Directed By - Ryan White
Release Date - September 6th 2013
Running Time - 86 Minutes

This is a really fascinating one as, rather than directly focusing on our fabulous foursome, why not hear the story of the secretary of the Beatles Fan Club, Freda Kelly? This is worth watching, as Freda comes across as a very likeable, modest lady, and she gives out some really charming and sometimes heart-warming Beatle stories. She was the secretary for The Beatles Fan Club from 1962-1974, and she was the lady who oversaw publication of the monthly Fan Club magazine. After leaving the Fan Club once the band broke up, Kelly became very reluctant to talk about her past with The Beatles, but following the tragic death of her son, and the birth of her grandson, she finally agreed for a documentary about her time as the Beatles 'Fan Club secretary to be made with longtime family friend, Ryan White, on director's duty. Financing for the film was raised via KickStarter, and it premiered in 2013 at the SXSW Film Festival in Austin, Texas, to positive reviews. The film's title actually comes from the 1963 Beatles Flexidisc single, given out to Fan Club members, in which George gives Freda a shout-out for her hard work, and the other three Beatles call out *"Good Ol 'Freda!"*

It is the first independent movie to have successfully licensed original recordings of The Beatles, and even features a proper non-archival appearance from Ringo Starr at the end of the film. It is absolutely worth seeing, and a fascinating look at the life and perspective of Freda and her journey with The Beatles.

The Night That Changed America: A Grammy Salute To The Beatles (2014)

Directed By - Gregg Gelfand
First Broadcast - February 9th 2014
Running Time - 150 Minutes

Hosted by the rather unlikely choice of old school hip-hop legend, LL Cool J (who's still hard as hell!). He is also joined by Johnny Depp, Eric Idle, Kate Beckinsale, Anna Kendrick, Jeff Bridges and Sean Penn. This all-star Grammy tribute to the Fab Four was made to commemorate their first official appearance on American soil, which happened 50 years earlier. Performed at the Los Angeles Convention Center's West Hall a day after the 56th Annual Grammy Awards, we get covers of Beatles songs by contemporary artists such as Ed Sheeran, Katy Perry, Alicia Keys, John Legend and Pharrell Williams, alongside old favourites such as Stevie Wonder, Jeff Lynne and The Eurythmics. Closing the show are sets from Ringo Starr and Paul McCartney with Paul and Ringo joining in for the grand finale, performing 'With A Little Help From My Friends 'and 'Hey Jude '- probably the closest thing ever to a proper Beatles reunion. Great stuff!

The Nation's Favourite Beatles Number One (2015)

Directed By - Stephen McGinn and John Piper
First Broadcast - November 11th 2015
Running Time - 120 Minutes

Part of the long-running "list show" series on ITV, *The Nation's Favourite*, which has been running since 2010. This special had the British public vote for their favourite Beatles song that made it to No.1 in the UK Singles Chart, with the winner being...' Revolution 9'! Just kidding, it was 'Hey Jude'!

Narrated by actor Alison Steadman, we also get opinions from a large array of British stars including Michael Palin, David Tennant, Ronan Keating,

Noel Gallagher, Corinne Bailey Rae, Jools Holland, Jake Bugg, Twiggy, Bjorn Ulvaeus, Ken Dodd, Giles Martin and many more, as well as an appearance from both Paul McCartney and Ringo Starr at the end of the programme to thank everybody.

Eight Days A Week (2016)

Directed By - Ron Howard
Release Date - September 15th 2016
Running Time - 106 Minutes

Directed by none other than Ron Howard, who was best known for being Richie Cunningham in the famous sitcom *Happy Days* and is now known for directing some of Hollywood's blockbusters such as *Apollo 13*, *The DaVinci Code* series, *Splash* and *Solo - A Star Wars Story*. It's basically a summary of the touring years of The Beatles, with the bulk of the film focusing on 1962-1966, and it was produced in cooperation with Macca, Ringo, and John and George's widows, Yoko and Olivia. It was announced on Hulu on the 4th May 2016, and premiered on the 15th September of that year. Critical reception was generally positive, and it even won a Grammy for Best Music Film in 2017, as well as two Emmys. It did however attract some controversy, as the estate of Sid Bernstein, the promoter of the Shea Stadium concert, sued Apple Music and Subafilms Ltd for the master recordings of the show. Apple retaliated claiming the lawsuit to be "frivolous" citing an agreement that he made for the film rights, and that he never made any claim during his lifetime.

This documentary is a great introduction piece to The Beatles for people who are not familiar with them, and want to know their story in under two hours, unlike the six part *Anthology* series, which will take a few sittings. As well as interviews with the surviving Beatles, we get interviews from celebrities such as Whoopi Goldberg, Sigourney Weaver, Eddie Izzard and Howard Goodall singing the praises of our fab foursome.

Beatlefacts

* The premiere in Leicester Square in London was attended by both surviving Beatles, Paul and Ringo, as well as Yoko Ono. Also in attendance were huge Beatle fans Noel and Liam Gallagher from Oasis, a very popular band that's very much influenced by our Fab Four, and a great group in their own right.

John & Yoko - Above Us Only Sky (2018)

Directed By - Michael Epstein
Written By - Joss Cowley
First Broadcast - November 24th 2018
Running Time - 90 Minutes

A retrospective of John's solo album *Imagine*, with its underlying message of radical engagement being just as relevant today as it was back in 1971. We also explore how the art, politics and music of John and Yoko are beautifully intertwined, and how the album and its iconic title track created a music movement that marked an era full of hope, justice, empathy and love.

The Beatles: Get Back (2021)

Directed By - Peter Jackson
Release Date - August 27th 2021

As stated earlier, *Let It Be* was a bit of a sombre affair - but apparently, what went on during that time wasn't all doom and gloom. Enter Peter Jackson, the acclaimed director of the *Lord Of The Rings* trilogy, and, distributed by Disney, *The Beatles: Get Back* is *Let It Be*, though this time, it's smiles and not frowns!
Announced in February 2019, and scheduled for release in August 2021, this film is going to revise history!

Chapter Ten
Solo Film and TV Projects

As well as being film and TV stars as The Beatles, John, Paul, George and Ringo (and Pete Best) have all done individual projects for film and TV. One thing you will learn in this chapter is that The Beatles were never inactive in film and television, as well as musically, once they parted ways in 1970.

In terms of being a genuine actor, Ringo Starr was the most prolific, with his acting abilities well-received in his films with The Beatles. This led him to star in many popular films from the late 1960s right up to the early 1980s. Paul's career in film and TV was mainly restricted to cameo appearances both as an actor and in documentary films being interviewed, but he did have a hand as a producer, a director, and even scored some films.

John's solo film projects were usually in collaboration with his wife, Yoko, and were mainly arthouse films for acquired tastes. Yoko had gained attention prior to meeting John with her rather unusual 1966 film *Bottoms*, which featured a parade of 365 naked bottoms, warts and all.

Probably the most successful Beatle in terms of solo film projects would arguably be George Harrison with his company, Handmade Films, which he set up with Denis O'Brien. With humble beginnings, as a way to finance the Monty Python masterpiece *The Life Of Brian*, Handmade Films would end up being one of the most successful independent film companies in the UK, with George serving as executive producer on 23 of the films, and making several cameo appearances in them. The company has made countless successful films, the latest one, *127 Hours*, being made in 2010.

Regarding movies made under George's Handmade Films company, I will only be including films where either George served as director, executive producer or had an acting role. With a few notable exceptions, I am also not including music videos or concert films for solo projects, unless the video in question was directed by one of The Beatles.

Not Only . . . But Also (1965-1966)

Written By - Peter Cook and Dudley Moore
First Broadcast - January 9th 1965 and December 26th 1966
Beatle Involved - John Lennon

Not Only...But Also was a popular pioneering BBC2 sketch comedy series featuring the legendary Peter Cook and Dudley Moore. Sadly, a lot of the episodes were wiped out during the 1970s archival cull at the BBC, but thankfully some of the shows that survived the cull featured none other than John Lennon. His first appearance was broadcast in January 1965, and featured him promoting his book *In His Own Write*.

The second was broadcast in December 1966. In this sketch, he played a character called Dan, who is the doorman of a nightclub that's located in an underground gentlemen's lavatory in London. It was filmed on a quiet Sunday morning on the 27th November 1966. It's a great series that spawned many a funny man (and funny lady), and if you can find an episode, it's worth checking out.

The Family Way (1966)

Directed By - John and Ray Boulting
Written By - Bill Naughton, Ray Boulting and Jeffrey Dell
Running Time - 115 Minutes
Release Date - December 18th 1966
Beatle Involved - Paul McCartney

A comedy drama about newlyweds living in a crowded house with the husband's family, starring Sir John Mills and daughter Hayley Mills. The movie got a lot of publicity for breaking Hayley Mills 'contractual purity by having her in a brief nude scene - even the film's tagline is *"Hayley Mills isn't playing kids games anymore"*.

The film's soundtrack was a collaboration between Paul McCartney and George Martin, while Macca was still in The Beatles. This helped the movie's financial earnings tremendously. Recorded two weeks prior to the film's premiere, the soundtrack was released in January 1967, and in many ways was the first "solo" album for Macca; but in actuality, the performance of the score is credited to The George Martin Orchestra. Despite not charting, Macca won an Ivor Novello Award in 1967 for Best Instrumental Theme.

Beatlefacts

* The movie's soundtrack was released on Decca Records - the very record label that turned down The Beatles back in January 1962!

The Defeat of The Dog (1966)

Directed By - Paul McCartney
Written By - Paul McCartney
Running Time - Unknown
Release Date - 1966
Beatle Involved - Paul McCartney

One of two experimental movies made by Paul in 1966, which was only shown to close friends. This film preceded John's experiments into avant-garde weirdness by two years, and according to *Punch* magazine: *"They were not like ordinary people's home movies. There were over-exposures, double-exposures, blinding orange lights, quick cuts from professional wrestling to a crowded car park to a close-up of a television weather map. There were long still shots of a grey cloudy sky and a wet grey pavement, jumping Chinese ivory carvings and affectionate slow-motion studies of his sheepdog Martha and his cat. The accompanying music, on a record player and faultlessly synchronised, was by the Modern Jazz Quartet and Bach"* [8]

The Next Spring Then (1966)

Directed By - Paul McCartney
Written By - Paul McCartney
Running Time - Unknown
Release Date - 1966
Beatle Involved - Paul McCartney

Like *The Defeat Of The Dog*, there is little to no information about this super-obscure experimental film by Macca made just for his friends. Any more info about this film would be totally fab!

How I Won The War (1967)

"I saw a film today oh boy - the English army had just won the war"

Directed by - Richard Lester
Release Date - October 18th 1967
Running Time - 109 Minutes
Beatle Involved - John Lennon

John's first major acting gig outside of The Beatles' films. This is a movie based on the novel of the same name, and Mr. Lennon plays the role of Musketeer Gripweed (who looks a bit like Harry Potter, thanks to his haircut and Lennon's trademark granny glasses), though the main star of the film is Lieutenant Ernest Goodbody played by Michael Crawford, best known for playing the loveable buffoon Frank Spencer in the BBC sitcom *Some Mothers Do 'Ave 'Em*. Crawford's character in the film is very similar to that of Spencer. Set in WWII, the film centres around Goodbody, and his mishaps, which sometimes lead to some sticky situations, and the film's humour can be quite macabre and surreal at times - like a black comedy version of popular BBC sitcom *Dad's Army*.

Directed by Beatle movie veteran Richard Lester and filmed in Lower Saxony in Germany and the Almeria in Spain in the autumn of 1966, Lennon did find filming boring, so Ringo flew by to keep him company, though he did find working on it a refreshing change from the chaos that was Beatlemania. He was pleased that he was treated as a normal person instead of a "demigod". The film would receive a shout-out in the *Sgt. Pepper* closing track 'A Day In The Life 'as shown with the quote above.

The movie received a mixed reception from critics, and Lennon himself is just a secondary character in a larger ensemble, but because of his Beatle fame, he is centre stage on the film's poster and home video release sleeves. If you are a fan of Michael Crawford, you will enjoy this film; but for Lennon fans, it's pretty ephemeral.

Beatlefacts

* Lennon wrote the classic 'Strawberry Fields Forever 'while this movie was being shot in Spain.
* Beatle buddy and roadie, Neil Aspinall, has an uncredited cameo as a dead soldier.

Two Virgins (1968)

Directed By - Yoko Ono
Written By - John Lennon, Yoko Ono
Release Date - 1968
Running Time - 19 Minutes
Beatle Involved - John Lennon

Everybody remembers John and future wife Yoko Ono's infamous experimental album *Two Virgins*, especially for its controversial cover, where they are both seen completely full-frontal nude. When it was distributed, it was covered up in a brown paper bag. A companion piece to the album of the same name, this "film" consists of J&Y playing the two virgins (which Lennon said they both felt like), madly in love, making silly faces and then making out for about 10 minutes. Thankfully this time they keep their clothes on!

No.5 AKA Smile (1968)

Directed By - Yoko Ono
Written By - John Lennon, Yoko Ono
Release Date - November 14th 1968
Running Time - 52 Minutes
Beatle Involved - John Lennon

52 minutes of John Lennon's face and nothing else, going from deadpan to a full on smile very, very, very, very slowly - at least it's clean and tasteful, unlike his later film *Self Portrait*, which we'll get to later in the book, which focuses on another, much more intimate part of Lennon's body!

Beatlefacts

*   The camera was shot at the insanely slow 20,000 frames per minute. Originally, the length was going to be four hours, though even the completed film's 52 minute running time is enough for most people!
*   When the movie premiered at the 1968 Chicago Film Festival, more than half the audience had left the cinema after 30 minutes.
*   Footage from this film was later reused in the 1996 "reunion" single music video, 'Real Love'.

The Smothers Brothers Comedy Hour (1968)

Created By - Marty Pasetta
Directed By - Various
First Broadcast - November 17th 1968
Running Time - 60 Minutes
Beatle Involved - George Harrison

A comedy variety show for CBS in the US that was famous for its topical and satirical humour. It was hosted by Tom and Dick Smothers, and it ran from 1967-1969. Beatle George was a massive fan, and this was shot during a seven-week stay in Los Angeles, when he was producing tracks for Jackie Lomax's debut album *Is This What You Want?*. Wearing a leather jacket, a frilly yellow shirt and green striped trousers, George's appearance for the show was filmed in front of a live studio audience, and he was also joined by Donovan, The Committee Dion and Jennifer Warnes.

"He came over and we spent a lot of time watching some of the old tapes and some of the newer shows together," remembers Tommy Smothers. *"He was very charming but a little uncomfortable by himself on the show."* Dick also added *"Back then in that year, The Beatles were the biggest thing in the entire universe. And to have George Harrison just stop on by to wish us luck and say 'Go on, keep doing it, 'it was a real coup."* [6]

Candy (1968)

Directed By - Christian Marquand
Written By - Terry Southern, Mason Hoffenberg and Buck Henry
Release Date - December 17th 1968
Running Time - 124 Minutes
Beatle Involved - Ringo Starr

Adapted from a 1958 novel of the same name, this tame softcore sex comedy film satirises erotic novels, and is told though the eyes of Candy (played by Ewa Aulin). Ringo Starr appears as a character called Emmanuel - a horny Mexican gardener, who gives Candy a bit of slap and tickle on a pool table. It's very cringy seeing Ringo, a Caucasian Liverpudlian, pretending to be a Mexican. He disappears in the film after that scene, and doesn't show up again until the end of the film. Also appearing is none other than the Hollywood legend himself, Marlon Brando, playing another stereotype - a randy Eastern Guru. Not quite *The Godfather* if you ask me (but at least you can tell what he is saying!).

It was the 18th highest grossing film of 1968 (which says a lot about cinema tastes at the time), but it did receive healthy reviews back in the day. Nowadays, it has something of a so-bad-it's-good reputation.

Thingumybob (1968)

Written By - Kenneth Cope
Release Date - 1968
Running Time - 45 Minutes Each
Beatles Involved - Paul McCartney and John Lennon

Short-lived sitcom for ITV franchise LWT (London Weekend Television) starring Stanley Holloway, who played a mischievous old age pensioner called Bob Bridge who was always hatching crazy schemes. Paul McCartney wrote the theme tune (credited as Lennon-McCartney), and it was recorded by The Black Dyke Mills band, a Yorkshire-based brass band, who were one of Apple Records 'first signings, and who had the first single for the iconic label.

Sadly, the series is currently lost in the archives.

Wonderwall (1969)

Directed By - Joe Massot
Written By - Gerard Brach and Guillermo Cabrera Infante
Release Date - January 12th 1969
Running Time - 92 Minutes
Beatle Involved - George Harrison

A far-out psychedelic film that stars 1960s sex symbol Jane Birkin, who funnily enough plays a character called Penny Lane (which is also a street in Liverpool and the name of a Beatles song, but you probably already know that!).

The film follows a mad scientist called Oscar Collins (played by Jack McGowan) who discovers a beam of light streaming through a hole, leading to his neighbour's house, and sees Penny Lane doing some modelling. Oscar becomes infatuated with her, and turns into a Peeping Tom. Penny then splits from her boyfriend, and ends up taking pills and passing out, but Oscar comes in to rescue her.

The only reason why people still remember this bizarre (and somewhat perverted) movie is because the soundtrack was provided by none other than George Harrison, who was approached by the film's director, Joe Massot, especially for the project. This resulted in George's debut solo album *Won-*

derwall Music; this was the first solo album by a Beatle. Unlike his later albums, this was more inspired by Indian Ragas, and received a mixed reception at the time, but is now considered an influential album.

The movie got mixed reviews, but is available on DVD.

Beatlefacts

* The title of the famous song by Oasis 'Wonderwall 'was a shout out to the soundtrack album.

Bed Peace AKA Honeymoon (1969)

Directed By - John Lennon and Yoko Ono
Release Date - March 25th 1969
Running Time - 70 Minutes
Beatle Involved - John Lennon

A 70 minute documentary of John and Yoko's (and Yoko's daughter from a previous marriage, Kyoko) honeymoon and their famous bed-in for world peace at the Amsterdam Hilton in the Netherlands. As this was a massive event that happened in 1969, it is definitely worth watching for historical purposes, plus we get to hear an early version of 'Because'. As well as chronicling the Amsterdam bed-in, we get to see a clip of the Montreal bed-in in Canada, where John and Yoko perform 'Give Peace A Chance'.

This is one of their more interesting "arthouse" film projects. All we are saying is 'Give Peace A Chance!'

Rape (1969)

Directed By - Yoko Ono
Written By - John Lennon, Yoko Ono
Release Date - August 22nd 1969
Running Time - 77 Minutes
Beatle Involved - John Lennon

A very strange and somewhat disturbing movie, released on the 22nd August 1969. It's basically a cameraman following a woman down the streets of a city, then chasing after her, knocking her over in a symbolic form of filmic assault. According to John himself regarding the film's message: *"We are showing how all of us are exposed and under pressure in our contemporary world. This isn't just about the Beatles. What is happening to this girl on the screen is happening in Biafra, Vietnam, everywhere."* [10]

Thankfully, there is no actual rape scene in the movie, and the rape itself is metaphorical.

Very tragically, the lead actress in the film (Hungarian actress Eva Majlath) was murdered in 2008.

Self-Portrait (1969)

Directed By - Yoko Ono
Written By - John Lennon, Yoko Ono
Release Date - September 10th 1969
Running Time - 42 Minutes
Beatle Involved - John Lennon

Not sure what to say about this "film"! It's basically a 42 minute single shot of a very intimate part of John Lennon's anatomy ending with - I shouldn't really say but it's very naughty! It was shown at the ICA (Institute of Contemporary Arts) in 1969 alongside the other Lennon/Ono Arthouse films *Two Virgins*, *Smile* and *Honeymoon*. Ono wanted to film the audience reaction to use it for a future re-cut of the film with a spit screen. The film has never been shown to the public since its premiere. Regarding the film, Lennon recalled in a TV interview for Michael Parkinson:" *That was a joke really. I made a film called 'Self Portrait', you know, and at that time I was a bit of a prick!"* [4]

Walden AKA Diaries Notes And Sketches (1969)

Directed By - Jonas Mekas
Release Date - December 1969
Running Time - 177 Minutes
Beatle Involved - John Lennon

John and Yoko make an appearance in this journalistic film directed by experimental filmmaker Jonas Mekas. The film is divided into four sections showing a chronicle of events in Mekas 'life, and him mingling with his celebrity friends. It is considered a classic of avant-garde cinema.

123

Did Britain Murder Hanratty? (1969)

Directed By - John Lennon and Yoko Ono
Release Date - Made on December 10th 1969 but shown February 17th 1972
Running Time - 36 Minutes
Beatle Involved - John Lennon

This was a vox pops feature about a convicted murderer called James Hanratty, who had been hanged for supposed rape and murder on the A6 highway near Bedfordshire back in 1961, one of the most famous crimes and trials of the decade. By 1965, the death penalty was waived for the crime of murder, but the story of the A6 crimes never really went away and there were several books asserting that Hanratty was in fact innocent, and was framed.

John and Yoko made this short feature in cooperation with Hanratty's parents; while made in 1969, it wasn't screened to the public until 1972 in the crypt of St. Martin-in-the-Fields church in London. In 2002, Hanratty was in fact proven guilty thanks to some DNA tests, though there are some who believe that the final result was based on the use of a spoiled sample.

Beatlefacts

* Neither John nor Yoko were credited during the end credits of this short film.

The Magic Christian (1969)

Directed By - Joseph McGrath
Written By - Terry Southern and Joseph McGrath
Release Date - December 12th 1969
Running Time - 92 Minutes
Beatles Involved - Ringo Starr and Paul McCartney

Loosely adapted from the 1959 novel of the same name, this is a goofy comedy movie in which Ringo plays a homeless man named Youngman, who is adopted by a man named Sir Guy Grand (played by Peter Sellers), the richest man in the world, and they overindulge in the high life, while getting into some bizarre scenarios, pranking and scamming people along the way. The movie's final third takes place on the aforementioned Magic Christian voyage, and all hell breaks loose!

The film had a huge all-star cast including Goon Spike Milligan, Monty Python's John Cleese and Graham Chapman (who also helped with the screenplay), Richard Attenborough, Christopher Lee (playing his most famous role of Dracula), legendary pin-up Raquel Welch and Roman Polanski.

One of the best things about the movie is the soundtrack, which is provided by the criminally underrated (and very Beatle-esque) band Badfinger who were signed to Apple Records, and it includes the song 'Come And Get It' written and produced by none other than Paul McCartney.

It's silly and it is campy, and is kind of like a middle-class version of the *Carry On* movies. Despite its critical bashing at the time (it's probably not the greatest film out there!), it's an entertaining one nonetheless, and you are bound to get at least one or two laughs out of it. Be warned, there is some outdated language and attitudes in the film too, which might feel uncomfortable for our modern world.

Beatlefacts

* The French title of the movie was *Un Beatle Au Paradis* which translates to *A Beatle In Paradise* - an obvious marketing ploy to sell the film to French Beatles fans.
* John and Yoko make a brief appearance in the film during a newsreel segment showing them enter The Magic Christian voyage. They are however played by doubles.
* The movie contains the final chord of 'A Day In The Life' from the *Sgt. Pepper* album (covered by Ken Thorne) near the end of the film in a scene featuring London's Tower Bridge.
* The movie would later inspire the *Simpsons* episode 'Homer vs Dignity', in which Mr. Burns adopts Homer Simpson as his prank monkey.

Will The Real Mr. Sellers . . . (1969)

Directed By - Tony Palmer
First Broadcast - December 18th 1969
Running Time - 48 Minutes
Beatles Involved - John Lennon, Paul McCartney and Ringo Starr

A documentary about the comedian Peter Sellers filmed around the time of *The Magic Christian*, narrated by fellow member of The Goons, Spike Milligan. All the Beatles (except for George Harrison) make brief appearances in this feature, as well as Paul's wife, the late Linda McCartney.

Man Of The Decade (1969)

First Broadcast - December 30th 1969
Running Time - 60 Minutes
Beatle Involved - John Lennon

At the end of the 1960s, John Lennon was nominated, alongside US President John F. Kennedy and Ho Chi Min, as 'Man Of The Decade 'in this special.

It was shown on ATV on the 30th December 1969 with John's segment being last. It begins with a mixture of archival clips, ranging from The Beatles performing 'Some Other Guy 'at the Cavern Club, The Beatles arriving at JFK Airport in February 1969, clips from *A Hard Day's Night* and *Help!*, Shea Stadium, The Beatles performing 'Hey Jude', John being arrested for dope possession, and a clip of crowds singing 'Give Peace A Chance 'during an anti-war demonstration near the White House.

After the archive clips, we get a new interview with Lennon conducted by anthropologist Desmond Morris, with John describing his education as being a waste of time, saying how little he learnt in his school days, apart from reading and writing. He also says that many musicians find success outside of the mainstream system and conventional values, and then goes on to talk about modern music's journey from the rock & roll days, the psychedelic era and back down to earth. It also shows Lennon having an optimistic look at the future, praising festivals such as Woodstock and the Isle of Wright Festival and saying that the 1970s will be good (whether they were in reality is debatable).

Thankfully, this programme still exists in the TV archives.

Beatlefacts

* When the interview for the documentary was being filmed, a separate camera crew from the BBC was taking footage of John being interviewed for a different documentary. They would later film more footage of John in a number of locations, which would be used in the 1988 documentary film *Imagine: John Lennon*.

Rowan & Martin's Laugh-In (1970)

Directed By - Mark Warren
First Broadcast - February 23rd 1970
Running Time - 60 Minutes
Beatle Involved - Ringo Starr

A rapid fire US comedy sketch show hosted by Dan Rowan and Dick Martin, which lasted from 1967-1973. Ringo appears in various sketches in an episode broadcast on the 23rd February 1970. This was filmed in LA, while he was promoting his film *The Magic Christian*, and was a coup, as all The Beatles were fans of the show. However, none of Ringo's appearances lasted longer than 30 seconds.

Who Goes There? (1970)

Directed By - Ringo Starr
Release Date - August 30th 1970
Running Time - 11 Minutes
Beatle Involved - Ringo Starr

A short, moderately amusing 11-minute comedy skit directed by Ringo (who also acted in it). It starred Maurice Gibb from The Bee Gees, Martin Lickert and Ringo's son, Jason Starkey. This short home movie only exists nowadays as a poor-quality bootleg, and was discovered during the 1st Andy Gibb Foundation Auction Sale.

Apotheosis (1970)

Directed By - John Lennon, Yoko Ono
Written By - John Lennon, Yoko Ono
Release Date - 1970
Running Time - 18 Minutes
Beatle Involved - John Lennon

Shot in Lavenham, a village in Suffolk, this is an 18-minute short, consisting of a balloon ascending and rising into the clouds, which I have to admit looks pretty, but nothing of note really happens. John and Yoko appear at the start of the film dressed in dark cloaks and hoods. It was originally made in 1969, featuring a helicopter, but they were unhappy with the finished result, so it was re-filmed in 1970.

Fly (1970)

Directed By - John Lennon, Yoko Ono
Written By - John Lennon, Yoko Ono
Release Date - December 1970
Running Time - 25 Minutes
Beatle Involved - John Lennon

A literal "Fly On The Wall" film about a fly zooming around the naked body of New York actress Virginia Lust, set to Yoko Ono's tune of the same name. For very acquired tastes! The film's goal is meant to be a celebration of the human body, but I'm not so sure about that!

Freedom (1970)

Directed By - John Lennon, Yoko Ono
Written By - John Lennon, Yoko Ono
Release Date - December 1970
Running Time - 1 Minute
Beatle Involved - John Lennon

Yoko struggles to take her bra off, and the film cuts off before it's undone. To quote one of Spider-Man creator Stan Lee's favourite sayings "" –*nuff said!*"

Dynamite Chicken (1971)

Directed By - Ernest Pintoff
Produced By - Ernest Pintoff
Written By - Ernest Pintoff
Release Date - January 20th 1971
Running Time - 76 Minutes
Beatle Involved - John Lennon

Directed, produced and written by Winsor McCay award winner, Ernest Pintoff, this American comedy movie staring the wonderful comic Richard Pryor was partially funded by, and featured a brief appearance from, both John Lennon and his wife, Yoko Ono. This compilation of sketches, spoofs, musical performances and film clips centres around the peace movement of the 1960s and 1970s put together in a rather patchwork way.

The Point (1971)

Directed By - Fred Wolf
Written By - Harry Nilsson, Carole Beers, Norm Lenzer, Fred Wolf.
First Broadcast - February 2nd 1971
Running Time - 90 Minutes
Beatle Involved - Ringo Starr

Harry Nilsson was a popular if somewhat underrated singer-songwriter, who was a good pal of our Fab Four, probably best known for his hits 'Everybody's Talkin' and 'Without You', and he was also known for his eclectic back catalogue, covering everything from pop to rock and even crooning.

December 1970 saw the release of his acclaimed album *The Point*, which was a concept album about a child called Oblio, who was the only round-headed person in the Pointed Village, where, by law, everything and everyone must have a point. It's a story that teaches people a lesson in tolerance and acceptance. It was adapted by Fred Wolf as a delightful animated TV special, and was broadcast on ABC Television as their 'Movie Of the Week'. While Dustin Hoffman was the narrator during the original broadcast, when it was issued for home video, Ringo came in and did the narrating (as well as playing the role of the father, who tells the story to his son). This is a fantastic animated feature that will entertain people of all ages, and Ringo's soothing narration really fits in well with the animation and Nilsson's beautiful tunes.

Beatlefacts

* Fred Wolf, the special's director, would later see success producing many acclaimed cartoon shows of the 1980s, most notably *DuckTales, Alvin and the Chipmunks* and *Teenage Mutant Ninja Turtles*.
* When the kids start selecting players for the game of triangle toss, they call for Harry, Fred and Richard. This is a reference to Harry Nilsson, who wrote the story and songs, Fred Wolf the film's director, and Richard is of course a reference to Richard Starkey AKA Ringo Starr!

Blindman (1971)

Directed By - Ferdinando Baldi
Written By - Vincenzo Cerami and Pier Giovanni Anchisi
Release Date - November 15th 1971
Running Time - 105 Minutes
Beatle Involved - Ringo Starr

A spaghetti western film about a blind but deadly gunman named Blindman, played by Tony Anthony, who has been hired to escort 50 mail order brides to their miner husbands. When he is double crossed by his buddies and a Mexican bandit, he retreats to Mexico to settle some scores and save the women. This film would have probably faded to obscurity if it wasn't for the fact that Ringo played the role of a character called Candy (which is funny, since old Ritchie had previously played a Mexican character in a film of the same name!), but it does have something of a healthy cult following.

Beatlefacts

* Posters of the film feature the caption 'Good Day Sunshine', which is in fact a song from the 1966 Beatles album *Revolver* - ironically, it's not one on which Ringo sings!

200 Motels (1971)

Directed By - Frank Zappa and Tony Palmer
Written By - Frank Zappa and Tony Palmer
Release Date - November 20th 1971
Running Time - 98 Minutes
Beatle Involved - Ringo Starr

Frank Zappa was a wonderfully quirky and very talented singer, guitarist, record producer, film director and anti-censorship activist, who pretty much played every single music genre known at the time. He was an early signee to The Beatles 'Apple Records label, recording for the Zapple sub-label, which was tailor made especially for him.

This 1971 surrealist musical is a trippy account of life on the road, and is mainly a series of left field nonsensical vignettes and Terry Gilliam-esque animation, interspersed with concert footage of his band, The Mothers Of Invention. Ringo plays the role of Larry The Dwarf, as well as a fictional version of Zappa himself. Ringo's chauffeur at the time, Martin Lickett, plays the role of a bass guitarist.

Despite the movie receiving a mixed reception from critics, it still inherits a cult following, as a DVD and Blu-Ray release came out in 2019.

Beatlefacts

* The movie never received proper distribution in the United Kingdom.

Raga: A Film Journey Into The Soul Of India (1971)

Directed By - Howard Worth
Written By - Nancy Bacal
Release Date - November 23rd 1971
Running Time - 97 Minutes
Beatle Involved - George Harrison

George shows up in this documentary about Norah Jones 'dad, the late great Indian sitar legend, Ravi Shankar, and it is narrated by Ravi himself. It follows his life from the late 1960s to the early 1970s following him on his return to India to revisit his guru, Baba Allauddin Khan. It also explores his life and influence in the western world, and of course his association with Mr. Harrison. The movie received very positive reviews.

Erection (1971)

Directed By - John Lennon, Yoko Ono
Written By - John Lennon, Yoko Ono
Release Date - 1971
Running Time - 20 Minutes
Beatle Involved - John Lennon

Thankfully this is NOT what you think it might be about (unlike *Self Portrait*)! It is basically a time lapse of the London International Hotel being built, hence the so-called "erection".

Up Your Legs Forever (1971)

Directed By - John Lennon, Yoko Ono
Written By - John Lennon, Yoko Ono
Release Date - 1971
Running Time - 70 Minutes
Beatle Involved - John Lennon

Basically a cleaner version of Yoko's 1966 film *Bottoms*, which was a film consisting of close-ups of 365 naked derrières for each day of the year. This film was 367 panning shots of bare legs - nothing more, nothing less, until the film ends with Lennon and Ono mooning themselves on camera. This was later spoofed in The Beatles parody *The Rutles: All You Need Is Cash* as '1000 Feet of Film'.

Clock (1971)

Directed By - Yoko Ono
Written By - John Lennon, Yoko Ono
Release Date - 1971
Running Time - 71 Minutes
Beatle Involved - John Lennon

A lost film - this was a one hour study of a clock face that was shot in the lobby of the St. Regis Hotel in New York in September 1971. John even recorded a soundtrack to this film, consisting of acoustic rock & roll covers. Quite literally rocking around the clock!

The Concert For Bangladesh (1972)

Directed By - Saul Swimmer
Release Date - March 23rd 1972
Running Time - 103 Minutes
Beatles Involved - George Harrison and Ringo Starr

George Harrison organised this fantastic benefit concert on the 1st August 1971 at Madison Square Gardens in New York to help raise humanitarian relief funds for the refugees of Bangladesh during the war of 1971. George is also joined on stage by Ravi Shankar, Bob Dylan, Eric Clapton, Billy Preston, Leon Russell, Klaus Voorman, Badfinger and Ringo Starr - totally epic! The concert received rave reviews, and sales from the concert film's DVD and album are still supporting UNICEF to this day.

Beatlefacts

* This concert could have been something of a Beatles reunion. Paul McCartney turned down the opportunity to take part, because of the bad feelings caused by The Beatles 'legal issues on their disbandment. John Lennon initially agreed to take part in the concert without the presence of Yoko, as Harrison had apparently stipulated - John supposedly had an argument with Yoko, and as a result of the agreement with George, he unfortunately had to bail out.

John & Yoko in Syracuse, New York (1972)

Directed By - Takahiro Iimura
First Broadcast - May 11th 1972
Running Time - 18 Minutes
Beatles Involved - John Lennon and Ringo Starr

A short documentary made for American Television about Yoko Ono's art exhibition at the Eversen Museum in Syracuse, New York, which opened on the 19th October 1971. This was Yoko's most prestigious exhibition, and also appearing in this short are Bob Dylan, Frank Zappa, Andy Warhol, John Cage, Dick Caveat, Spike Milligan, Phil Spector, Allen Klein and Ringo Starr and his wife, Maureen.

The Basil Brush Show (1972)

Written By - George Martin (no not THAT George Martin!)
First Broadcast - June 24th 1972
Running Time - 30 Minutes
Beatle Involved - Paul McCartney

Basil Brush is a fox puppet who has been a staple of children's television in the UK since the end of the 1960s, and who is still going strong to this day; probably best known for his catchphrase *"Boom! Boom!"*. In the CBBC series *The Basil Brush Show*, Paul McCartney and his band, Wings, appeared in a 1972 episode miming to 'Mary Had A Little Lamb 'interspersed with some low-budget animated sequences illustrating the words, in a break from Basil's antics. They were slightly bemused with their newfound position being children's entertainers!

133

Monty Python's Flying Circus (1972)

Directed By - Ian MacNaughton
Written By - Graham Chapman, John Cleese, Terry Gilliam, Eric Idle, Terry Jones and Michael Palin
First Broadcast - October 26th 1972
Running Time - 30 Minutes
Beatle Involved - Ringo Starr

What can I say about Monty Python - they are basically the comedy world's own answer to The Beatles. Their *Flying Circus* TV series, which ran from 1969 to 1974, is arguably the greatest comedy series of all time, and their movies such as *Monty Python And The Holy Grail* and *The Life Of Brian* (which we'll get to later in the book) are just as, if not more, iconic than the TV shows that preceded them. All The Beatles were fans of Monty Python (Lennon once said he would have rather been a Python than a Beatle), and Ringo himself made an appearance in a series 3 episode 'Mr. and Mrs. Brian Norris 'Ford Popular'. At the very end of the episode, there is a post-credits mock chat-show sketch hosted by the "It's" Man (an old man played by Michael Palin, who, when he says the word "It's", the show's title sequence begins) and Ringo and popular singer Lulu appear as guests. When the "It's" man arrives and says that word - the title sequence begins before the sketch could even start, making Lulu and Ringo walk off in disgust!

Eat The Document (1972)

Directed By - Bob Dylan
Release Date - November 30th 1972
Running Time - 54 Minutes
Beatle Involved - John Lennon

John makes a brief appearance in this documentary about the legendary singer/songwriter (and friend of our Fab Four) Bob Dylan and The Hawks (later to be known as The Band) on the infamous 1966 Judas tour of the UK. John's brief segment was filmed on Friday 27th May 1966 in a limousine, featuring John and Dylan on a journey (possibly under the influence of something) from John's home at the time in Weybridge to the Mayfair Hotel in London. Humorously, the raw footage for this sequence shows them struggling to engage in a coherent conversation. The uncut footage ends with Dylan unwell and needing to vomit - gross!

The movie has never seen a home video release, but bootleg versions have been circulating among Dylan (and Lennon) fans.

Born To Boogie (1972)

Directed By - Ringo Starr
Release Date - December 18th 1972
Running Time - 67 Minutes
Beatle Involved - Ringo Starr

Ringo Starr's solo directorial debut, this is a concert film about the band T.Rex performing at the Empire Pool (now known as The Wembley Arena). The film is also interspersed with the band recording, with Ringo and Elton John at the Apple Studios in Saville Row, with some sketches similar to those in the infamous *Magical Mystery Tour* film, shot at Denham and Tittenhurst Park in Sunninghill.

It received positive reviews from critics at the time. The movie got a DVD release in 2005 with an array of extras, not anything of Beatle note.

Beatlefacts

* The Mad Hatter's Tea Party sequence was shot at John Lennon's house, where the video for his solo single 'Imagine 'was filmed.

Imagine (1972)

Directed By - John Lennon, Yoko Ono
Written By - John Lennon, Yoko Ono
First Broadcast - December 23rd 1972
Running Time - 83 Minutes
Beatles Involved - John Lennon and George Harrison

A 1972 TV film directed by and starring John and Yoko, filmed mostly at their home in Tittenhurst Park in Ascot and centring around John's 1971 classic album of the same name. It also features some original songs and tunes from Yoko's 1971 album, *Fly*. There isn't much of a story, and it's mainly a collection of promo clips of Lennon's solo songs, interspersed with some fantasy and gag sequences. Watch out for a cameo from George in a scene where John and his "celebrity buddies" Fred Astaire, Jack Palance, Dick Cavatt and of course George escort Yoko over and over through a doorway. The film is widely available on DVD, and was even given a limited theatrical run in September 2018.

Beatlefacts

*   Other people starring in this film uncredited included jazz legend Miles Davis, Andy Warhol and more infamously, Phil Spector and Allen Klein.

James Paul McCartney (1973)

Produced By - Gary Smith
First Broadcast - May 10th 1973
Running Time - 50 Minutes
Beatle Involved - Paul McCartney

A television special featuring that loveable charmer, James Paul McCartney, which was produced by ATV Productions in 1973. Featuring his current band at the time, Wings, this was a combination of live performances and some rather cheesy "variety" segments, such as a Busby Berkeley-esque musical segment featuring some dancers dressed in half man/half woman costumes dancing to 'Gotta Song, Gotta Dance'. It's very 1970s at times, but at least the music is very good.

It was finally released on DVD in 2018, remastered as part of the deluxe reissue of the Wings album *Red Rose Speedway*.

That'll Be The Day (1973)

Directed By - Claude Whatham
Written By - Ray Connolly
Release Date - May 13th 1973
Running Time - 91 Minutes
Beatle Involved - Ringo Starr

Named in tribute to the Buddy Holly & The Crickets song of the same name (a favourite among The Beatles 'earlier incarnation, The Quarrymen), this is a period drama set in the 1950s during the rock & roll era, about a character named Jim Maclaine (played by David Essex), who is rejecting society's conventions and entering a world of sex and hedonism. This film was a cash-in on the 1950s nostalgia craze that was prevalent during the 1970s. Ringo appears in this film playing a barman named Mike, who helps Jim to lose his virginity, but unfortunately it makes him addicted, leading to a dark path.

The film was a commercial success and was one of the most popular films of 1973 at the UK box office, and was nominated for two BAFTAs. A sequel to the film was made in 1975 called *Stardust* and Ringo was offered the opportunity to reprise his role as Mike. Despite the character's larger screen time in the sequel, for whatever reason Ringo declined, and the role went to singer Adam Faith, who received critical acclaim for his portrayal of Mike the barman.

Beatlefacts

* As well as the song's title being a reference to a song that The Quarrymen used to play, the movie opens with a guitar instrumental called 'Raunchy', the song George Harrison played to John Lennon as an audition piece for The Quarrymen.

Live and Let Die (1973)

Directed By - Guy Hamilton
Release Date - July 12th 1973
Running Time - 121 Minutes
Beatle Involved - Paul McCartney

The eighth instalment in the very long-running James Bond film franchise, and the first one to star Roger Moore as 007; it got a polarising reception from critics, with many people considering it to be a blaxploitation film slapped with the Bond logo. As we all know, the producers get whoever is currently popular to do the title theme, and Paul and his band at the time, Wings, do not disappoint - the track being regarded as one of the series 'best. It is so successful that it has had a life beyond the film, being covered by the likes of Guns N 'Roses, and Paul still plays it at his gigs. Many younger people today don't even know that it came from a Bond movie! It was produced by George Martin, and reached No.9 in the UK singles chart, and even No.1 in the US, making it the most successful Bond theme of all time.

Beatlefacts

* Interestingly, when Paul first played the track to the film producer, Harry Saltzman, he thought it was just a mere demo, and suggested Thelma Houston should record it! George Martin insisted that Paul McCartney's version was strong enough to use.

The Holy Mountain (1973)

Directed By - Alejandro Jodorowsky
Written By - Alejandro Jodorowsky
Release Date - November 27th 1973
Running Time - 115 Minutes
Beatle Involved - John Lennon

John and Yoko helped fund this popular Mexican cult classic, about an alchemist being a Jesus-like messianic character, hoping to achieve enlightenment. The movie is filled with religious and sacrilegious imagery, as well as some sex, extreme violence, frightening scenes, and some profanity. Definitely not for children!

It was produced by The Beatles 'ex-manager, Allen Klein.

Beatlefacts

* George was a big fan of Jodorowsky, and wanted to play the thief character, but declined, as it would have involved him having to take his kit off, much to the disappointment of Beatle fangirls.

Cheech and Chong - Basketball Jones (1973)

Directed By - Paul Gruwell
Written By - Cheech Martin and Tommy Chong
Release Date - December 12th 1973
Running Time - 4 Minutes
Beatle Involved - George Harrison

George Harrison (and Beatle buddies, Billy Preston, Klaus Voorman, Tom Scott and Carole King) perform on this novelty single by comedy act, Cheech and Chong. The track is probably best known for being covered by Barry White and Chris Rock for the Looney Tunes film *Space Jam*. The Beatles make a cameo appearance in the animated music video singing along with the song, which was later featured in the 1979 Peter Sellers comedy classic *Being There*.

Beatlefacts

* This rather unusual collaboration came together because Lou Adler, the song's producer, played the track to George Harrison, who was recording in the studio next door, and George enjoyed the song and wanted to be a part of it.

* One of Chong's ambitions was to smoke a joint with all The Beatles. He has done so with all of them except for Macca.

The Zoo Gang (1974)

Produced By - Herbert Hirschman
Release Date - April 5th 1974 - May 10th 1974
Running Time - 49-51 Minutes Each
Beatle Involved - Paul McCartney

A drama series produced by ITC Entertainment and broadcast by ITV, based on the 1971 book by Paul Gallico. The show was about four people who worked together during the Second World War, who were known as The Zoo Club because their code names were those of animals. Thirty years on, they still work on various adventures.

The show's theme music was composed by both Paul and Linda McCartney, and it was the B-side to Wings 'hit single 'Band On The Run'. It would later be reissued several times with the latest being on the 2010 rerelease of the *Band On The Run* album. The series is currently available on DVD.

Son Of Dracula (1974)

Directed By - Freddie Francis
Written By - Jennifer Jayne
Release Date - April 19th 1974
Running Time - 90 Minutes
Beatle Involved - Ringo Starr

Bram Stoker's Dracula stories have been entertaining and frightening people since the end of the 19th century, and there have been countless adaptations of this iconic novel over the years. In 1974, Apple Films made an all-star musical version of the 1943 film *Son Of Dracula* that featured Ringo Starr as Merlin, alongside Harry Nilsson as Count Downe (Dracula's Son), Freddie Jones, Suzanna Leigh, Peter Frampton, Keith Moon and Dan Meaden as Count Dracula.

This film was made during the short period in the early 1970s when Ringo wanted to concentrate on filming and acting, and he also served as the film's producer. The movie was complete in November 1972, but was postponed for a year and a half. Soon after the film's completion, Ringo called in Monty

Python's Graham Chapman (who at the time was working with Douglas Adams and Bernard McKenna on a Ringo Starr themed TV special) to rewrite the script and overdub the dialogue, as well as giving it a more Pythonesque soundtrack, but this was later shelved. The completed film's screenings have been limited to the midnight movie circuit, and there (as of writing) hasn't been an official home video or DVD or Blu-Ray release, but it has made it onto the bootleg circles.

Little Malcolm and His Struggle Against the Eunuchs (1974)

Directed By - Stuart Cooper
Written By - David Halliwell and Derek Woodward
Release Date - June 1974
Running Time - 109 Minutes
Beatle Involved - George Harrison

The first movie for which George Harrison served as executive producer, and it was a project of Apple Films. This comedy drama was adapted from the stage play of the same name, starring legendary actor Sir John Hurt playing Malcolm Scrawdyke, an art student who is kicked out of college, and who forms a political party called The Party Of Dynamic Erection - a chauvinistic and fascistic sect that attracts a band of misfits. The movie was primarily shot in Lancashire in the UK during February-March 1973, and George provided the incidental music for the film's soundtrack, with the band Splinter (recommended by former Beatle roadie, Mal Evans) providing the song 'Lonely Man 'for inclusion in a pivotal scene.

Production on the movie was troubled, thanks to the ongoing lawsuits regarding the breakup of The Beatles, and ties with their former manager, Allen Klein. It was eventually released in 1974, and went on to win a gold medal at the Atlanta Film Festival, receiving a short run at London's West End in 1975. The movie received positive reviews, and got a DVD and Blu-Ray release in 2011.

Beatlefacts

* The late Sir John Hurt would also appear in the promo video for Paul McCartney's solo single 'Take It Away'.

Lisztomania (1975)

Directed By - Ken Russell
Written By - Ken Russell
Release Date - October 10th 1975
Running Time - 103 Minutes
Beatle Involved - Ringo Starr

A surrealistic film directed by Ken Russell, whose acclaimed films include *Women In Love*, *The Devils* and *Altered States* as well as a movie for The Who, *Tommy*. This was a biopic musical about the famous 19th century classical composer, who was considered the first "pop star", Franz Liszt, starring Roger Daltrey from The Who as Liszt and Ringo Starr as the Pope. The film follows his bawdy lifestyle and is devoted to Liszt's "friendship" with Richard Wagner. He also falls in love with Princess Carolyn of St. Petersburg (played by Sara Kestelman), but the Pope forbids them to marry.

The movie is known for being very, very weird.

Beatlefacts

* The first movie to use the Dolby Stereo sound system technique.

Saturday Night Live (1975-Present)

First Broadcast - October 11th 1975-Present
Running Time - 90 Minutes each
Beatles Involved - Paul McCartney, George Harrison and Ringo Starr

Ultra-famous US variety comedy sketch series that has been running since 1975. It kick-started the careers of many big comedians such as Bill Murray, Mike Myers, Dan Ackroyd, Chris Rock, Eddie Murphy, and many more. In an episode broadcast on April 24th 1976, the producer of the show, Lorne Michaels, gave The Beatles an outstanding offer of... $3000 to reunite and perform on the show. The Beatles didn't respond, and a month later, he upped the ante to $3200 - an extra $50 each. It is also the programme where we get the famous sketch where Eddie Murphy claims to be the fifth Beatle!

George, Paul and Ringo have all appeared on the show. George appeared in an episode broadcast on the 20th November 1976, where he performed four songs duetting with the guest host, Paul Simon. Ringo even hosted the show, and in one episode in an act of self-mockery on the 8th December 1984, he auctioned himself off in a memorabilia auction: a guitar pick used by John

141

went for $45,000, Paul's toothbrush was bought for $110,000 but poor Ringo went for a mere $800 - though to fair, Ringo is priceless!

Paul has appeared on *SNL* multiple times in 1980, 1993, 2010 and 2012 as a music guest, and made a cameo appearance in a 2006 episode. The Beatles were impersonated many times in the show, for example, a 1978 'A Framework for the Reunion of The Beatles 'sketch had John Belushi playing John Lennon and Bill Murray playing Paul McCartney. There was also a parody version of The Beatles done in a cuban style called 'Los Beatolos Cubanos', which appeared in an episode broadcast on the 17th November 1979, best known for their hits 'Jesterday', 'Resolution 'and 'Norwegian World'.

Rutland Weekend Television (1975)

Written By - Eric Idle
First Broadcast - December 26th 1975
Beatle Involved - George Harrison

Eric Idle's first comedy sketch project after *Monty Python 's Flying Circus* and made after filming *Monty Python and the Holy Grail*. This was a parody of a no budget regional television service, and also appearing in the series on a regular basis was a friend to both The Beatles and the Pythons, Neil Innes, who would often sing the musical numbers. George Harrison appeared in the 1975 Christmas Special playing himself, and performing as a character named Pirate Bob.

The series is probably best known for begetting The Rutles - arguably the most famous parody version of the Fab Four. The first Rutles sketch featured a character named Ron Lennon (later renamed to Ron Nasty, played by Neil Innes) suffering from a condition that makes him sing love songs, leading to the Beatle parody 'I Must Be In Love'. We get to see the Rutles perform a pastiche of 'A Hard Day's Night'. Ron Lennon would also appear performing a song in a later sketch called 'The Children of Rock-N-Roll 'which would evolve into the Rutle song 'Good Times Roll'. The success of these sketches would lead to the creation of the TV movie *The Rutles: All You Need Is Cash*, which we will cover later in the book.

Because of rights issues, and as it was made during an unhappy time in Eric Idle's life, the series has never seen an official video or DVD release.

Beatlefacts

*   In the Rutland Weekend Television incarnation of The Rutles, Eric Idle plays Stig (The George Harrison character), while in the film version, he plays Dirk (the Paul McCartney character). Dirk in this version is played by David

Battley. Barry (Ringo) is also known as Kevin, and The Rutles in this earlier incarnation hail from Rutland itself rather than Liverpool, as in the film version.

The Beach Boys: It's OK (1976)

Directed By - Gary Weis
Release Date - August 5th 1976
Running Time - 60 Minutes
Beatle Involved - Paul McCartney

The Beach Boys are one of the greatest musical acts of the 1960s, comparable in quality to The Beatles themselves. *It's OK* was a TV special that was broadcast in 1976, which combined interview segments, comedy skits and concert footage from Brian Wilson's return to the stage after his infamous "wilderness" period. Paul and Linda McCartney make a short appearance in a scene that documents Brian Wilson's birthday party.

Fire In The Water (1977)

Directed By - Peter Whitehead
Written By - Peter Whitehead, Marc Sursock
Release Date - 1977
Running Time - 90 Minutes
Beatle Involved - John Lennon

John Lennon makes an appearance in this film about a man in a remote cabin in the Scottish Highlands who decides to edit a documentary about the swinging 60s. The film also revolves around the man's girlfriend wandering though the back of the woods, encountering many animals, living and dead. The film's soundtrack includes many well-known artists such as Pink Floyd and The Doors, and it also features an appearance from world famous artist David Hockney.

Empty Hand (1977)

Directed By - David Litchfield
Release Date - 1977 (Unreleased)
Running Time - 32 Minutes
Beatle Involved - Paul McCartney

A short film about a karate tournament hosted by Geoff Britton, where Paul served as the producer and provided some percussive background music. The film was never released commercially, and very little information about the project exists, so if anybody could help me for a possible future edition of this book, it would be very much appreciated!

Sextette (1978)

Directed By - Ken Hughes
Release Date - March 3rd 1978
Running Time - 91 Minutes
Beatle Involved - Ringo Starr

One of the biggest sex symbols of the first half of the 20th century was a lady named Mae West, known for her hourglass figure and sensual voice; she was the master of the double entendre - but could she pull it off in 1978? Well, at that stage, Mae West was a frail old lady of 84, who was forty years past her prime, heavily made up, with a lot of dental work, and she still acted like she was in her 20s or 30s! This film is based on the play of the same name, and it was her final movie appearance before her death in 1980.

Ringo plays the role of Laslo Karolny, one of Marlon Manners '(West's character) many husbands - she was 84, he was 38 - young enough to be her grandson! The movie received universally negative reviews at the time, but oddly does have something of an ironic cult following.

Ringo (1978)

Directed By - Jeff Margolis
Written By - Neal Israel and Pat Proft
First Broadcast - April 26th 1978
Running Time - 60 Minutes
Beatles Involved - Ringo Starr and George Harrison

A really "campy" 1978 made-for-TV primetime variety special for NBC in America, featuring Ringo Starr and his fictional half brother, Ognir Rrats (Ringo Starr backwards) in a loose adaptation of *The Prince and the Pauper*. This special featured an all-star cast including Art Carney, John Ritter, Carrie Fisher, Peter Cullen, and George Harrison. It begins with a fake press launch where George Harrison comes in and says *"I think it was the trousers"* refer-ring to the contemporary Beatles parody film *The Rutles: All You Need Is Cash*. George, while battling a barrage of questions from the press, also says that he's there to clear up any rumours surrounding Ringo's upcoming concert.

The next hour consists of cheesy acting and loads of song and dance num-bers including a duet between Thomas The Tank Engine and Princess Leia on the song 'You're Sixteen '- yep, we're not making this up! Probably the pin-nacle of really "naff" 1970s variety specials, but it is hilarious because it is so beautifully wacky.

Beatlefacts

* As stated previously, Carrie Fisher and Ringo duet - probably the closest thing to a crossover between two of my favourite things, *Star Wars* and The Beatles, not to mention Opitmus Prime from the Transformers (Peter Cullen) is in this special too!

The Kids Are Alright (1979)

Directed By - Jeff Stein
Release Date - June 15th 1979
Running Time - 101 Minutes
Beatle Involved - Ringo Starr

This is a really fun, well-received rockumentary film about one of my favour-ite bands of the 1960s that is not named The Beatles - The Who.

Ringo makes a short appearance featuring him in conversation with their wild and crazy drummer, Keith Moon, who very sadly passed away less than a year after this film came out.

Monty Python's The Life Of Brian (1979)

Me with the incredible Michael Palin during one of our meetings, good friend to George Harrison and part of the legendary Monty Python team.

Directed By - Terry Jones
Written By - Graham Chapman, John Cleese, Terry Gilliam, Eric Idle, Terry Jones and Michael Palin
Release Date - August 17th 1979
Running Time - 94 Minutes
Beatle Involved - George Harrison

Comedy team Monty Python's most famous (and most controversial) film would have to be *The Life Of Brian*, which was about a man named Brian Cohen (played by Graham Chapman), a Jewish man who lived around the time of Jesus Christ, who joins a resistance group, and ends up fleeing the Romans, while being mistaken for the Messiah (he is in fact a very naughty boy!). The film is controversial for its criticism of organised religion, and some organisations mistook it for being a mockery of Jesus and his teachings (Jesus is, in fact, in the film and is portrayed with upmost respect). It was banned in many places at the time (in fact on the poster it said it was so funny, it was banned in Norway!).

Because of the controversial subject matter, the film was rejected by many studios, but it was saved by the miracle of George Harrison, who set up a new film company called Handmade Films just so he could see it! With £3million funding from George, Eric Idle from the Pythons described the film's budget as being the *"world's most expensive cinema ticket"*. As a way of saying thanks, the Pythons gave George a small cameo role as Mr. Papadopulous, owner of the Mount, and he was even given a word of dialogue (*"hullo!"* over-dubbed by Michael Palin).

Unless you are easily offended, this is one of the funniest and most thought-provoking films you will ever see. Thank you George Harrison - without you, we wouldn't have had this masterpiece!

The Long Good Friday (1980)

Directed By - John Mackenzie
Written By - Barrie Keeffe
Release Date - November 3rd 1980
Running Time - 114 Minutes
Beatle Involved - George Harrison

A popular gangster movie starring Bob Hoskins and Dame Helen Mirren, set during the Northern Ireland troubles. The movie got a great reception from critics, and even appeared at No.21 on the British Institute's list of BFI Top 100 British Films. It was a production of George Harrison's Handmade Films, and he was executive producer.

Barrie Keefe would write a sequel called *Black Easter Monday*, but it was never made.

Beatlefacts

* The cinematic debut of actor Pierce Brosnan, better known as James Bond. In this film, he plays an IRA terrorist.

Eric Clapton And His Rolling Hotel (1980)

Directed By - Rex Pyke
Release Date - 1980
Running Time - 62 Minutes
Beatle Involved - George Harrison

A documentary about guitar whiz Eric Clapton's European tour of 1978. When he performs the number 'Further On Up The Road', he is joined by George Harrison and Elton John. Despite being completed in 1980, it has never been released commercially, but bootleg copies have surfaced over the years.

Caveman (1981)

Directed By - Carl Gottlieb
Written By - Carl Gottlieb and Rudy De Luca
Release Date - April 17th 1981
Running Time - 91 Minutes
Beatle Involved - Ringo Starr

A goofy romantic comedy film, where a caveman named Atouk (played by our Ringo) seeks revenge on a larger rival named Tonda (John Matuszak) for the hand of a beautiful cavewoman, Lana (played by Barbara Bach). The filming was mainly shot in Mexico in locations such as the Sierra de Organos National Park, Durango and the Churubusco Studios. The movie was both a critical and commercial failure, but some critics did enjoy some of the film's humour, especially a scene with an unconvincing "special effects" dinosaur. The film saw a US DVD release in 2002 by MGM Home Entertainment, and a Blu-Ray release by Olive Films in 2015.

Beatlefacts

*   The movie's dialogue is more or less entirely in caveman language. Some showings of the film had the audiences issued with a pamphlet for 30 caveman words, so that people could understand what was going on.
*   The movie opens up with the caption "One Zillion B.C. - October 9th", this was a shout out to the late John Lennon's birthday, which was on October 9th 1940.
*   Barbara Bach (Lana) first met Ringo on the set of this film and a year later they got married, and are still married today - probably the best thing to come out of the film.

Time Bandits (1981)

Directed By - Terry Gilliam
Written By - Terry Gilliam and Michael Palin
Release Date - July 16th 1981
Running Time - 90 Minutes
Beatle Involved - George Harrison

A popular and successful comedic fantasy film with involvement from several of the Monty Python members. This revolves around a kid accidentally joining a troupe of travelling dwarves, as they jump between various time periods looking for treasure to steal. Produced by George's Handmade Films, he was also executive producer, and it featured his song 'Dream Away 'during the film's end credits.

Monty Python Live at the Hollywood Bowl (1982)

Directed By - Ian McNaughton and Terry Hughes.
Written By - Graham Chapman, John Cleese, Terry Gilliam, Eric Idle, Terry Jones and Michael Palin
Release Date - June 25th 1982
Running Time - 77 Minutes
Beatle Involved - George Harrison

A collection of some of Monty Python's classic sketches (Parrot Sketch not included!) and some new material in a hilarious live show performed at the Hollywood Bowl back in 1980. The film also contains friend to both The Beatles and Pythons, Rutle Neil Innes, performing a couple of musical numbers. George Harrison was an uncredited executive producer and it was co-produced between George's Handmade Films and Python (Monty) Pictures.

Beatlefacts

*   According to the Monty Python documentary *Almost The Truth - The Lawyer's Cut* John Lennon and Yoko Ono attended one of the shows.
*   The Beatles themselves played at The Hollywood Bowl back in 1964.

149

The Cooler (1982)

Directed By - Lol Creme and Kevin Godley (of Godley and Creme and 10CC fame)
Release Date - July 29th 1982
Running Time - 11 Minutes
Beatles Involved - Paul McCartney and Ringo Starr

A short promotional film that was originally made to promote the song 'Private Property 'from Ringo's solo album *Smell The Roses*. It was filmed in South West London in the middle of January 1981. The film was conceived by Macca, and Ringo plays a prisoner who is caught, and then thrown into the cooler, where he fantasises about his circumstance and the commandant, played by Barbara Bach, who is in fact Ringo's wife. The film also had appearances from both Paul and Linda McCartney, with Paul playing a prisoner, a musician and a cowboy on horseback, while Linda played a prison camp warden.

It was the official British entry in the short film category at the Cannes Film Festival on the 24th May 1982.

Scrubbers (1982)

Directed By - Mai Zetterling
Written By - Susannah Buxton, Roy Minton, Jeremy Watt and Mai Zetterling
Release Date - September 24th 1982
Running Time - 90 Minutes
Beatle Involved - George Harrison

Handmade Films (George Harrison's company) distributed this crime drama based on the novel of the same name. The movie is about women serving in Borstal Prison, and it got a mixed reception, due to having actresses who were at least in their twenties playing characters who were meant to be in their teens. George was executive producer.

The Missionary (1982)

Directed By - Richard Loncraine
Written By - Michael Palin
Release Date - November 5th 1982
Running Time - 83 Minutes
Beatle Involved - George Harrison

A Handmade Films comedy set in 1905, where a missionary (played by Michael Palin) is recalled to England to minister London's hookers. The film also starred a friend to both The Beatles and the Pythons, Neil Innes, who played a small role as a singer in Gin Palace. George was executive producer.

Privates On Parade (1983)

Directed By - Michael Blakemore
Written By - Peter Nichols
Release Date - March 18th 1983
Running Time - 100 Minutes
Beatle Involved - George Harrison

George was an executive producer on this adaptation of the Peter Nichols play about a gay military entertainment group called The Song And Dance Unit Southeast Asia (SADUSEA) assembled to entertain troops during the Malayan Emergency, who fall in and out of love, while trying to avoid Malayan Communist bullets during the late 1940s. It received mixed reviews.

Bullshot (1983)

Directed By - Dick Clement
Written By - Ronald E. House, Dick White and Alan Shearman
Release Date - October 27th 1983
Running Time - 85 Minutes
Beatle Involved - George Harrison

A parody of the Bulldog Drummond books by H.C. McNeile - this was another Handmade Films project where George was executive producer. This film was a comedy about a dashing (if somewhat buffoonish) World War I ace fighter pilot called Captain Hugh "Bullshot" Crummond, who must save the world from the evil Count Otto van Bruno (Ronald E. House) and win the heart of a beautiful young lady. The movie had an all-star cast featuring the likes of Billy Connolly, Nicholas Lyndhurst and Mel Smith.

Princess Daisy (1983)

Directed By – Waris Hussein
Written By - Judith Krantz and Diana Hammond
First Broadcast - November 6th and 7th 1983
Running Time - 90 Minutes Each
Beatle Involved - Ringo Starr

Not a film about the Super Mario character of the same name, this is a two-part TV miniseries based on the novel of the same name by Judith Krantz. Daisy (played by Merete Van Kamp) is the daughter of a Russian Prince (played by Stacy Keach) and an American movie actress. After her parents ' death, she flees from her half-brother and becomes a model, and falls in love with the modelling agency's president, but her half-brother finds out, and is ready to blackmail her and wreck her life. Ringo Starr is in this TV film playing a character named Robin Valerian.

Beatlefacts:

*   Waris Hussein is probably best known for directing the very first *Doctor Who* episode 'An Unearthly Child 'back in 1963, which was broadcast the day after the LP *With The Beatles* was released.

Rupert and the Frog Song (1984)

Directed By - Geoff Dunbar
Written By - Paul McCartney, Linda McCartney and Geoff Dunbar
Release Date - May 3rd 1984
Running Time - 13 Minutes
Beatle Involved - Paul McCartney

Rupert Bear has been in the hearts of British children since 1920. Created by Mary Tourtel, he first appeared as a comic strip in the *Daily Express* newspaper on 8th November 1920. Since he was a tyke, Macca has been a huge fan of this cuddly bear, and ever since the 1970s has been wanting to make his own Rupert film. One day, after the disbandment of the Fab Four, Paul's company, McCartney Productions Ltd (MPL), acquired the film rights - interestingly, his song 'Little Lamb Dragonfly 'was originally intended for the proposed film, but it ended up on his *Red Rose Speedway* album.

With animator Geoff Dunbar in the director's chair, production officially began in 1981, and was completed in 1983. It was finally released in 1984, and was an accompaniment to Macca's *Give My Regards to Broad Street* film. It is probably best known for containing the single 'We All Stand Together ' (AKA 'The Frog's Chorus'), which ended up being a massive commercial success, despite its mixed critical reception, reaching No.3 in 1984. The singing voices were provided by the St. Paul's Choir & The King's Singers.

Whilst not to everyone's taste, it's a great film for children, and is a good way of getting them into The Beatles; plus the animation is superb.

Gasoline (1984)

Directed By - John Jopson
Release Date - June 15th 1984
Running Time - 89 Minutes
Beatle Involved - George Harrison

George Harrison makes a brief appearance in this documentary about the life of Grand Prix racing drivers on the Formula One circuit.

Thomas The Tank Engine & Friends (1984-1986)

Directed By - David Mitton
Written By - The Rev W. Awdry, Christopher Awdry, Britt Allcroft, David Mitton
First Broadcast - October 9th 1984 - December 23rd 1986
Running Time - 5 Minutes Each
Beatle Involved - Ringo Starr

The Rev. Wilbert Awdry's *Railway Series* (AKA the *Thomas The Tank Engine* books, as they are more commonly known) is a series of very popular children's books about a railway with talking steam engines that reside on the Island of Sodor, lasting from 1945 to 2011. It remains an iconic piece of children's literature - part of the continued success lies within the live action model television adaptation of these stories, which began all the way back in 1984, and to this day remains on the air.

Britt Allcroft (who created the TV adaptation) was looking for a suitable narrator to read the stories (rejects included Johnny Morris and Willie Ruston, both of whom narrated Thomas audiobooks previously), and after hearing Ringo Starr's voice during a television interview, she thought he would be the perfect fit; as she puts it herself, his vocal tones have a *"railway voice"*. Ringo was initially reluctant (as he put it, he was more of a *Beano* man) as he wasn't familiar with the original *Railway Series* books, but after being enthralled on reading them, he finally accepted the gig. Ringo narrated the initial series in an eight day (a week) period, but had to re-do four episodes because of the tone of his voice.

The show was an instant critical and commercial success, and thanks to Britt Allcroft's genius of including Ringo as the show's narrator, it brought the wonderful stories of The Rev. W. Awdry to a new generation of fans. Ringo even did a promotional appearance for the series at the Didcot Railway Centre heritage railway site.

When he was asked to return for a third series of *Thomas*, Ringo declined, due to his work with his All-Star Band, and he was replaced by the late actor Michael Angelis (who coincidentally was the brother of Paul Angelis, the man who voiced Ringo in *Yellow Submarine*).

For classic children's shows from the past, it doesn't get any better than this, and it is highly recommended for the young and the young at heart, especially the first two series with Ringo's warm, cozy, Liverpudlian tones and the stories being very faithful to the original books.

Beatlefacts

* The show's iconic theme song's beat (composed by Mike O'Donnell and Junior Campbell) was inspired by The Beatles song 'Mean Mr. Mustard 'from the *Abbey Road* album. O'Donnell once considered doing an extended 3 minute version, with Ringo on vocals.

* A character figurine of Ringo appears as a workman in the episode 'The Flying Kipper '(first broadcast December 11th 1984).

A Private Function (1984)

Directed By - Malcolm Mowbray
Written By - Alan Bennett and Malcolm Mowbray
Release Date - November 9th 1984
Running Time - 92 Minutes
Beatle Involved - George Harrison

George Harrison was executive producer of this successful comedy film starring Michael Palin and Maggie Smith set in 1947 during the aftermath of the

154

Second World War, when food rationing continued, leading to a married couple becoming involved in the booming bacon black market. The movie received positive reviews and won three BAFTAS - one for Maggie Smith (best actress), another for Liz Smith (best supporting actress) and one for Denholm Elliot (best supporting actor). It was adapted into a musical for the West End in April 2011, under the new name of *Betty Blue Eyes*.

Beatlefacts

* In a scene where the guest list for the banquet is being discussed, there is a mention of inviting somebody named Starkey. This is of course a reference to Richard Starkey, the real name of Ringo Starr, possibly inserted as an in-joke by either George or one of the scriptwriters.

Give My Regards To Broad Street (1984)

Directed By - Peter Webb
Written By - Paul McCartney
Release Date - November 28th 1984
Running Time - 108 Minutes
Beatles Involved - Paul McCartney and Ringo Starr

Basically a 1980s reimagining of *A Hard Day's Night* that focuses on Paul... except nowhere near as beloved. Written by Paul himself and very loosely based on a true story, this film focuses on an unusually bad day in the life of Paul McCartney, in which Macca is recording a new album, complicated by the fact that the master tapes have gone missing, interspersed with some surreal dream and fantasy sequences.

This film was a pet project of Paul McCartney's for a long time. Since he (like myself) has been a lifelong film-buff, he wanted to get back into the world of film and acting again, after his success with the films he did with The Beatles. Filming of this flick began in November 1982, after the completion of his *Pipes of Peace* album, with production carrying on until July 1983. During the interim period, the *Pipes of Peace* album came out, and the film was eventually released in autumn 1984.

When it came out, it unfortunately got a critical bashing and flopped big time commercially (grossing $1.4million against a $9million budget)... oh and Ringo makes an appearance too (as well as their respective wives, Linda and Barbara, and also George Martin)! On a positive note, the soundtrack album was a big commercial success. The song 'No More Lonely Nights' was even nominated for a Golden Globe Award and a BAFTA Film Award for Best Original Song - Motion Picture.

It even received a video-game adaptation with the storyline taking place after the events of the film. It came out on the Commodore 64 and the Sinclair ZX Spectrum home computers in 1985. It was developed by Argus Press Software.

The movie has never seen a recent DVD release, except in 2004 in North America only.

Water (1985)

Directed By - Dick Clement
Written By - Bill Persky, Dick Clement and Ian La Frenais
Release Date - January 11th 1985
Running Time - 115 Minutes
Beatles Involved - George Harrison and Ringo Starr

A satire of the early 1980s Falkland Islands invasion. This was an all-star comedy film about a UK diplomat to a West Indian island finding his normal idyllic existence thrown into confusion when a big US drilling company finds a large source of natural mineral water there. The cast for this film featured many big stars of the time including Michael Caine, Billy Connolly, Eric Clapton and Ruby Wax, as well as George Harrison and Ringo Starr playing small roles as members of The Singing Rebels 'Band (so technically a half-Beatles reunion!). Despite some positive reviews, the film was a commercial failure.

Beatlefacts

*   Prior to joining The Quarrymen (the band that would end up being The Beatles), George was, in fact, in a band called The Rebels.

Billy Connolly: An Audience With Billy Connolly (1985)

Directed By - Alasdair Macmillan
First Broadcast - October 26th 1985
Running Time - 60 Minutes
Beatle Involved - Ringo Starr

Ringo and his wife Barbara Bach are in the audience in this wonderful stand-up comedy show with the Big Yin. Not much of Beatle note, but a hilarious show nonetheless.

156

Alice In Wonderland (1985)

Directed By - Harry Harris
Written By - Lewis Carroll
First Broadcast - December 29th 1985
Running Time - 187 Minutes
Beatle Involved - Ringo Starr

The classic tale of *Alice in Wonderland* by Lewis Carroll has been adapted for TV and film as many times as The Beatles have had a hit record. This 1985 adaptation was made for TV by CBS, starring Natalie Gregory as the titular character, and was separated into two 90-minute episodes. This version had an all-star cast, and Ringo played the role of The Mock Turtle. The film was moderately successful, and was later released on VHS in 1986, and again on DVD in 2006.

Beatlefacts

*   The original *Alice in Wonderland* book was a favourite of John Lennon, as proven in the Beatles classic 'I Am The Walrus'.

Billy Joel: A Matter of Trust (1986)

Directed By - Neil Jordan
Written By - Neil Jordan and David Leland
Release Date - July 9th 1986
Running Time - 4 Minutes
Beatles Involved - Paul McCartney and Ringo Starr

Paul and Ringo make brief cameo appearances in the promotional video for Billy Joel's hit single 'A Matter of Trust '- Macca is shown leaning against a wall, and Ringo is standing on a street outside a window.

Shanghai Surprise (1986)

Directed By - Jim Goddard
Written By - Tony Kenrick, John Kohn and Robert Bentley
Release Date - August 29th 1986
Running Time - 97 Minutes
Beatle Involved - George Harrison

Adapted from the novel *Faraday's Flowers*, George Harrison's Handmade Films produced this critically and commercially slammed movie starring Madonna and Sean Penn, when they were an item. George performs five tunes on the album's soundtrack, while Madonna performs none, much to the disappointment of many of her fans. George also has a cameo in the film, performing in a nightclub scene, while wearing a white suit.

The picture was nominated for six Razzies, and Madonna even won a Razzie for Worst Actress for this film (and another one for *Who's That Girl* the following year). Definitely one of Madge's (and George's) lowest moments.

Mona Lisa (1986)

Directed By - Neil Jordan
Written By - Neil Jordan and David Leland
Release Date - September 19th 1986
Running Time - 104 Minutes
Beatle Involved - George Harrison

A Handmade Films production, where George was executive producer. It is a film noir starring Bob Hoskins, Michael Caine and Cathy Tyson about an ex-convict who becomes entangled in the life of a high-class hooker - not really kids' stuff!

Also starring in the film are Robbie Coltrane, Clarke Peters, Kate Hardie and Zoe Nathenson.

The movie got great reviews from critics such as Roger Ebert, and won many prestigious awards, including a BAFTA, a Golden Globe Award, a Cannes Film Festival Award, and many more, with the lion's share of the award wins going for Bob Hoskins 'portrayal of the character George.

To The North of Kathmandu (1986)

Directed By - Terence Ryan
Written By - Terence Ryan
Release Date - 1986 (Unreleased)
Beatle Involved - Ringo Starr

A 1986 comedy TV special about Max Boyce taking part in the 1986 World Elephant Polo Championships starring Ringo, his wife, Barbara Bach, as well as the comedian Billy Connolly.

The special was never shown, and information about it is very scarce, so any future historians who could give me some more information on this - your efforts would be very much appreciated!

The Return Of Bruno (1987)

Directed By - Jim Yukich
First Broadcast - February 7th 1987
Running Time - 56 Minutes
Beatle Involved - Ringo Starr

A fake comedic US TV documentary (or mockumentary, if you will) about Hollywood badass Bruce Willis as his fictitious alter ego, Bruno Radolini, who is a legendary blues singer/musician, influencing many big names in popular music. As well as featuring the likes of Michael J. Fox, Elton John, Phil Collins, Brian Wilson, Jon Bon Jovi, The Bee Gees, Graham Nash and Steven Stills, one of the people appearing on the special, paying tribute to Radolini, is none other than Ringo Starr. The film was nominated for a 1988 ACE award (Award for Cable Excellence) in the category Writing a Musical Special or Series.

Withnail and I (1987)

Me with Liverpudlian actor Paul McGann, who played Marwood in 'Withnail and I' and who also presented 2019's 'The Cavern Club: The Beat Goes On', which featured Paul McCartney.

Directed By - Bruce Robinson
Written By - Bruce Robinson
Release Date - April 10th 1987
Running Time - 107 Minutes
Beatle Involved - George Harrison

Another Handmade Films production with George as executive producer. This cult comedy classic stars Richard E. Grant in his breakthrough role as Withnail and Paul McGann (best known for being the 8th incarnation of *Doctor Who*) as Marwood. It is about two drugged up out of work actors retreating to the countryside for a holiday that ends up becoming a disaster. The movie proved to be very popular, and these days is considered a cult classic.

Beatlefacts

* Because the movie was produced under George's Handmade Films, they were able to secure the rights to the Beatles classic 'While My Guitar Gently Weeps 'for the soundtrack.

Eat The Rich (1987)

Directed By - Peter Richardson
Written By - Peter Richardson and Pete Richens
Release Date - August 17th 1987
Running Time - 90 Minutes
Beatle Involved - Paul McCartney

Mr. Macca has a cameo in this cult comedy classic as a banquet guest sitting on a dining table. A fight emerges, and he is escorted away by security. The film contained many famous alternative comedians from The Comedy Strip circuit and musicians of the time, such as Rik Mayall, Ade Edmondson, Nigel Planer, Dawn French, Jennifer Saunders, Jools Holland, Robbie Coltrane, and even an appearance from Lemmy from Motörhead.

Despite being a commercial failure, the movie has received somewhat of a following, and provided a good critique of Thatcher-era Britain.

The Lonely Passion of Judith Hearne (1987)

Directed By - Jack Clayton
Written By - Brian Moore and Peter Nelson
Release Date - December 23rd 1987
Running Time - 110 Minutes
Beatle Involved - George Harrison

Starring Bob Hoskins and Maggie Smith and set in 1950s Dublin, this film features a broke middle-aged spinster scraping by, giving out piano lessons, while she makes a sad final bid for love with a man who resides at her rundown boarding house. George was an executive producer and it was made by Handmade Films.

The Real Buddy Holly Story (1987)

Directed By - Richard Spence
Release Date - 1987
Running Time - 86 Minutes
Beatle Involved - Paul McCartney

Paul was the producer of this documentary movie about the man who made wearing glasses sexy - the late, great rock & roll legend Buddy Holly, who had many hits including 'That'll Be The Day '(a favourite of the proto-Beatles, The Quarrymen, and probably their first recording), 'Peggy Sue', and of course 'Words Of Love 'as covered by our fabulous foursome on their album *Beatles For Sale*. This was made as a response to the biopic *The Buddy Holly Story* starring Garry Busey as Buddy, as Macca wanted to show a more faithful account of what really happened in Buddy Holly's very short lived life which had a massive impact around the world.

Bellman and True (1988)

Directed By - Richard Loncraine
Written By - Desmond Lowden, Richard Loncraine and Michael Wearing
Release Date - May 12th 1988
Running Time - 112 Minutes
Beatle Involved - George Harrison

A Handmade Films production where George served as executive producer. This bank heist film is about a computer hacker named Hiller, who was bribed by a group of bank robbers to obtain details of a security system at a newly-built bank. Having obtained all the necessary information, he thought that he'd seen the last of the robbers, but now they have traced him and his son to London, and hold Hiller and his son hostage, forcing him to decode the information about the alarm and take part in the robbery.

The Raggedy Rawney (1988)

Directed By - Bob Hoskins
Written By - Bob Hoskins and Nicole De Wilde
Release Date - April 21st 1988
Running Time - 103 Minutes
Beatle Involved - George Harrison

Starring the likes of Bob Hoskins and Zoe Wanamaker, George was executive producer for this Handmade Films drama set in WWII, about a boy escaping from the army after a traumatic combat experience. He dressed up in women's clothes and joined a passing gypsy caravan, who thought he was a young girl. Falling in love with a gypsy girl only led to problems with the gypsy band, especially when the wounded commanding officer eventually tracked him down. It was Bob Hoskins 'directorial debut, and it also featured a small role for popular punk/new wave singer, Ian Dury.

Track 29 (1988)

Directed By - Nicolas Roeg
Written By - Dennis Potter
Release Date - July 12th 1988
Running Time - 91 Minutes
Beatle Involved - George Harrison

Dramatic film about a lady named Linda who is tormented by giving up her baby for adoption at the age of only 15. Her husband is preoccupied with model trains, his mistress, and being a doctor. George was executive producer in this Handmade Films production.

Bread (1988)

Directed By - Robin Nash
Written By - Carla Lane
Release Date - October 20th 1988
Running Time - 70 Minutes
Beatle Involved - Paul McCartney

Popular BBC sitcom that ran from 1986 to 1991 about a working class family in Liverpool called the Boswells. The seventh episode of the fourth series has the character of Billy going to the opening of an animal refuge by Linda

McCartney (in reality, Linda was a great friend of writer Carla Lane). Billy gets her autograph, and starts chatting, and he invites her for some tea when she's in the area. Linda actually does show up for the tea, and the character of Nellie (who isn't aware of who she is) asks if her husband is at work – only to have Macca showing up in person to collect Linda!

Shining Time Station (1989-1993)

Created By - Britt Allcroft and Rick Siggelkow
Written By - The Rev W. Awdry, Christopher Awdry, Britt Allcroft and David Mitton
First Broadcast - January 29th 1989 - June 11th 1993
Running Time - 30 Minutes Each
Beatle Involved - Ringo Starr

An Americanised adaptation of *Thomas The Tank Engine & Friends* in a format not too dissimilar to shows such as *Sesame Street* and *Mister Rogers' Neighborhood*. In each episode, the people at Shining Time Station learn about special life lessons, and a magical 18 inch miniature railway guard named Mr. Conductor (played by Ringo) reads stories from the world of *Thomas The Tank Engine* adapted from the original 1984 series, but with British Railway terminology replaced with American terms (and the character of The Fat Controller is always being referred to by his proper name of Sir Topham Hatt).

The show received critical acclaim, and high ratings, though after the first series Ringo was replaced, due to his musical commitments, with the unlikely choice (which still worked really well) of the blue (but very funny) stand-up comedian George Carlin (don't worry, Carlin cleaned up his act for the kiddies!).

The series was later adapted as a movie in 2000 as *Thomas & The Magic Railroad* with Alec Baldwin as Mr. Conductor and Peter Fonda as the depressed character Burnett Stone; it had a poor reception at the time, but these days it has a cult following.

Beatlefacts

* One episode features Ringo singing the first verse of the famous non-kid-friendly Monty Python song 'Lumberjack Song'. He gets the words wrong, but that could just be for copyright reasons!

Powwow Highway (1989)

Directed By - Jonathan Wacks
Written By - David Seals, Janey Heaney and Jean Stawarz
Release Date - February 24th 1989
Running Time - 87 Minutes
Beatle Involved - George Harrison

A Handmade Films production, where George was executive producer in this well-received drama about the struggles of reservation-dwelling Native Americans. Buddy Red Bow, our protagonist, is trying to seek pride and identity through both traditional and mystical means of gathering power. The film is notable for having many actors who were unknown at the time in minor roles, before ending up doing bigger things, such as Amanda Wyss, Wes Studi and Graham Greene. It won the filmmaker's trophy at the Sundance Film Festival, and Best Picture, Best Director and Best Actor (for A Martinez, who plays Buddy) at the Native American Film Festival.

Ten For Two: The John Sinclair Freedom Rally (1989)

Directed By - Steve Gebhardt
Release Date - April 1st 1989
Running Time - 78 Minutes
Beatle Involved - John Lennon

This was a recording of an all-star benefit concert in aid of John Sinclair, who was arrested for possessing marijuana in 1969, which led to several protests in the hippie community. This massive concert was held at the Crisler Arena in Michigan, and featured the likes of John and Yoko and Stevie Wonder as well as several famous speakers. Shortly after the concert, Sinclair was eventually released, and in 2019 he became the first person to purchase the old wacky baccy when it was legalised in December of that year.

It wouldn't make sense for John to have produced a film that came out in 1989, but this film was actually made in 1972, and both John and Yoko served as producers. The movie received its premiere at the Royal Oak in Michigan on April Fools Day 1989 (this wasn't an April fool!), but the film has never seen a public release, because it shows John on one of his off-days (it was, after all, during his dark, paranoid phase of the early 70s), but it is available on the bootleg circuit.

Checking Out (1989)

Directed By - David Leland
Written By - Joe Eszterhas
Release Date - April 21st 1989
Running Time - 96 Minutes
Beatle Involved - George Harrison

Critically panned comedy about a man named Ray (played by Jeff Daniels) who is obsessed with his own mortality. George Harrison has an uncredited cameo appearance playing a janitor. He was also the movie's executive producer and it was a Handmade Films production.

How To Get Ahead In Advertising (1989)

Directed By - Bruce Robinson
Written By - Bruce Robinson
Release Date - May 5th 1989
Running Time - 94 Minutes
Beatle Involved - George Harrison

A black comedy starring Richard E. Grant. This film, where George was executive producer, made under his Handmade Films company, is about a pessimistic advertising executive having writer's block at work, leading to a meltdown. He is spiralling out of control, and strangely enough develops a boil on his shoulder that talks to him! The movie received a mixed reception from critics, but it did get some praise, most notably from actor Jim Carrey, praising Richard E. Grant's work on this film.

The Movie Life Of George (1989)

Directed By - Charles Brand
First Broadcast - December 1st 1989
Running Time - 52 Minutes
Beatle Involved - George Harrison

As you can tell from this book, George Harrison had a hugely successful second career with his film company, Handmade Films... all because EMI refused to produce the Monty Python masterpiece *The Life Of Brian*! This documentary was made to coincide with the 10th anniversary of Handmade Films' founding, and among those interviewed includes George himself, the Monty

Python team, Michael Caine, Billy Connolly, Bob Hoskins and Robbie Coltrane.

The Simpsons (1989-Present)

"What are The Beatles?" Millhouse Van Houten

"They wrote all the songs on Maggie's baby records" Bart Simpson

Season 14 Episode 21, Bart of War (first broadcast, 2003)

Directed By - Various
Created By - Matt Groening
First Broadcast - December 17th 1989 - Present
Running Time - 30 Minutes
Beatles Involved - Ringo Starr, George Harrison and Paul McCartney

I think most people living in the world today know who Homer, Marge, Bart, Lisa and Maggie Simpson are - they are probably the most successful animated family in television history, who have been on our screens since 1987. When the characters graduated from being short one-minute sketches on *The Tracy Ullman Show* to a series proper in 1989, it took off big time.

This show has the unique distinction of having three of the four Beatles guest starring, with the first Beatle to appear in the show being Ringo in the Season 2 classic 'Brush With Greatness'. In this episode, Marge Simpson rediscovers her lost dream of painting pictures, after Homer finds portraits of Ringo Starr lying in the attic. Marge sent one of them to Ringo in the 1960s, but never received a reply until 1991, where Ringo finally sends one, praising her art - so much, that he hung it on his wall. *"We were so excited that we got Ringo Starr coming in to do the show, and we recorded him over at the Complex in West Los Angeles,"* recalls Matt Groening. *"We were given a list of rules about what we couldn't do to Ringo, such as 'Don't touch him', 'Don't approach him', and 'Don't ask for his autograph'. But of course when he shows up in this big limo, Brian brings out a big poster and asks him to sign it!"* [5]. Brian K Roberts, who wrote the script, recalled that he had not received the rules for the guidelines, so he showed up with a copy of the script cover for Ringo to sign. Matt Groening asked him if he wanted to be either animated in the way he was in the King Features Beatles TV Cartoon or the way he was in the *Yellow Submarine* film, and Starr chose the latter. Unfortunately, over time, as we know in 2008, Ringo wasn't quite as generous when it came to fan mail, because he found out that too many dealers and "fans" were selling his autographs online for stupid prices.

The next Beatle to appear in the show was George Harrison - this time in the Season 5 premiere episode 'Homer's Barbershop Quartet'. This episode is, in fact, a 22-minute affectionate spoof of the Fab Four's career, with the episode being about the rise and fall of Homer's (and his friends, Barney, Apu and Principal Skinner) barbershop quartet, The Be-Sharps, whose career parallels that of The Beatles. There are LOADS of Beatles references, from Chief Wiggum being the Pete Best of the band, Moe's Tavern being originally called 'Moe's Cavern', Barney dating a Japanese conceptual artist, who is very similar to Yoko Ono, to their final album being called *Bigger Than Jesus* and the cover featuring the band walking on water, *Abbey Road* style. The real George Harrison shows up at the afterparty of the 1986 Grammys, where The Be-Sharps' hit single 'Baby On Board' won the award for Best Soul, Barbershop or Spoken Word album. Homer is thrilled at meeting George, as he shows him a table full of brownies. At the end of the episode, where The Be-Sharps play one last show on the roof of Moe's Tavern, George comes in responding with *"It's been done!"*. Matt Groening recalls that George was *"pretty glum"* in the recording studio, and only perked up when a staff member asked him a question about his obscure experimental soundtrack album *Wonderwall Music*, but he did however say that George was super nice and very sweet to the staff.

The third Beatle to make his mark on the show was Paul. His appearance (with his late wife, Linda McCartney) was in the Season 7 episode 'Lisa The Vegetarian' back in 1995, where Lisa is put off eating meat and becomes a vegetarian. In the episode, Apu Nahasapeemapetilon, the man who runs the Kwik-E-Mart, is also revealed to be vegetation, and on the roof of the Kwik-E-Mart, they meet Macca and Linda, and Paul reveals that he has been friends with Apu since his days when The Beatles were in India with the Maharishi. We also get some ribbings of the "Paul Is Dead" urban myth, as well as Apu doing a tuneless rendition of 'Sgt. Pepper's Lonely Hearts Club Band'. Thanks to McCartney, Lisa has permanently remained a vegetarian on the show. David Mirkin, who was the show runner at the time, said that working with the McCartneys was one of the most amazing experiences of his life.

The Beatles would be referenced in many future episodes to come, with the episode 'Bart of War' revealing that Homer's deeply Christian neighbour, Ned Flanders, is a closet collector of Beatles memorabilia, and John Lennon makes an unofficial "appearance" in a 2008 'Treehouse of Horror' Halloween special. The Simpsons' hometown of Springfield also has the "claim" of being the birthplace of The Beatles in a ploy to attract more tourists.

All three episodes where a Beatle appears are highly recommended, and are definitely episodes not to miss.

Beatlefacts

* In *The Simpsons* episode with Paul, according to Homer and Bart, you don't win friends with salad - whether this is true is debatable.

Nuns on the Run (1990)

Directed By - Jonathan Lynn
Written By - Michael White
Release Date - March 16th 1990
Running Time - 89 Minutes
Beatle Involved - George Harrison

A Handmade Films production; George Harrison was the executive producer for this goofy Ealing-esque comedy film starring Eric Idle (as Brian) and Robbie Coltrane (as Charlie) cross-dressing as nuns. The plot revolves around this duo of misfits wanting to get out of the criminal world, but their boss kills those wanting to leave. Critical reception was mixed.

Beatlefacts

* The movie's soundtrack features the 1979 George song 'Blow Away'.

Cold Dog Soup (1991)

Directed By - Alan Metter
Written By - Stephen Dobyns and Thomas Pope
Release Date - February 14th 1991
Running Time - 87 Minutes
Beatle Involved - George Harrison

The final film for the Handmade Films company with direct involvement from George Harrison. It was an adaptation of the novel of the same name by Stephen Dobyns. This is a dark romantic comedy film about a Zen Buddhist taxi driver, played by Randy Quaid, whose passenger is trying to get rid of his date's dead dog, Jasper.

Ghosts of the Past (1991)

Directed By - Anne Paul
First Broadcast - October 4th 1991
Running Time - 77 Minutes
Beatle Involved - Paul McCartney

You may not know this, but Paul McCartney is, in fact, a classical music buff, and his first Oratorio took place at the Liverpool Cathedral in June 1991, composed in collaboration with Carl Davis, to commemorate the Royal Liverpool Philharmonic Orchestra's 150th anniversary. This Oratorio in eight movements got a large amount of media attention back in the day, and is a loose telling of Paul McCartney's own life with the character of Shanty being based on him. In this documentary, we get a great behind-the-scenes look at how it was all put together, and Paul also takes his collaborator, Carl Davis, on a grand tour of Liverpool, showing him all the places that appear in the story of the Oratorio.

Daumier's Law (1992)

Directed By - Geoff Dunbar
Release Date - May 1992
Running Time - 15 Minutes
Beatle Involved - Paul McCartney

Paul and Linda McCartney were executive producers of this short adaptation from the drawings of 19th century artist Honore Daumier. This satirical black and white animated short flick tells the story of a man in a bookstore reading an allegorical story about a man who has been wrongly accused, who must feed a giant named Gargantua until salvation arrives. Production on this short was four years in the making, and Paul also provided the film's soundtrack, which sounded very un-Paul-like, although it actually fits the short really well. It was nominated for Best Short at the Cannes Film Festival in 1992.

Appaloosa (1994)

Directed By - Barry Chattington
Release Date - July 16th 1994
Running Time - 26 Minutes
Beatle Involved - Paul McCartney

A short documentary about a beautiful horse named Appaloosa, who was owned by Paul and Linda McCartney, which showcases Appaloosa training for a dressage competition. Being a horse lover and rider myself, this is right up my street. The short was narrated by Linda, and was produced by both Linda and Paul.

Help! War Child (1995)

Directed By - Geraldine Dows
First Broadcast - September 11th 1995
Running Time - 60 Minutes
Beatle Involved - Paul McCartney

Paul and Linda McCartney (as well as daughter Stella) appear in this documentary about the making of the 1995 charity album *Help* (not to be confused with The Beatles album of the same name) to help raise funds for the charity War Child, which provided aid to war-torn countries like Bosnia and Herzegovina. Paul also recorded a new version of 'Come Together 'for the album as part of a supergroup called The Smokin 'Mojo Filters, which included Macca, Paul Weller from The Jam, Noel Gallagher from Oasis, Steve Craddock from Ocean Colour Scene, Steve White and Carleen Anderson from acid jazz band The Young Disciples. An epic collaboration for an epic cause.

Devour The Earth (1995)

Directed By - Tim Phillips
Written By - Tony Wardle
Release Date - 1995
Running Time - 22 Minutes
Beatle Involved - Paul McCartney

Paul McCartney narrates this short documentary about the global consequences of meat consumption. It was produced by the Vegetarian Society.

Grateful Dead (1995)

Directed By - Paul McCartney
Release Date - 1995
Running Time - 114 Minutes
Beatle Involved - Paul McCartney

A compilation of still photos taken by Paul's wife, Linda, of the band The Grateful Dead at their house in Haight-Asbury, and at a gig in Central Park in New York - both from the band's formative days. The photos are transitioned using panning, and other techniques, as well as using excerpts from Grateful Dead songs as background music.

The Rolling Stones Rock and Roll Circus (1996)

Directed By - Michael Lindsay-Hogg
Release Date - October 12th 1996
Running Time - 66 Minutes
Beatle Involved - John Lennon

Oasis vs Blur, Britney vs Christina, The Rolling Stones vs The Beatles - there have always been two similar factions throughout music history, but thankfully, the relationship between The Beatles and their biggest rivals, The Rolling Stones, has always been a friendly and diplomatic one, and in my humble opinion, both bands are awesome!

Despite being shot on the 11th December 1968, this concert was shown to the public nearly 28 years later. Set in a makeshift circus stage, the gig, as well as The Stones, featured John, his soon-to-be-wife Yoko, Eric Clapton, Mitch Mitchell (of the Jimi Hendrix Experience) and Keith Richards forming a one-off supergroup called Dirty Mac, performing the Beatles song 'Yer Blues' from *The White Album* - probably the closest thing you will get to a group that combines both The Beatles and The Stones.

It is also known for being the final appearance of Stones founder, Brian Jones, several months before his tragic death in 1969.

Beatlefacts

* Michael Lindsay-Hogg has directed many Beatles projects, notably the film *Let It Be*, and the promo clips for 'Paperback Writer', 'Rain', 'Hey Jude' and 'Revolution', as well as the made-for-TV fictionalised account of John and Paul *Two Of Us* in 2000.

172

Tropic Island Hum (1997)

Directed By - Geoff Dunbar
Written By - Paul McCartney and Geoff Dunbar
Release Date - October 10th 1997
Running Time - 13 Minutes
Beatle Involved - Paul McCartney

Delightful Disney-esque animated short film written by Paul McCartney. The story is about a character named Wirral The Squirrel, who is almost killed by soldiers. A character named Froggo helps him, and they retreat to a tropical island where various animals take refuge, and sing the aforementioned 'Tropic Island Hum'. Wirral falls in love with another squirrel named Wilhelmina (voiced by Linda McCartney). While not the deepest animated movie out there, it's a really charming short that will entertain your little ones.

'Tropic Island Hum' was released in September 2004 as a single, reaching the modest but healthy position of No.21 in the UK singles charts.

Beatlefacts

* Paul and Linda McCartney provided all the character voices. It was Linda's final project before her unfortunate passing from cancer in April 1998.

Paul McCartney's Standing Stone: The Documentary (1997)

Directed By - Christopher Swan
First Broadcast - December 26th 1997
Running Time - 51 Minutes
Beatle Involved - Paul McCartney

Made for the BBC, and broadcast on BBC1 in the UK and PBS in America, this was a behind-the-scenes look at Paul McCartney's second foray into classical music, *Standing Stone*, following on from the success of his 1991 Liverpool Oratorio, and issued shortly after the release of his solo pop album *Flaming Pie*. The concert itself was also shown on the British TV station Channel 5 and both the concert and documentary would later be released on DVD in 1999.

Christopher Reeve: A Celebration Of Hope (1998)

Directed By - Louis J. Horvitz
First Broadcast - March 1st 1998
Running Time - 30 Minutes
Beatle Involved - Paul McCartney

Macca contributed a video message for this TV special dedicated to the actor Christopher Reeve (best known for playing Superman) who was unfortunately paralysed after a horse riding accident. He also plays a version of the song 'Calico Skies 'from the McCartney solo album *Flaming Pie*. Reeve tragically passed away in 2004 - a much missed person.

Tuesday (2001)

Directed By - Geoff Dunbar
Written By - David Wiesner
Release Date - September 4th 2001
Running Time - 13 Minutes
Beatle Involved - Paul McCartney

An animated adaptation of the award-winning book of the same name by David Wiesner, about a night when frogs are flying on their lily pads, passing through a town, and going into a house to watch TV, where they encounter a dog who joins in their adventure. When dawn appears, the frogs return to their normal life... only to find lily pads all over the town!

The animated version was made in 2001, and was released in 2002 as part of the anthology project *Paul McCartney: Music & Animation* which also includes *Rupert & The Frog Song* and *Tropic Island Hum*. Voices were provided by Paul himself and famous US actor Dustin Hoffman. Both Macca and Geoff Dunbar, who directed this short, were nominated for a British Academy Award. A really beautiful animated short with a feel not too dissimilar to the Christmas animated shorts of Raymond Briggs like *The Snowman*.

Beatlefacts

* The film is dedicated to the memory of Linda McCartney, who passed away three years prior to the film's completion.
* Geoff Dunbar had also directed the three previous animated short films of Paul McCartney, *Rupert & The Frog Song*, *Daumier's Law* and *Tropic Island Hum*.

174

Britain's Brilliant Prodigies (2002)

First Broadcast - August 26th 2002
Beatle Involved - Paul McCartney

Paul McCartney and Davina McCall co-hosted this talent series featuring stars of the future. Those featured on the show included Louise Redknapp, Lisa-Scott Lee from Steps and Vanessa White, who would later end up being in the popular girl group The Saturdays. The show would return again in 2003 presented by Bob Geldof, Sarah Ferguson and Robin Gibb, and was most notable for introducing the world to a lady named Jessica Cornish, who would later end up reinventing herself as the lovely Jessie J!

Brian Wilson On Tour (2003)

Directed By - John Anderson
Release Date - March 17th 2003
Running Time - 77 Minutes
Beatle Involved - Paul McCartney

This candid look at The Beach Boys legend Brian Wilson on tour features footage of Paul McCartney inducting Brian Wilson into the Songwriter's Hall of Fame - an achievement well deserved from one genius to another.

Ringo Rama (2003)

Directed By - Ringo Starr, Brent Carpenter and Mark Hudson
Release Date - March 23rd 2003
Running Time - 41 Minutes
Beatle Involved - Ringo Starr

Have you ever wanted to hang about with Ringo Starr? The answer is obviously yes, but the chances are usually about the same as winning the lottery, so here is the next best thing!

This documentary directed by old Richie himself (and his friends, Brent Carpenter and Mark Hudson) was made in 2003 to promote his album of the time *Ringo Rama*, and it has a very intimate feel to it, kind of like hanging about with the man himself! We get a very up-close-and-personal look at the recording process, with Ringo collaborating with his famous rock music friends, including Eric Clapton, Willie Nelson and Pink Floyd's David Gilmour. It was included as a bonus DVD, in the deluxe edition of his *Ringo Rama* album. Great stuff.

Concert for George (2003)

Directed By - David Leland
Release Date - October 10th 2003
Running Time - 146 Minutes
Beatles Involved - Paul McCartney and Ringo Starr

Performed on the 29th November 2002 at the Royal Albert Hall in London, one year after the tragic passing of our good pal, George Harrison. This was a wonderful tribute concert in aid of the Material World Charitable Foundation, and was organised by his widow Olivia and his son Dhani, arranged under the musical direction of Eric Clapton. Appearing on the bill were Ravi Shankar and his daughter, Anoushka, Monty Python (sans John Cleese) performing the delightfully offensive 'Sit On My Face 'and 'The Lumberjack Song', joined by Python regulars Carol Cleveland, Neil Innes, The Fred Tomlinson Singers and even famous Hollywood actor Tom Hanks.

The remainder of the show featured "George's Band" which included the two surviving Beatles, Paul and Ringo, as well as Dhani Harrison, Eric Clapton, Jeff Lynne, Tom Petty, Billy Preston, Jools Holland, Albert Lee, Sam Brown, Gary Brooker, Joe Brown, Ray Cooper, Andy Fair-weather-Low, Marc Mann, Dave Bronze, Klaus Voorman, Jim Keltner and many other musicians who had worked with George over the years. They performed songs from both George's years in The Beatles, as well as songs from his solo years. Joe Brown closed the show with a poignant rendition of 'I'll See You In My Dreams 'played on the ukulele - one of George's favourite instruments.

Temples of Rock (2003)

Directed By - Carlo Gennarelli
Written By - Carlo Gennarelli and Steven Stern
Release Date - November 2003
Beatle Involved - Ringo Starr

Presented by the organist of The Doors, Ray Manzarek, Ringo Starr is interviewed alongside the likes of Graham Nash, Johnny Ramone and Smokey Robinson in this film looking at some of the most influential clubs, studios and theatres in the history of rock & roll such as Sun Studio, The Cavern Club (obviously!), Motown's Hitsville Studio, Whisky a Go-Go, Fillmore Auditorium, CBGB and the Fillmore East.

Not In My Name (2007)

Release Date - 2007
Running Time - 14 Minutes
Beatle Involved - Paul McCartney

A teaching tool for high schools in the UK - Paul McCartney alongside Joanna Lumley, Martin Shaw, Chrissie Hynde and Jerome Flynn speak from the heart to condemn the controversial process of factory farming, containing some disturbing and powerful footage.

The Rocker (2008)

Directed By - Peter Cattaneo
Written By - Maya Forbes, Wallace Wolodarsky and Ryan Jaffe
Release Date - October 17th 2008
Running Time - 102 Minutes
Beatle Involved - Pete Best

A comedy film about a failed drummer getting a second chance at fame, which featured big stars such as Will Arnett, Emma Stone, Bradley Cooper, Josh Gad, Christina Applegate and more. It received a mixed reception from film critics, and was a commercial failure, grossing only $8million against its $15million budget.

The reason for mentioning this is because the film aptly featured a short cameo appearance by none other than the original drummer from The Beatles, Pete Best, who sits reading an issue of *Rolling Stone* magazine at a bus stop.

Britain's Got The Pop Factor . . and Possibly a New Celebrity Jesus Christ Soapstar Superstar Strictly On Ice (2008)

Directed By - Peter Kay
Written By - Peter Kay
First Broadcast - October 12th 2008
Running Time - 120 Minutes
Beatle Involved - Paul McCartney

A (mostly) affectionate parody of late-2000s UK reality TV talent shows, most notably *The X Factor*, created by the hilarious British stand-up comic, Peter Kay. Paul McCartney (a friend of Kay) makes a small appearance, mentoring the main protagonist of the special, Geraldine McQueen (played by Kay) by jamming to the theme tunes of the game show *Blankety Blank* and the Australian soap *Home and Away*. It's hilarious stuff!

As a nod to Macca's past, Geraldine later performs 'We All Stand Together 'in this special.

All You Need Is Klaus (2009)

Directed By - Jorg Bundschuh
Release Date - May 7th 2009
Running Time - 90 Minutes
Beatles Involved - Paul McCartney and Ringo Starr

A journey into the life of The Beatles 'good friend and all-round good egg, Klaus Voormann, who they have known since the early Hamburg days, who also designed the iconic cover of the *Revolver* album. Both Paul and Ringo are featured, and we also get appearances from Astrid Kirchherr and Yoko Ono.

Brüno (2009)

Directed By - Larry Charles
Written By - Sacha Baron Cohen
Release Date - July 10th 2009
Running Time - 81 Minutes
Beatle Involved - Paul McCartney

Sacha Baron Cohen is a very popular British comedian best known for his outrageous fictional characters, including "wigga" Ali G, the Kazakhstani journalist Borat and the flamboyantly gay Austrian fashion reporter, Brüno (which this film focuses on). He decides to come to America to become the *"biggest Austrian superstar since Hitler"*. Like all of Sacha Baron Cohen's work, it is known for being extremely controversial, but also very funny. Paul has a very brief cameo scene, where he is watching a fashion show in Milan, where Brüno is also in attendance.

Al's Brain in 3-D (2009)

Directed By - "Weird Al" Yankovic
Written By - "Weird Al" Yankovic
Release Date - July 16th 2009
Running Time - 10 Minutes
Beatle Involved - Paul McCartney

"Weird Al" (or Alfred) is probably the world's greatest song parodist. He's had a career that has spanned over 40 years, and is the most successful comedy recording artist of all time. His affectionate ribbings of classic pop and rock tunes have earned him both critical and commercial acclaim, even if he is more of a cult figure outside of his native America.

In 2009, Al produced a 10 minute short that was shown at the Orange County Fair in California, which teaches people about the brain and how it functions in an entertaining way. Macca makes a brief cameo appearance as 'First Man On The Street'.

Beatlefacts

* Weird Al had considered doing a parody version of Paul's solo hit 'Live and Let Die 'called 'Chicken Pot Pie 'with a clucking chicken chorus. With Paul obviously being a veggie, the song fell through.
* Weird Al had previously affectionately ribbed Paul McCartney in a mock "interview" for his show *Al TV* back in the 1990s. He did a similar one with George Harrison in the 1980s.

Oh My God (2009)

"Peace And Love!"

Directed By - Peter Rodger
Release Date - October 16th 2009
Running Time - 93 Minutes
Beatle Involved - Ringo Starr

Ringo Starr makes an appearance in this poignant film that asks the question 'What Is God?' Many well known celebrities share their opinions on God and religion, such as Hugh Jackman, Seal, Bob Geldof, Baz Luhrmann and many more.

At the end of the day, regardless of whether you are Christian, Muslim, Buddhist, Jew, Hindu, atheist, whatever, you can enjoy the music of The Beatles!

Peter Kay's Animated All Star Band: The Official BBC Children In Need Medley (2009)

Directed By - Tim Harper
Written By - Peter Kay
First Broadcast - November 21st 2009
Running Time - 6 Minutes
Beatle Involved - Ringo Starr

An epic 2009 charity single/animated music video for the UK charity Children In Need organised by UK comedian Peter Kay and the BBC, featuring a huge array of beloved characters from UK children's TV shows (and US cartoons *Ben 10*, *Scooby Doo* and *Spongebob Squarepants*) singing a medley of classic pop songs. Ringo reprises his role as Thomas The Tank Engine, singing the song 'Jai Ho 'from the movie *Slumdog Millionaire* while The Fat Controller stuffs himself with cake. The medley ends with all the characters singing the end portion of 'Hey Jude 'mashed with 'One Day Like This 'by Elbow. The medley was a huge success, and sold over 452,000 copies in the UK, going straight to No.1.

Beatlefacts

* The physical release of the single features a cover in tribute to *Sgt. Pepper's Lonely Hearts Club Band*.

With Great Power: The Stan Lee Story (2010)

Directed By - Terry Dougas, Nikki Frakes and Will Hess
Release Date - July 24th 2010
Running Time - 80 Minutes
Beatle Involved - Ringo Starr

Stan "The Man" Lee was a really awesome individual who was the head hon-
cho behind Marvel Comics, and was the co-creator of such iconic publications
as *Spider-Man*, *Captain America*, *The Punisher* and *Wolverine*. Ringo Starr is
interviewed in this documentary about Grandpa Badass, talking about the su-
perheroes he would like to be, and the impact Stan's comics had on his own
career.

Beatlefacts

*   As much as we would have liked it to happen, Stan Lee never made any
cameos in any of The Beatles' films.

Smithy To The Rescue (2011)

First Broadcast - March 18th 2011
Running Time - 93 Minutes
Beatles Involved - Paul McCartney and Ringo Starr

A really funny comedy skit for the 2011 Comic Relief Red Nose Day telethon
for BBC, starring the character of Smithy played by James Corden. This
sketch is probably best known for starting his famous 'Carpool Karaoke 'rou-
tine, with the first person to participate being George Michael. The centrepiece
of the sketch revolves around a roundtable crisis meeting between Smithy and
his many celebrity friends including Rupert Grint, Kiera Knightley, Justin
Bieber, JLS, Robert Winston, former Prime Minister Gordon Brown and of
course Paul and Ringo.

Beatlefacts

*   James Corden and Paul McCartney are good friends in real life. Paul appeared on a very well-received 'Carpool Karaoke' segment in 2018.

Bee Gees: In Our Own Time (2011)

Directed By - Skot Bright
Release Date - April 14th 2011
Running Time - 94 Minutes
Beatles Involved - Paul McCartney and Ringo Starr

Paul and Ringo are interviewed in this documentary about the famous brothers Gibb AKA The Bee Gees, who went from being a popular 1960s Beatle-esque trio known for their harmonies, to 1970s disco megastars known for their high-pitched falsetto voices.

Lady Gaga Presents: The Monster Ball Tour At Madison Square Garden (2011)

Directed By - Laurieann Gibson
Release Date - May 7th 2011
Running Time - 117 Minutes
Beatle Involved - Paul McCartney

Macca comes out as a "little monster" (affectionate term for Gaga fans), as he is in the audience of this filmed performance of Gaga's show at New York's Madison Square Gardens.

Annie Nightingale: Bird On The Wireless (2011)

Directed By - Simon Brook
Release Date - May 20th 2011
Running Time - 60 Minutes
Beatle Involved - Paul McCartney

Paul McCartney is interviewed alongside the likes of big beat DJ legend Fatboy Slim (who was once Macca's next door neighbour in Brighton), Mick Jones from The Clash, Paul Weller and rapper Tinchy Stryder, singing the praises of famed BBC Radio 1 DJ, Annie Nightingale MBE.

The Love We Make (2011)

Directed By - Bradley Kaplan and Albert Maysles
Release Date - September 9th 2011
Running Time - 89 Minutes
Beatle Involved - Paul McCartney

The awful attacks on the World Trade Center in New York on September 11th 2001 were a deep tragedy for the world, leaving a very bitter aftertaste that still lingers to this day. This documentary film, which came out almost 10 years to the day after the tragedy, looks at Paul McCartney organising the benefit gig The Concert For New York City that took place at Madison Square Gardens in New York City on the 20th October and featured the likes of David Bowie, The Who, Elton John, Mick Jagger, Keith Richards, Destiny's Child, Jay-Z, James Taylor, The Backstreet Boys and many more.

The film premiered at the Toronto Film Festival on the 9th September, and was released theatrically on the same day.

Beatlefacts

* The film's title is a reference to a line from The Beatles song 'The End '- *"And in the end, the love you take is equal to the love you make"*.

God Bless Ozzy Osbourne (2011)

Directed By - Mike Fleiss and Mike Piscitelli
Release Date - September 16th 2011
Running Time - 94 Minutes
Beatle Involved - Paul McCartney

Ozzy Osbourne from the band Black Sabbath is an odd but very talented chap, known for his foul mouth and his bizarre taste in food! Macca is interviewed in this documentary, which takes viewers inside the complex mind of the rock legend.

Glass Walls (2012)

Written By - Bruce Friedrich and Phillip Stein
Release Date - January 26th 2012
Running Time - 13 Minutes
Beatle Involved - Paul McCartney

Narrated by Macca. After watching this, I don't think you will ever want to eat anything with a head again! This is an anti-meat propaganda film to show that if abattoirs had glass walls, everybody would become veggie.

BB King: The Life Of Riley (2012)

Directed By - Jon Brewer
Release Date - October 10th 2012
Running Time - 123 Minutes
Beatle Involved - Ringo Starr

Ringo is interviewed in this great documentary movie about the late Mississippi Blues guitar legend, BB King, who was given a shout-out in The Beatles song 'Dig It'. It is narrated by probably the most badass elder statesman on the planet who isn't an ex-Beatle - Morgan Freeman.

To The Arctic (2013)

Directed By - Greg MacGillivray
Release Date - February 13th 2013
Running Time - 40 Minutes
Beatle Involved - Paul McCartney

Narrated by Meryl Streep, this is a 3D film made for IMAX cinemas. It's a story about the lives of a mother polar bear and her two young cubs as they navigate the changing Artic wilderness they call home. Paul McCartney provided some music for this film about the effects of climate change.

Sound City (2013)

Directed By - Dave Grohl
Written By - Mark Monroe
Release Date - February 18th 2013
Running Time - 107 Minutes
Beatle Involved - Paul McCartney

Directed by the famed drummer and all-round nice guy, Dave Grohl (Nirvana, Foo Fighters), this documentary is a history of the famous recording studio, Sound City in California, and how it's struggling to keep up with the modern age, and follows Grohl's attempts to bring it back to its former glories. Ten minutes of the film feature Paul McCartney recording the song 'Get Me Some Slack 'with former Nirvana members, Grohl, Krist Novoselic and Pat Smear. The song premiered at the Concert for Sandy Relief benefit concert, and it won the award for Best Rock Song at the 56th Grammy Awards in 2014.

12-12-12 (2013)

Directed By - Amir Bar-Lev and Charlie Lightening
Release Date - November 1st 2013
Running Time - 105 Minutes
Beatle Involved - Paul McCartney

Paul was the executive producer on this documentary about a benefit concert for victims of Hurricane Sandy, featuring an all-star lineup including The Rolling Stones, The Who, Roger Walters, Chris Martin, Kanye West, Alicia Keys, Bon Jovi, Eric Clapton and more.

Finding Fela! (2014)

Directed By - Alex Gibney
Release Date - January 17th 2014
Running Time - 119 Minutes
Beatle Involved - Paul McCartney

Paul McCartney makes a brief audio interview appearance in this comprehensive documentary about the Nigerian funk music legend, Fela Kuti, who, during his lifetime, was considered a dangerous revolutionary to the government of the time. Macca and Kuti crossed paths during the making of Wings '*Band On The Run* album, which was recorded in Nigeria, which unfortunately didn't go down well, as Kuti publicly accused the band of being in Africa to exploit and steal African music after they once visited his club.

The Powerpuff Girls: Dance Pantsed (2014)

Directed By - David P. Smith
Written By - Craig McCracken, William Mata, Chris Mitchell and David P. Smith
First Broadcast - January 20th 2014
Running Time - 23 Minutes
Beatle Involved - Ringo Starr

The Powerpuff Girls is a very popular US cartoon superhero series that initially ran from 1998-2005. 2014 saw the broadcast of a reboot special named 'Dance Pantsed', which was announced in late 2012, when Ringo Starr confirmed via YouTube that he was doing some voice work for the show. Broadcast in January 2014, the special had Ringo play a flamboyant mathematician named Fibonacci Sequins. His name is a pun on the Fibonacci sequence.

Ringo recorded a song for the special entitled 'I Wish I Was A Powerpuff Girl', but it was not featured in the programme.

Beatlefacts

* The creator of *The Powerpuff Girls*, Craig McCracken, is a well known Beatles fan, and had previously spoofed them in an episode entitled 'Meet The Beat-Alls', which had lots of references to The Beatles. A great episode for Beatle fans, which is covered later in this book.

BoJack Horseman (2015)

Directed By - JC Gonzalez
Written By - Joe Lawson
First Broadcast - July 17th 2015
Running Time - 24 Minutes
Beatle Involved - Paul McCartney

Paul McCartney makes a cameo appearance in this adult animated series for Netflix about a washed up actor named BoJack Horseman (an anthropomorphic horse) who was a big star in a sitcom called 'Horsin 'Around 'in the 1980s and 1990s.

Appearing in the Season 2 episode 'After The Party', the episode focuses on BoJack, Princess Carolyn, Diane and Mr. Peanutbutter learning some important lessons about love in the wake of a surprise birthday party. The episode ends with Paul jumping out of a birthday cake at Diane's 35th birthday party to an empty room, disappointed that, by then, everybody had left!

Beatlefacts

* In the 2014 episode 'BoJack Hates The Troops', BoJack reads a newspaper with the headline 'The Beetles call it quits 'featuring a spoof of the album cover of *A Hard Day's Night*, but with bugs.

Jimi Hendrix - Electric Church (2015)

Directed By - John McDermott
Release Date - September 4th 2015
Running Time - 89 Minutes
Beatle Involved - Paul McCartney

Macca is interviewed in this documentary about guitar king Jimi Hendrix's awesome and historic performance that took place at the Atlanta Pop Festival to a massive crowd of over 200,000 people. Two months later, Hendrix would tragically no longer be with us.

Some Mothers Do 'Ave 'Em - Sport Relief Special (2016)

Directed By - Dominic Brigstocke
Written By - Michael Crawford, Raymond Allen and the Dawson Brothers
First Broadcast - March 18th 2016
Running Time - 12 Minutes
Beatle Involved - Paul McCartney

A classic BBC UK sitcom originally running from 1973-1978, starring Michael Crawford as the well meaning but disaster-prone Frank Spencer, who often got himself into sticky situations with plenty of slapstick (all performed by Crawford himself), much to the suffering of his loyal wife Betty (ooh Betty!).

The series had a one-off revival for the Sport Relief charity telethon in 2016, featuring big names such as comedian David Walliams, football manager Arsene Wenger and Mayor of London at the time (and future Prime Minister), Boris Johnson. Paul McCartney himself makes an appearance (as himself) walking in a park on his phone, while Spencer is on his bike telling him to get out the way. Macca jumps into a bush, stands up again and yells at him *"Bloody kids!"* (despite the fact that Crawford was 74 at the time!). A very fun special that kept the spirit of the original series alive.

Beatlefacts

*   In the original series, Spencer only said his famous catchphrase, "ooh, Betty!" once.

Pure McCartney VR (2016)

Directed By - Tony Kaye
Release Date - June 10th 2016
Running Time - 45 Minutes
Beatle Involved - Paul McCartney

A collaboration between Paul McCartney and the Jaunt Virtual Reality mobile phone app - a leading producer of fully-immersive cinematic virtual reality experiences. This is an episodic series of virtual reality (VR) documentary programmes, to coincide with the 2016 compilation *Pure McCartney*, with each of these VR experiences delving into the stories behind the most iconic songs from Paul McCartney's solo years.

Filmed in Macca's private home studio, these shorts took fans on a personal journey with Paul, recollecting memories and anecdotes related to the songs, including classics such as 'Mull of Kintyre 'and 'Coming Up 'to more recent songs like 'Dance Tonight 'and 'My Valentine'. It also marked the first time Paul McCartney's music had been remastered using the Dolby Atmos sound technique.

If you haven't met Paul McCartney in person, this is the next best thing!

Popstar: Never Stop Never Stopping (2016)

Directed By - Akiva Schaffer and Jorma Taccone
Written By - Akiva Schaffer, Jorma Taccone and Andy Samberg
Release Date - August 26th 2016
Running Time - 87 Minutes
Beatle Involved - Ringo Starr

A 2016 'mockumentary 'film starring Andy Samberg, Akiva Schaffer and Jorma Tacconne. It's a spoof of the modern music industry and the modern celebrity climate, focusing on a rapper named Conner4real, formally of Style Boyz, who finds success as a solo artist, only to live a reckless high life surrounded by soulless "yes men", losing touch with his friends. Despite the movie's positive reception, it was a commercial failure, grossing only $9million against its $20million budget.

Ringo Starr makes a brief cameo as himself alongside Ed Sheeran, Rihanna, Justin Bieber, Katy Perry, P!nk, Snoop Dogg, Usher, Nas, 50 Cent, Danger Mouse, Mariah Carey, Akon, Carrie Underwood, Seal and many more.

Ethel & Ernest (2016)

Directed By - Roger Mainwood
Written By - Raymond Briggs
Release Date - October 29th 2016
Running Time - 94 Minutes
Beatle Involved - Paul McCartney

Written by Raymond Briggs, best known for the graphic novels *The Snowman* and *Father Christmas*. This is an acclaimed animated movie, based on the graphic novel of the same, and is the true story of Briggs 'parents, detailing their life from the 1920s to the 1970s, and accounts the extraordinary events occurring during that time. Paul McCartney contributed a song for the closing credits entitled 'In The Blink Of An Eye'.

Pirates of the Caribbean: Dead Men Tell No Tales AKA Salazar's Revenge (2017)

Directed By - Joachim Ronning and Espen Sandberg
Written By - Jeff Nathanson
Release Date - May 26th 2017
Running Time - 129 Minutes
Beatle Involved - Paul McCartney

Based on the famous Disneyland ride, *The Pirates of The Caribbean* films have been a series of swashbuckling adventure movies, which began in 2003 and feature Johnny Depp as the charismatic loveable rogue, Captain Jack Sparrow. The fifth film of the franchise (*Dead Men Tell No Tales*) was released in 2017, and, like Keith Richards appearing as Captain Jack's dad, Captain Teague, Macca makes a small appearance as Jack's uncle called Uncle Jack (how confusing). Macca is actually real life buddies with Depp, as he appeared in three of Macca's solo videos including 'My Valentine '(also with Natalie Portman) as well as the videos for 'Early Days 'and 'Queenie Eye'.

One Day A Week (2017)

Directed By - Baptiste Rouget-Luchaire
Release Date - November 2nd 2017
Running Time - 5 Minutes
Beatle Involved - Paul McCartney

A short narrated by Paul about the devastating impact of animal agriculture on climate change. This was made in collaboration with Macca's Meat Free Monday and also features Emma Stone and Woody Harrelson.

Wish You Weren't Here: The Dark Side Of Roger Walters (2018)

Directed By - Ian Halperin
Written By - Ian Halperin
Release Date - July 10th 2018
Running Time - 82 Minutes
Beatle Involved - Paul McCartney

Paul McCartney was interviewed in this documentary about Pink Floyd legend Roger Walters and his controversial views about modern day Israel.

Carpool Karaoke: When Corden Met McCartney - Live From Liverpool (2018)

Directed By - Ben Winston
First Broadcast - August 20th 2018
Running Time - 60 Minutes
Beatle Involved - Paul McCartney

An extended special version of Paul McCartney's 'Carpool Karaoke 'segment in the long-running TV series *The Late Late Show with James Corden*. In this fantastic special, James Corden is in Macca's home town of Liverpool for a special day with the Beatle legend, exploring Paul's childhood haunts including his home, where he wrote several of his songs with John Lennon, and an impromptu gig in a local pub. We also get Corden and Macca doing some karaoke to several Beatles hits.

This is a fantastic and hilarious special, and is highly recommended. A shortened version is on James Corden's YouTube account.

Echo In The Canyon (2018)

Directed By - Andrew Slater
Release Date - September 20th 2018
Running Time - 83 Minutes
Beatle Involved - Ringo Starr

Ringo is interviewed in a look at the music scene in Los Angeles 'Laurel Canyon, featuring the likes of The Byrds, Buffalo Springfield, The Mamas and the Papas and The Beach Boys.

The Bruce McMouse Show (2019)

Directed By - Barry Chattington
Release Date - January 21st 2019
Running Time - 53 Minutes
Beatle Involved - Paul McCartney

This is a concert film with a difference. Set during Paul McCartney's 1972 tour with his new band at the time, Wings, this is a partially animated film with the storyline centring around how they came to meet the inimitable impresario, Bruce McMouse, an anthropomorphic cartoon mouse, and a family of mice living under the concert stage. The character voices were provided by

Paul and Linda McCartney as well as Deryck Guyler, Pat Coombs and Derek Nimmo. The animated footage is interspersed back-and-forth with Wings concert footage from their European tour.

Despite the project starting in 1972, this film was in development hell for some time. It was eventually completed in 1977, but by that stage, Wings ' line-up had changed, and music at the time changed with it. It eventually got remastered in 2018 alongside a brand-new audio mix and had a limited theatrical run in January 2019.

The Cavern Club: The Beat Goes On (2019)

Directed By - Christian Francis-Davies and John Keats
Release Date - September 7th 2019
Running Time - 70 Minutes
Beatle Involved - Paul McCartney

Narrated by the charming and charismatic actor Paul McGann, this is a celebration of the famous Cavern Club in Liverpool, which was founded in 1957 by jazz buff Alan Synther, before becoming the premier venue for rock & roll music, and of course the host of 292 gigs by The Beatles! Paul McCartney is one of the many people who are interviewed in this fascinating documentary.

Idris Elba Meets Paul McCartney (2020)

First Broadcast - December 19th 2020
Running Time - 60 Minutes
Beatle Involved - Paul McCartney

The famous actor/singer/writer/producer/rapper/DJ Idris Elba talks to our Macca in this BBC retrospective of his life and career, and to promote his album at the time, *McCartney III*. Nice, relaxed interview with both Paul and Idris (who is a good friend of Paul's daughter, Stella) comfortable in each other's company.

Billy Connolly: It's Been A Pleasure (2020)

First Broadcast - December 28th 2020
Running Time - 60 Minutes
Beatle Involved - Paul McCartney

An ITV retrospective of Scotland's greatest stand-up comedian, whose life on the stage has been sadly cut short after contracting Parkinson's disease. One of the people interviewed in this emotional documentary is none other than Paul McCartney, who shares his fond thoughts on "The Big Yin" and his wonderful career.

High In The Clouds (TBA)

Directed By - Timothy Reckart
Written By - Paul McCartney, Jon Crocker, Phillip Ardagh, Geoff Dunbar and Josh Klausner
Release Date - TBA
Beatle Involved - Paul McCartney

An adaptation of Paul's children's story of the same name from 2005 in collaboration with Phillp Ardagh, about a young squirrel named Wirral, whose woodland home is destroyed by human development. Guided by the final words of his mum and aided by some new animal friends he meets along the way, he must make his way to the secret utopia known as Animalia. The plot of the book centres around the theme of preserving nature and letting animals live free and in their natural habitat.

This project has been in development hell since 2013. Originally, it was going to be made through Unique Pictures and RGH Entertainment with Tony Bancroft serving as producer, with a theatrical release in 2015. Move forward to 2019, and now Timothy Reckart is going to be serving as director with Macca acting as producer and songwriter, composing some original songs for the film (with one of the songs being rumoured to be a collaboration with Lady Gaga).

The film is still in pre-production as of writing.

Untitled Paul McCartney X Rick Rubin Project (TBA)

First Broadcast - TBA
Beatle Involved - Paul McCartney

A six-part documentary series that was teased in December 2020, made in collaboration with Paul McCartney and legendary hip-hop producer Rick Rubin, best known for being the co-founder of Def Jam Recordings (Run-DMC, Public Enemy, Beastie Boys etc). More details to follow soon!

Chapter Eleven
Unfinished/Shelved Beatles Related Films

Not every Beatle film eventually made it onto the screen, and some ideas just ended up on the cutting room floor. As The Beatles were the hottest ticket of the 1960s, everybody wanted to jump in on the Beatle gravy train, and filmmakers were no exception - loads of budding movie directors wanted The Beatles in their films.

Whether this was for the better, I'll leave it up to you to decide.

The Yellow Teddy Bears AKA Gutter Girls (1963)

Directed By - Robert Hartford-Davis
Release Date - July 1963

This was the boys 'first ever movie offer. An exploitation B-Movie about a group of British teenage schoolgirls who wear a small teddy bear on their uniform to signify that they have lost their virginity. The Beatles were offered cameo appearances in the film, but they turned it down, as they would have had to either perform songs written by somebody else, or have their songs copyrighted by the people making it. Their role was given to a singer and guitarist named Malcolm Mitchell. [26]

A Talent For Loving (1966, made in 1969)

Directed By - Richard Quine
Release Date - 1969

In 1965, when *Help!* was being made, the third Beatle movie announced was going to be a comedic western movie entitled *A Talent For Loving*, and it would have started shooting the following year. The plot was about a gamer named Patten, who wins the deeds to a ranch in Mexico, but finds out that a curse has been placed on it. Richard Condon, who wrote the screenplay (and based it on his novel of the same name) had envisioned The Beatles as a crew of pioneering Liverpudlians who had travelled west. The Beatles ultimately rejected doing the film, but it did eventually come out in 1969 under the name *Gun Crazy*, and featured Richard Widmark, Chaim Topol, Cesar Romero (AKA The Joker from the 1960s *Batman* TV show) and Genevieve Page. [26]

Up Against It (1967)

Written By - Joe Orton

In January 1967, a writer named Joe Orton was approached by Walter Shenson about writing a screenplay for The Beatles, as his darkly comical way of writing appealed to them. Shenson paid him an advance of £5000 to come up with a screenplay. The script was adapted from his novel *The Silver Bucket* and it also combined another of his novels called *Head to Toe*. Unlike *A Hard Day's Night* and *Help!*, which were family-friendly affairs, *Up Against It* was more intended for an adult audience, with themes of political assassination, guerrilla warfare and transvestism. The script was handed over to Brian Epstein, but Orton never heard back from either Epstein or The Beatles. He then revised the script by cutting the protagonists down to three (with Mick Jagger and Ian McKellen being considered for two of the leads) and he even planned a meeting with former Beatle director, Richard Lester, to discuss filming options. Tragically, on August 9th 1967, just 18 days before the harrowing death of Brian Epstein, Joe Orton was murdered at home by his partner, Kenneth Halliwell - he was only 34 years old.

The script did however see a second life in 1979, when it was finally published, and it was adapted into a musical in 1989 with music by Todd Rundgren. It was even adapted into a radio play in 1997 for BBC Radio 3 with the cast including Prunella Scales (Sybil Fawlty from *Fawlty Towers*) and Damon Albarn from the Britpop band Blur. [26]

Shades Of A Personality (1967)

Directed By - Michelangelo Antonioni
Written By - Owen Holder

Originally with the rather generic working title of 'Beatles 3', this was to be shot in Malaga in Spain and was going to be directed by Michelangelo Antonioni, who directed the award-winning film *Blow Up*. The plot was going to be about a man (played by John) who suffers from a split personality - each of these personalities (Paul, George and Ringo) would emerge in separate sub plots. Sounds pretty interesting and is somewhat like the Pixar film *Inside Out*.

Because of *Sgt. Pepper* and *Magical Mystery Tour* getting in the way, the project had to be shelved. [27]

Captain Blood (1969)

Ringo was allegedly set to star(r) in a film which was also going to feature comedian Tommy Smothers. Shooting was to start in March 1969 in Jamaica, but the film never materialised. [27]

Death May Be Your Santa Claus (1969)

Directed By - Frankie Dymon Jr.
Release Date - 1969
Running Time - 36 Minutes

John Lennon and Yoko Ono were set to make a guest appearance in this film about the dystopian visions of a young, black European militant. They made it onto the set, but the director, Frankie Dymon Jr, didn't show up, so they didn't end up being in the film! [27]

The Lord Of The Rings (1969)

In the mid 1960s there were rumours that John Lennon was enthusiastic about adapting J.R.R. Tolkien's timeless fantasy novel *The Lord of The Rings*. Things were getting closer to reality in 1968; Denis O'Dell, who ran Apple Films, entered negotiations for a new Beatles film. Since *Yellow Submarine* wasn't part of their three film contract with United Artists, he considered adapting the classic book as a multimedia musical extravaganza. Richard Lester wasn't up for the director's chair, so O'Dell shortlisted David Lean, Robert Bolt, Michelangelo Antonioni and Stanley Kubrick. The project ultimately never materialised, and *Let It Be* ended up being the third film in the contract with United Artists. *Lord Of The Rings* would finally be adapted for the big screen in 2001, with Peter Jackson as director, and ended up being a gigantic hit. Coincidentally, Jackson also directed the 2021 Beatles documentary *Get Back*. [26]

The Three Stigmata of Palmer Eldritch (196X or 197X)

Written By - Phillip K.Dick

John Lennon once considered doing an adaptation of Phillip K.Dick's 1965 science fiction novel, set in the then-far-flung future of 2016, with a plot similar to the 2010 Christopher Nolan film *Inception*. It was one of Lennon's favourite books, and he even wanted to buy the rights to the novel and film it, but he never got round to doing so.

Many of Phillip's works have been adapted into many successful feature films including *Blade Runner*, *Total Recall* and *Minority Report*. [27]

Paul McCartney's Sci-Fi Movies (197X)

When Paul McCartney set up his MPL Communications company in 1969, Macca, in an act of coming out of the geeky closet, wanted to make a few science fiction movies. With his wealth increasing, he could afford to hire some top writers to prepare scripts from his basic ideas, and he even approached Isaac Asimov to write a screenplay around the premise of extraterrestrials who came to earth and took on the appearance of his band, Wings. Asimov wrote a script, but Macca wasn't 100% happy with it, and after a further rewrite, it fell through. He even approached the creator of *Star Trek* himself, Gene Roddenberry, to make a movie with him. It was announced in the press but ultimately nothing came from it! [27]

Working Class Hero (197X)

Presumably based around the popular John Lennon solo track of the same name from his 1970 album *John Lennon/Plastic Ono Band*. A lot of film was shot for it, but nothing ever materialised. [27]

Oh! Calcutta! (1972)

Directed By - Jacques Levy
Written By - Kenneth Tynan
Release Date - June 1972

Based on the very controversial Broadway musical comedy revue written by the famous British drama critic Kenneth Tynan, probably best known for allegedly being the first person to say the F-word on British TV. John Lennon contributed a sketch to this film about a very inappropriate recreational activity, often associated with 13-year-old boys, which was cut out of the finished movie. [28]

Harry and Ringo's Night Out (1974)

Written By - Harry Nilsson and Ringo Starr

A collaboration project between the legendary singer/songwriter Harry Nilsson and Ringo Starr. Very little is known about the project, and it never materialised. [27]

The Three Musketeers (1974)

Directed By - Richard Lester
Release Date - March 29th 1974

Back in the 1960s, Richard Lester approached The Beatles about doing the millionth film based on the old classic French novel from 1844 *The Three Musketeers* by Alexandre Dumas. The Beatles eventually declined, as they thought they were not suited to the characters of the Musketeers. Also being considered was their favourite celeb crush of the time, French sex kitten Brigitte Bardot, as Milady de Winter. It was eventually made in 1974 without them (obviously, as they had disbanded by then) with the cast including the likes of Michael York, Raquel Welch and Spike Milligan. [26]

Our Show For Ringo Starr (1975)

Written By - Graham Chapman and Douglas Adams

A collaboration between Monty Python's Graham Chapman and Douglas Adams, best known for writing *The Hitchhiker's Guide To The Galaxy* - the duo teamed up to create a TV movie based around Ringo's solo album *Goodnight Vienna*. It was a science-fiction story about Ringo playing an office worker, whose increasingly boring life suddenly becomes interesting when a robot mistakes him for his outer-space counterpart, Rinog Trars, and grants him the power to travel through space and time, and even destroy the universe itself with a wave of his hand.

Despite it being pitched to various American television networks, nobody was interested in producing it. However, the script was eventually made public

199

in 1999 in the book *OJRIL: The Completely Incomplete Graham Chapman*. [29]

Band On The Run (1980)

Presumably based around the 1973 Wings album of the same name, this Paul McCartney film was going to be about an old rock star fed up with the life-style, retreating from the rock & roll rat race to join a group of unknown musicians. The basic storyline was written by Macca, and Willie Russell, the playwright responsible for the award winning play *John, Paul, George, Ringo . . . and Bert*, was hired to fatten up the storyline and make a script. Despite the script being complete, the film was never finished. [26]

Strawberry Fields Forever (Unknown)

A rumoured sequel to the beloved animated classic *Yellow Submarine* - all that is known about this film comes from a book called *The 50 Greatest Movies Never Made* by Chris Gore. Apparently it was planned to be the first computer animated motion picture (the first one would end up being 1995's *Toy Story* by Pixar). Allegedly, 10 minutes of footage was made, but has never been publicly released. [30]

3 Days In The Life (2007)

Directed By - Anthony Cox
Running Time - 120 Minutes

A fly-on-the-wall account of John Lennon at his house at Tittenhurst Park in London back in 1970. Compiled from 10 hours' worth of intimate footage of John and Yoko shot by Yoko's ex-husband, Anthony Cox. The film contained footage of Lennon smoking dope with civil rights activist Michael X, writing songs (which later evolved into the Lennon solo hits 'Mind Games 'and 'Remember') and discussing putting LSD in Richard Nixon's tea.

It was pulled from public release by Yoko, as she had a clear and absolute agreement with Cox that the footage would never be commercially released, and the people who were going to be releasing the film were breaching their agreement. [31]

The Beatles - The Lost Concert (2012)

Directed By - Steve Cole
Intended Release Date - May 17th 2012
Running Time - 92 Minutes

A documentary that was to focus on their first ever US concert appearance on the 11th February 1964 at the Washington Coliseum. As well as featuring new interviews with Paul and Ringo, a slew of famous people were scheduled to appear in this documentary including Chuck Berry, Steven Tyler from Aerosmith, Mark Ronson, Duffy and Paul Gambaccini. Unfortunately, the film was never released because of a legal dispute between its producers and Sony/ATV Music Publishing, which owns the copyright of the eight Beatles tracks that were featured in the concert. [32]

Yellow Submarine Remake (2012)

Directed By - Robert Zemeckis

Back in 2009, Disney, Apple and Imagemovers Digital announced a motion-capture remake of the 1968 animated classic at the D23 Expo, and the release date was planned for 2012, to coincide with the 2012 Summer Olympics in London. It was to be directed by Robert Zemeckis (*Who Framed Roger Rabbit*, *Back To The Future*, *Forrest Gump* etc.), who was also known for making films in this CGI motion-capture style such as *The Polar Express* and *A Christmas Carol* (he also directed 1978's Beatle inspired movie *I Wanna Hold Your Hand*), and the roles of The Beatles would have been played by the tribute band, The Fab Four, with Paul's voice provided by Peter Serafinowicz, John being voiced by Dean Lennox Kelly, Cary Elwes as George, and Adam Campbell as Ringo. *Doctor Who*'s David Tennant was in talks to play the Chief Blue Meanie, and if the film was successful, it was to have been adapted into a Broadway Musical and a Cirque de Soleil Show. Because of the commercial failure of the aforementioned *Christmas Carol* film and another of Zemeckis', *Mars Needs Moms*, and Disney shutting down Imagemovers Digital, the project was scrapped. By 2012, Zemeckis had no interest in continuing the project. All that remains of the film are some concept art and some animation tests. [33]

The Fifth Beatle (2013)

Based on the acclaimed graphic novel by Vivek Tiwary, this TV drama was going to tell the story of The Beatles 'manager, Brian Epstein, who is often considered to be the fifth member of The Beatles. It was announced in 2013, and the rights were optioned by Sonar Entertainment. It was going to be a multi-part television series and Vivek Tiwary, who wrote the original graphic novel, was going to serve as both the series 'writer and executive producer. Despite the drama acquiring the rights to The Beatles' back catalogue from Sony, it ultimately never materialised, as of writing, and is assumed shelved. A similar project in the form of a film biopic was announced in 2020. [34]

Chapter Twelve
Beatle Biopics and Fictionalised Portrayals

Biopics, AKA biographical pictures - the subject of many an Oscar. They are basically dramatisations of real life people, with varying degrees of success and historical accuracy; and don't forget to give our main protagonists some obligatory grit and an angst upgrade. Before *Bohemian Rhapsody* and *Rocketman* were mega successes, The Beatles had their fair share of biopic movies made about them. Also included here are fictionalised versions of our fabulous foursome in other films and TV shows, including parody versions - some with actors, others using manipulated stock footage to put them into fictional situations. Expect in these fictional portrayals for John to get all the glory, Paul to get some, George to be sidelined to the back, and Ringo to get a line or two if he's lucky. Another trend with these pictures is that they will either focus on the formative years, or the turbulent final years, with the Beatlemania and psychedelic eras being entirely glossed over.

In 2020, a biopic based on the life of Beatles manager Brian Epstein was announced.

El Rey En Londres (1966)

Directed By - Anibal Uset
Written By - Roberto Campbell, Roger Dunton and Jorge A.Zerda
Release Date - October 11th 1966
Running Time - 85 Minutes

Translated into English as *The King In London*, this is an Argentinian musical comedy movie featuring singers Palito Ortega and Graciela Borges playing themselves, taking a trip to London, and meeting several popular artists of The British Invasion via the cost-saving method of archival clips.

The Beatles make an "appearance" at the end of this film, via stock footage of them performing 'She Loves You 'at the ABC Cinema in Manchester from 1963, which was originally featured in the Pathe featurette *The Beatles Come To Town*. In the context of the film, The Beatles are actually the opening act for Palito Ortega, who closes the film playing his hit tune 'Tu Tienes Todo 'with an audience consisting of Beatles audience stock footage. During

203

the transition between the two acts, the stock footage Beatles are replaced with doubles, with John introducing Ortega. The continuity is very poor, as the doubles don't look like the real Beatles, John doesn't sound anything like John when he introduces Ortega, and he suddenly changes guitars.

Clips are available on YouTube.

Beatlefacts

* To fool people into thinking that The Beatles actually physically appear in the film, the Fab Four appear predominantly on the poster receiving top billing!

The Goodies Rule OK? (1975)

Directed By - Jim Franklin
First Broadcast - December 21st 1975
Running Time - 49 Minutes

The Goodies was a Pythonesque sitcom that was massively popular in the UK and ran from 1970-1982, starring Bill Oddie, Tim Brooke Taylor and Graeme Garden playing themselves.

The special begins with The Goodies (under the name of The Bootles) playing in The Cavern Club in 1961 to an audience of record company executives, only for rotten fruit to be thrown at them on stage. However, after leaving the stage, four young men come in and steal their songs and appearance, and end up becoming stars - The Beatles (who appear in the episode via well-coordinated stock footage and overdubbed voices)!

This special is readily available on DVD.

I Wanna Hold Your Hand (1978)

Directed By - Robert Zemeckis
Release Date - April 21st 1978
Running Time - 98 Minutes

The directorial debut of Robert Zemeckis, who would later direct classic films such as the *Back To The Future* trilogy, *Who Framed Roger Rabbit*, and *Forrest Gump*. It centres around a group of teenagers from New Jersey who run off to see our fabulous foursome perform on *The Ed Sullivan Show* back in 1964 in the hope of meeting them. Along the way, they learn new things regarding growing up and friendship.

The Beatles themselves don't really appear in the movie, but when we do get a glimpse, we only see their backs or their feet, a technique that would be repeated again when they "cameoed" in the 2015 CGI movie *Minions*.

Playing himself in the movie is DJ Murray The K, who infamously called himself 'the fifth Beatle'.

The movie was well-received, and the success of this film led to Robert Zemeckis being one of the most successful film-makers of all time.

Beatlefacts

*   It took nine months to secure the rights to The Beatles 'music.
*   Carrie Fisher, best known for playing Princess Leia in the *Star Wars* movies, and fresh from duetting with Ringo Starr in the infamous 1978 *Ringo* variety special, was going to play the part of Janis, but this fell through.

The Birth Of The Beatles (1979)

"Where are we going lads? To The top! What top? The very top!"

Directed By - Richard Marquand
Written By - John Kurland and Jacob Eskendar
Running Time - 104 Minutes
Release Date - November 23rd 1979

Produced by Dick Clark, and created by some of the team responsible for the Elvis Presley biopic *Elvis* starring Kurt Russell, this was the very first dramatic film based on the life of The Beatles, and was the only one made during the lifetime of John Lennon. It was directed by Richard Marquand, who directed none other than the timeless classic *Star Wars Episode VI - The Return Of The Jedi*. Unlike future Beatle biopics, which tend to focus on one particular member (usually John), this one attempts to have equal focus on all four members (and Pete Best and Stuart Sutcliffe too!) but to be fair, like most future Beatle biopics, John is centre stage. This film focuses on the formative years, spanning 1961-1964.

For something made in 1979 for no budget, it does what it sets out to do, and the actors do a halfway decent job at portraying the Fab Four (with John Altman AKA Nasty Nick from UK soap drama *Eastenders* playing George Harrison), even if John (played by Stephen MacKenna) is, in fact, played by an actor in his mid-30s, and their resemblance to the real Beatles is superficial. Paul is played by Rod Culbertson, Ray Ashcroft plays Ringo, Michael Ryan plays Pete Best, while David Wilkinson plays Stuart Sutcliffe.

The highlight would be the re-creation of the music that was provided by the band RAIN, who were one of the early Beatles tribute bands, and they do a fantastic job, sounding almost identical to the real Beatles. It even had some creative consulting from one of the actual Beatles - Pete Best, the original drummer for the band, who had a hand in making it, though the events reflected in the film do show a bias towards him, especially in regards to how he was fired from the band.

The film hasn't seen an official home video release, so the best place to find it would be via streaming if it's available or if you can find a third generation homemade VHS somewhere, but it is doing the rounds in the bootleg DVD circuit.

While it is showing its age, it's an admirable effort for the time period.

Beatlefacts

* The Beatles, with the exception of Pete Best, were opposed to this film being made, and wanted it to be scrapped, probably explaining why it has never been commercially released outside of bootlegs.

SCTV (1980)

Directed By - John Blanchard
Written By - Various
First Broadcast - September 19th 1980
Running Time - 30 Minutes

SCTV (AKA *Second City TV*) was a US sketch show series not too dissimilar to Eric Idle's *Rutland Weekend Television* which ran from 1976-1981. It revolved around a fictional TV station called *SCTV*, and the sketches were usually parodies of films and TV shows. In an episode broadcast on the 19th September 1980, Ringo Starr (played by Rick Moranis, who is probably best known for playing Louis Tully in *Ghostbusters*) forms a new band called Rings, and performs the title track from their debut album *Cause I Know That You'll Always Be*. In the middle of the song, he goes into a drum solo similar to that of The Beatles track 'The End'.

Beatlefacts

* The name 'Rings' is a mixture of a take-off of the name of Paul McCartney's band after The Beatles, Wings, and Ringo's many rings on his fingers.

Beatlemania (1981)

Directed By - Joseph Manduke
Written By - Bob Gill, Robert Rabinowitz and Lynda Obst
Release Date - July 1981
Running Time - 86 Minutes

Beatlemania was a successful Broadway show that focused on The Beatles ' success, which ran from May 1977 to October 1979, totalling 1006 performances at the Boston Colonia Theatre and the Winter Garden Theatre on Broadway. The musical was a massive success, despite not having an official opening night, and for the show's first six months, every ticket had sold out. The show is still going to this day.

Because of the stage show's success, a movie adaptation was produced by USA Video Production after 3 years of development. Production began in late 1980 (shortly before Lennon's horrific murder), and the film's cast consisted of David Leon as John, Mitch Weissman as Paul, Tom Teeley as George and Ralph Castelli as Ringo, and it was basically the stage show on film. The movie received a negative reception from critics, and plans for a follow up were immediately shelved.

Beatlefacts

* Many of the members of the stage show's cast would later join RAIN - a Beatles tribute band who had provided cover versions in the biopic film *Birth Of The Beatles*.

Spitting Image (1984-1996, 2020-Present)

Created By - Peter Fluck and Roger Law
First Broadcast - February 26th 1984-Present
Running Time - 25 Minutes

Very funny UK satirical sketch show series using some incredibly terrifying caricatured puppets of politicians and celebrities that was a mainstay of British television in the 1980s and 1990s. Paul and Ringo have been ribbed on the show on numerous occasions. Paul is portrayed as a small puppet, who only seems to sing bland sugary sweet songs, and who is desperate to have another chart hit, sometimes joined by his then-wife Linda.

Ringo is portrayed with an enormous nose and large Mick Jagger-esque lips. One skit featured Ringo taunting Yoko Ono before being kicked unconscious by her, while another one features him drunk, narrating 'Thomas the

Tanked Engine', featuring a boozed-up Thomas with a red nose, big lips and beard with Gordon The Big Engine taking him to the drying out shed, and then going completely off the rails!

John and Yoko: A Love Story (1985)

Directed By - Sandor Stern
Written By - Sandor Stern and Edward Hulme
First Broadcast - December 2nd 1985
Running Time - 146 Minutes

Made for American TV station NBC, this biopic primarily focuses on the love story between John Lennon and Yoko Ono, chronicling the years from 1966 to John's tragic murder in 1980. The first hour or so focuses on the Beatle years, while the rest of the film is more focused on John's solo years.

One thing that increases the credibility of this TV movie is the fact that it did have a great deal of cooperation from Yoko herself and the Lennon estate, but do expect some of the facts to be sanitised, although overall it's fairly accurate. The film also helps portray Ms. Ocean Child - a somewhat maligned figure in The Beatles story - in a more positive light, showing her troubles with sexism and racism, and you really do feel sad for her when she suffers from a heartbreaking miscarriage and later stillbirth. Another well-received aspect about the film is that it portrayed John in a rather accurate and more balanced way, without accentuating the stereotypes of John either being an unpredictable jerk or being St. John of Peace and Love.

Beatlefacts

*   The longest of The Beatles biopics to date, running at 146 minutes.
*   Peter Capaldi - who is known for playing the 12th incarnation of Doctor Who - plays George Harrison. Mark McGann - the actor who plays John - is the brother of Paul McGann, who played the 8th incarnation of The Doctor. The McGann brothers also have acting siblings in Stephen and Joe.
*   The role of John Lennon was initially considered for an actor named Mark Lindsay, but he had to pull out as his full name was none other than Mark Lindsay Chapman... so the role went to another Mark, Mark McGann, who had an uncanny resemblance to John, and even sounds a bit like him (it helps being a fellow Liverpudlian). Mark Lindsay Chapman would later portray John for real in the 2008 film *Chapter 27*, which is based around the murder of John Lennon.
*   Mike Myers (*Shrek, Austin Powers, Wayne's World* etc.) has a small un-credited appearance as a young deliveryman. Myers 'parentage is actually

from Liverpool. The last letter George Harrison wrote before he died was to Myers, praising his work on *Austin Powers*.

* Due to copyright reasons, the film was never screened in the UK on TV. When eventually released on VHS in the UK, it went for the rather silly price of £55 (around £168 in 2021!). It did however see a DVD release in 2006.

John Lennon: A Journey In The Life (1985)

Directed By - Ken Howard
First Broadcast - December 6th 1985
Running Time - 64 Minutes

Broadcast on BBC1 in the winter of 1985 to mark the fifth anniversary of John's tragic murder, this was part of the BBC documentary series *Everyman*. Ken Howard, the man who directed the film, was no stranger to the world of music, having written many songs for artists such as Dave Dee, Dozy, Beaky, Mick and Titch, and he even co-wrote a song for none other than Elvis Presley. This film was a combination of dramatised footage interspersed with archive footage from the real Lennon and performances made especially for the programme, including Roger Walters from Pink Floyd playing 'Across The Universe'. John Lennon is played by Bernard Hill (AKA Theoden from the *Lord Of The Rings* films), who coincidentally portrayed Lennon ten years previously in a stage play. The TV film also featured an appearance from The Beatles' press officer Derek Taylor playing himself.

The movie received praise from none other than John's widow Yoko Ono, but unfortunately because of the amount of copyrighted footage used, it is very unlikely to be appearing on home video or streaming anytime soon, which probably explains this film's obscurity.

Midnight Angel: Stuart Sutcliffe (1990)

Directed By - Andrew Piddington
First Broadcast - May 13th 1990
Running Time - 49 Minutes

Part of the London Weekend Television (LWT) documentary series *Celebration* which lasted from 1979-1993, this is a very obscure documentary/biopic hybrid about the life of The Beatles 'original bassist, the late Stuart Sutcliffe, which preceded *Backbeat* by four years!

This television drama was about the last six months of Stuart's life, and he is portrayed in this film by Peter Leeper, who is best known for playing Mr.

Parrott in the children's TV drama *Grange Hill*. Pauline Sutcliffe, Stuart's sister, served as technical consultant, and shooting took place in Hamburg, Glasgow and London, while Liverpool was represented by still photographs, and archive footage of The Beatles playing at The Cavern Club in 1962.

This TV drama has never been rebroadcast since its initial transmission, and while the programme hasn't been wiped, finding a copy of it via the bootleg circles is almost as rare as finding a genuine copy of The Beatles' experimental track 'Carnival Of Light'!

Beatlefacts

* With the exception of a sequence showing Stuart's paintings, the documentary was made entirely in black and white.
* When the movie was being shot, a fan of Stuart's work expressed anger at himself being filmed and protested *"The Beatles are famous, he's not famous!"* [7]. Harsh.
* Andrew Piddington would later direct the 2006 biopic about John Lennon's assassin *The Killing Of John Lennon*.

The Hours and Times (1991)

Directed By - Christopher Munch
Written By - Christopher Munch
Release Date - September 7th 1991
Running Time - 60 Minutes

This is a fictionalised dramatisation of a rumoured affair John Lennon had with The Beatles 'manager, Brian Epstein, back in 1963, set in a getaway weekend in Barcelona, Spain. Epstein is struggling to express his infatuation for Lennon, and John is torn between Epstein needing him, and revealing his suffering. They reflect on both their private and professional lives, and express the unique bond that they share.

The short film received positive reviews from critics, and it won a Special Jury Recognition award at the 1992 Sundance Film Festival as well as a nomination for the Grand Jury Prize at the same event.

The film saw a re-release in 2019 with a new restoration from Oscilloscope Labs, and was premiered at Sundance later that year.

Beatlefacts

* This is the first time Ian Hart would portray John Lennon. He would portray him again in 1994's *Backbeat* and 2013's *Snodgrass*.

Smashie and Nicey - the End Of An Era (1994)

Directed By - Daniel Kleinman
Created By - Harry Enfield and Paul Whitehouse
First Broadcast - April 4th 1994
Running Time - 45 Minutes

Hilarious UK BBC mockumentary about two ageing washed-up DJs from Radio FAB F.M. with Mike Smash played by Paul Whitehouse and Dave Nice played by Harry Enfield. The Beatles appear in an interview scene via manipulated stock footage (nabbed from an appearance in the 1963 news programme *Day By Day*) and Nicey (Enfield) ends up having a thing for Paul McCartney, and asks what he's doing after the show. Possibly due to clearance issues, The Beatles scene was cut out of the home video release.

Backbeat (1994)

Directed By - Iain Softley
Written By - Iain Softley, Michael Thomas and Stephen Ward
Release Date - April 11th 1994
Running Time - 100 Minutes

A biopic set in the early Hamburg days of The Beatles from 1960-62. The main focus of this film is on Stuart Sutcliffe (played by Stephen Dorff) and his relationship with John Lennon (Ian Hart, in the second time he's played him) and his girlfriend, photographer Astrid Kirchherr (played by Sheryl Lee). The original script that Iain Softley wrote was based on a series of interviews conducted in 1988 with the likes of the real Astrid Kirchherr and other people who were close to The Beatles in Hamburg, but after failing to secure funding, Stephen Ward came in to rewrite the script. The project was finally green-lit in 1993.

The movie received mostly positive reviews from critics; even though Paul McCartney had some reservations, he did enjoy Stephen Dorff's performance as Stuart Sutcliffe, but George Harrison wasn't impressed, and walked out during the premiere. People who praised the film included Astrid Kirchherr, Julian Lennon, Pete Best and Stuart's sister, Pauline. The movie appeared on *Entertainment Weekly*'s list of 'The Best 50 Movies You've Never Seen' in 2012.

The film was adapted into a stage musical in 2010, with another one appearing in 2011.

Beatlefacts

* This film actually does feature a real Beatles recording. When The Beatles perform 'My Bonnie 'with Tony Sheridan in a recording studio, it's actually the real recording used - a rarity for movies about The Beatles.
* George Harrison's mother, Louise, was played by none other than Freda Kelly, who was the manager of The Beatles fan club.
* The second time Ian Hart plays John Lennon - he played him previously in *The Hours And Times* in 1991 and would play him again in 2013 in *Snodgrass* - maybe these films take place in the same continuity??
* Gary Bakewell who plays Paul McCartney would return as Paul in the 2000 TV drama *The Linda McCartney Story*.
* Scott Williams, who plays Pete Best, is a massive Beatles fanboy, and even grew up in Penny Lane in Liverpool. As well as reprising his role six years later in *In His Life - The John Lennon Story*, he played a character named Macca (which is Paul McCartney's nickname) in the acclaimed *Lock, Stock and Two Smoking Barrels*, which was produced by Handmade Films and directed by Guy Ritchie.
* In the film, Stuart covers the Elvis Presley song 'Love Me Tender'. In 2011, a supposed recording of him from 1961 singing the song was released by the Stuart Sutcliffe Estate. It was however proven to be fraudulent thanks to detective work by fans, as it was revealed to be a low-quality version of a 1967 recording by The Boston Show Band.

Forrest Gump (1994)

Directed By - Robert Zemeckis
Written By - Eric Roth
Release Date - October 7th 1994
Running Time - 142 Minutes

Classic movie about a simple yet kind hearted man named Forrest Gump (played by Tom Hanks), who watches historical events from the 1950s-1980s unfold (using the art of archival clips), but his only desire is to be reunited with his hedonistic childhood sweetheart, Jenny. One of the people he encounters on his travels is John Lennon (obviously portrayed by stock footage with his voice overdubbed by Lennon impersonator, Joe Stefanelli) who meets Gump when they both appear on the *Dick Cavett Show* in 1970. The film implies that Gump helped inspire John to write the lyrics to his solo hit 'Imagine 'when Gump talks about his experiences in Mao era China - everything Gump says is worked into the song.

While there's not much there for Beatle fans other than this brief scene, this film is a classic, even if by modern standards the scenes where Gump interacts with historical figures look a bit obvious. Interestingly, the film's director, Robert Zemeckis, also directed the 1978 film *I Wanna Hold Your Hand*, which is about the early days of Beatlemania through the eyes of some fans - it was his first movie.

The Dana Carvey Show (1996)

Directed By - John Fortenberry
Written By - Dana Carvey
First Broadcast - March 12th 1996
Running Time - 30 Minutes

A short lived comedy sketch series starring *Saturday Night Live* comic Dana Carvey, who is probably best known for playing the loveable Garth Algar in the film *Wayne's World*. The first episode featured a sketch called 'Leftover Beatle Memories 'where George, Paul and Ringo (all played by Cavey) circa *Anthology* era, share some amusing anecdotes on The Beatles - Schwing!

Dark Skies (1996)

Directed By - Matthew Penn
Written By - Brent V. Friedman, Brad Markowitz and Bryce Zabel
First Broadcast - October 26th 1996
Running Time - 42 Minutes

An *X-Files* clone for NBC, set in the 1960s, about the political aide John Loengard (played by Eric Close) having a run-in with extraterrestrial forces, and ending up tracking a body-snatching alien invasion as part of a super secret agency - it was cancelled after one season.

In the episode 'Dark Days Night', John Loengard and Kim Sayers uncover a Hive Plot to use The Beatles 'US debut on *The Ed Sullivan Show* to induce a mass suicide. The episode also sees Loengard watching the Fab Four rehearse for their appearance on *The Ed Sullivan Show*, and he meets Sullivan, Brian Epstein (played by Carey Eidel) and even John Lennon himself (played by Joe Stefanelli, who had previously voiced him in *Forrest Gump*), who gives him a signed autograph and doodle. Tim McDougall plays Paul, Rick Pizana plays George while Carmine Grippo is Ringo - none of those three have any speaking lines.

Beatlefacts

*   The autograph and face doodle that John gives Loengard does not match his writing style from the time period, and is in fact more akin to his writing style from the 1970s, especially as the doodle shows John with long hair, which he didn't have until 1968!

A Spasso Nel Tempo - L'avventura Continua (1997)

Directed By - Carlo Vanzina
Written By - Carlo Vanzina
Release Date - December 11th 1997
Running Time - 95 Minutes

Translated to *Getting Around In Time - The Adventure Continues*, this is a sequel to an Italian sci-fi comedy about two tourists called Walter and Asciano getting into a real time machine, and getting lost in time, a bit like Bill and Ted. They travel to the 1960s, and Walter (played by Massimo Boldi, who's dressed a bit like Austin Powers) comes across The Beatles (sans Ringo, who's gone off briefly) crossing the famous Abbey Road crossing and meets up with them. Walter then substitutes for Ringo, and joins them in Abbey Road studios and they do a rendition of their hit 'She Loves You', followed by a medley consisting of 'Let It Be', 'If I Fell', 'Get Back 'and 'Strawberry Fields Forever 'before Ringo returns to the studio. The film didn't get a good reception from the critics.

Gary Gibson plays John, Lawrence Gilmour is Paul, James Lee Elgood is Ringo and Martin Powell is George.

Beatlefacts

*   The historical accuracy isn't good. John and Paul look like their early-1960s style, while George looks like he did during the *Abbey Road* period; not to mention different songs from different periods of The Beatles being played by Walter. Maybe it's a result of time travel messing up history?

Stella Street (1998, 2001)

Directed By - Peter Richardson
Written By - Peter Richardson, Phil Cornwell and John Sessions
First Broadcast - October 16th 1998
Subsequent Appearance - November 13th 2001
Running Time - 10 Minutes Each

Stella Street was a comedic BBC Two series that ran from 1997-2001, with a film version being made in 2004, and a web revival in 2008. The show was a mockumentary series about the aforementioned street in London, where famous celebrities have decided to take refuge. In this series, Mick Jagger and Keith Richards run a corner shop, and in the series two first episode 'Three Months Later . . .', they have a nightmare about losing their job to The Beatles.

The Fab Four returned in the first episode of the fourth series, broadcast in 2001, where we flash back to 1963, and The Beatles have moved to Stella Street jamming in a cafe, and filming 'Twist & Stab '(directed by Alfred Hitchcock) in the upstairs of a house, featuring scenes of graphic violence, by the request of Paul McCartney.

Phil Cornwell plays John and Ringo, while John Sessions plays Paul and George (and Yoko Ono).

Big Train (1998)

Directed By - Graham Linehan and Christopher Morris
Written By - Graham Linehan and Arthur Matthews
First Broadcast - November 9th 1998-February 11th 2002
Running Time - 30 Minutes

A very funny and underrated Monty Python-esque UK sketch show series written by the team behind *Father Ted* and featuring comedians who would end up doing bigger things, such as Simon Pegg and Catherine Tate. One of the sketches in the first series featured The Beatles 'producer George Martin (played by Kevin Eldon) being kidnapped by Iranian terrorists, while rambling about his history in The Beatles in the process. Don't worry, he gets freed in the end!

Rock Profile (1999-2000)

Directed By - Michael Cumming
Created By - Matt Lucas and David Walliams
First Broadcast - December 25th 1999-March 11th 2000
Running Time - 10 Minutes

A satirical comedy series written by Matt Lucas and David Walliams, who would team up again for the super successful sketch series *Little Britain*. It was a series of spoof interviews involving UKTV presenter Jamie Theakston (playing himself) with Matt and David playing parodies of famous rock and pop stars, often using weird or unflattering caricatures or often with fictional characteristics. Paul McCartney is portrayed as a man who is fed up with people asking him about his solo career, and pleased when people mention The Beatles. George Harrison is portrayed as having an Indian accent, and keeps a poppadum in his top pocket, while Ringo Starr claims to be Thomas The Tank Engine's representative on earth! Funny stuff.

Two Of Us (2000)

Directed By - Michael Lindsay-Hogg
Written By - Mark Stanfield
First Broadcast - February 1st 2000
Running Time - 89 Minutes

Directed by The Beatles' good friend Michael Lindsay-Hogg, who had previously directed *Let It Be* and several Beatles music videos, this VH1 US TV film is a fictionalised account of April 24th 1976, six years after the end of The Beatles, with John and Paul meeting up in New York discussing their lives and whether The Beatles should reform. It is also the day in which Lorne Michaels made a statement on the comedy programme *Saturday Night Live* inviting the Fab Four to reunite for the fee of... $3000!

Even if the lead actors don't really look or sound anything like the real John and Paul (in fact, one critic compared this film's version of John to Liam Gallagher from Oasis, who models himself on Lennon), this is forgiven as it is actually a pretty good TV film, and was well-received by Beatles fans. Because of their lack of resemblance, I was initially put off until a few minutes in, when I realised that this one is pretty decent. Definitely one of the better dramatisations, and worth checking out if you can find it.

Beatlefacts

*   Actor Aidan Quinn, who played Paul, stated in a 2004 interview that he met the real Paul McCartney after finishing the film, and Paul had enjoyed it, much to his relief.
*   In the real version of this event, both John and Paul's wives, Yoko and Linda, were also present - it was the last time that they met in person.
*   When John offers Macca some chocolate by saying *"Take this brother, may it serve you well"* - this is a reference to a line John said in that weird piece of noise known as 'Revolution 9'.

The Linda McCartney Story (2000)

Directed By - Armand Mastroianni
Written By - Christine Bernardo
First Broadcast - May 21st 2000
Running Time - 120 Minutes

A made-for-TV biopic for the American market - the central focus is on Paul McCartney's late wife, Linda Eastman McCartney, and it was adapted from the book *Linda McCartney The Biography*. The plot focuses on Linda's early years, snapping photographs for *Rolling Stone* magazine and rubbing shoulders with the Hollywood elite, and of course falling in love with Paul, their marriage and what follows.

Elizabeth Mitchell plays Linda while Gary Bakewell returns as Paul McCartney (having previously played the role in *Backbeat*) and it was shot in Vancouver in Canada. The Beatles covers used in the soundtrack to this biopic were performed by an acclaimed Californian tribute band called The Fab Four. The film received a mixed reception from the fanbase.

Beatlefacts

*   In the scene where The Beatles argue about who should manage them after Brian Epstein's death, they refer to a man named Bruce Grossman. In real life, his name was Allen Klein.
*   Tim Piper, who plays John, reprised his role in an internet series called 'Talks With Lennon Podcast' where Piper plays a version of what John would be like today talking about current events and his past in The Beatles.

In His Life: The John Lennon Story (2000)

Directed By - David Carson
Written By - Michael O'Hara
First Broadcast - December 3rd 2000
Running Time - 85 Minutes

Broadcast near to the 20th anniversary of John Lennon's passing. Like *Two Of Us* and *The Linda McCartney Story*, this TV film was made for the US market, and focused on John Lennon's teenage to early twentysomething years. The film focuses on John living with his Aunt Mimi, forming The Quarrymen, dealing with the abandonment by his father, meeting his first wife, Cynthia Powell, the early Hamburg years of The Beatles, and, like *The Birth Of the Beatles*, ends with The Beatles playing on *The Ed Sullivan Show*.

While a competent low budget TV film for the time, I would recommend *Backbeat* and *Nowhere Boy* (which we'll get to later in the book) over this one, but to its credit, it is arguably one of the more historically accurate Beatle dramatisations. It did however receive a nomination in 2001 by the American Cinema Editors for Best Edited Motion Picture For Commercial Television.

Beatlefacts

* The third made-for-TV Beatle related drama released in 2000. If 2000 was remembered for one thing, it would be the year of made-for-TV Beatle biopics!
* For Irish actor Philip McQuillan, who plays John Lennon, it was his first major acting role. It is his only filmed or televised acting role to date.
* The second time Pete Best is played by Scott Williams, who previously played him in *Backbeat*.

House Of Rock (2000)

First Broadcast - 2000-2002
Running Time - 10 Minutes

Hailed as Britain's answer to *South Park* by *The Guardian*, this was a Channel 4 adult animated series about dead celebrities, and what they get up to in the afterlife, while living in a large undone house. John Lennon appears (voiced by Gary Howe) in Series 2, and is portrayed as being both pompous and pretentious with a monotone voice. He comes with his very own *Yellow Submarine*, which he wears around his waist at all times.

Celebrity Deathmatch (2002)

Written By - Eric Fogel and Gordon Barnett
First Broadcast - April 25th 2002
Running Time - 21 Minutes

A claymation animated series that ran from 1998-2007, broadcast on MTV. In this show, well-known figures duke it out in a wrestling ring, and who ends up dying first, loses. In the episode 'The Missing Beatles Tape', the Fab Four pummel each other senseless in a humorous display of cartoon violence. George and Ringo unfortunately die, and John and Paul are about to kill each other, but Yoko Ono comes in to save the day by singing 'Amazing Grace', and John, Paul and Yoko end the match by singing a brand new Beatles song 'Revolution No.10'.

American Dream (2003)

Written By - Jonathan Price and Josh Goldstein
First Broadcast - January 5th 2003
Running Time - 60 Minutes

A *Wonder Years*-esque nostalgic look at the 1960s about a family from Philadelphia, who experience the life and struggles of the time, accompanied by well-known pop songs from the era. The show lasted from 2002-2005.

In the episode 'I Wanna Hold Your Hand', we get a re-enactment of The Beatles' first visit to America, which uses a clever combination of actors and archival stock footage. The plot of the episode partially focuses on the Pryor family getting to grips with Beatlemania.

My Dinner With Jimi (2003)

Directed By - Bill Fishman
Written By - Howard Kaylan
Release Date - February 16th 2003
Running Time - 90 Minutes

Written by actual Turtles member, Howard Kaylan, and made on the really low budget of $250,000, this is a relatively obscure comedic biopic centring around The Turtles, probably best known for the track 'Happy Together'. The plot focuses on events in the group's lives circa 1966-1967 ending up with a night in 1967 when the band encountered The Beatles, and Howard Kaylan

219

from the band having dinner with Jimi Hendrix, hence the title of the film, as well as encounters with the likes of Brian Jones from the Rolling Stones, Donovan, Frank Zappa, Mama Cass and Jim Morrison from The Doors. Despite its premiere in 2003 at the Santa Monica International Film Festival and some positive reviews, the film only had a very limited theatrical run in 2007, restricted to Toronto in Canada.

Brian Groh plays John, Quinton Flynn is Paul, Nate Dushku plays George and Ben Bode plays Ringo.

The Killing of John Lennon (2006)

Directed By - Andrew Piddlington
Written By - Andrew Piddlington
Release Date - July 15th 2006
Running Time - 114 Minutes

A biographical movie about Mark David Chapman, and his plot to murder our hero, John Lennon. Despite being made in 2006, and receiving a premiere at the Edinburgh Film Festival in July of that year, it didn't come out officially until 2008. Robert Sherman and Tom J. Raider both play John Lennon at different stages of his life, Yuka Sonobe and Yan Xi portray Yoko Ono, while Jonas Ball dons the role of Mark Chapman. The movie received mixed reviews.

Beatlefacts

* Andrew Piddlington had previously directed the very obscure TV Beatles biopic *Stuart Sutcliffe: Midnight Angel*.

The Peter Serafinowicz Show (2007-2008)

Written By - Peter and James Serafinowicz
First Broadcast - October 4th 2007-December 23rd 2008
Running Time - 30 Minutes

A short-lived sketch show created by comedian Peter Serafinowicz (AKA Darth Maul in *Star Wars Episode 1- The Phantom Menace* and Garthan Saal in *Guardians Of The Galaxy*). Two Beatle related skits were made. One was a reoccurring sketch called 'Ringo Remembers', which was a documentary series in which Ringo reflects on fictionalised moments in his career, such as writing the theme tune to *Goldfinger* in the style of his tune 'Don't Pass Me

By'; the struggles with going to the toilet during the *Let It Be* sessions; and John Lennon writing an early version of 'Imagine 'with boastful, ego tripping lyrics. Another sketch that Serafinowicz made was a news segment which revealed that it was John Lennon who thought of the iPod, originally called The BeatleBox (a cross between a dishwasher and a jukebox).

I'm Not There (2007)

Directed By - Todd Haynes
Created By - Todd Haynes and Oren Moverman
Release Date - December 21st 2007
Running Time - 135 Minutes

An unconventional, very loose biopic about the legendary singer-songwriter and good friend to the Fab Four, Bob Dylan, most notable for him being portrayed in the film by multiple actors (including Christian Bale, Heath Ledger and Ben Whishaw), representing different eras of Bob's life. We get a fantasised account of our pal Bob (in this sequence played by Cate Blanchett, we're not kidding) introducing The Beatles to something not-so-legal that makes them high and giddy. The Beatles are played by Johann St-Louis (John), Mike Caruso (Paul), Pierre-Luc Lebeau (George) and Jean-Nicolas Dery (Ringo).

Beatlefacts

* The final film to be released in Heath Ledger's lifetime before his extremely tragic premature death in January 2008.

Walk Hard: The Dewey Cox Story (2007)

Directed By - Joe Kasdan
Written By - Joe Kasdan and Judd Apatow
Release Date - December 21st 2007
Running Time - 96 Minutes

A satire of rock music biopics, which tells the story of Dewey Cox (played by John C. Reilly), whose music career spanned from the 1950s-1970s and who lived a life of Sex and Drugs and Rock & Roll. The movie was a success and is to this day considered a cult classic.

The Beatles appear in a scene (with Paul Rudd as John, Jack Black as Paul, Justin Long as George and Jason Schwartzman as Ringo) where Dewey visits

India, and they take LSD, leading to a *Yellow Submarine*-esque hallucination scene.

Chapter 27 (2008)

Directed By - Jarrett Schaefer
Written By - Jarrett Schaefer
Release Date - March 28th 2008
Running Time - 114 Minutes

Based on the book *Let Me Take You Down* by Jack Jones, like the previous film *The Killing Of John Lennon*, this film has the same plot, focusing on Mark Chapman's intentions to kill our beloved John. In this film, Chapman is portrayed by the usually handsome Jared Leto, who gained weight and made himself look more ugly to resemble the real life Chapman. The movie received a negative reception from critics, and was one of the most controversial films made in the 2000s. Yoko refused to comment or watch the film, and there were many petitions to have the movie banned, such as boycottchapter27.org. Despite the controversy, it did however win two awards at the Zurich Film Festival, one for director Jarrett Schaefer and another for Jared Leto.

Beatlefacts

* John is morbidly played by an actor named Mark Lindsay Chapman. He was originally considered to play him in the 1985 biopic *John and Yoko - A Love Story*, but bailed out because of his namesake.
* There isn't a 27th chapter in the book *The Catcher In The Rye*, the book that "inspired" Mark Chapman to kill John Lennon.

CollegeHumor Originals - Ringo Wants to Sing More (2009)

Release Date - August 4th 2009
Running Time - 3 Minutes

Made for the YouTube channel CollegeHumor, this funny short is a parody of The Beatles song 'Octopus 'Garden', in which Ringo complains about his lack of involvement in many of The Beatles songs, and that he could sing on more than just one of the tracks on the albums. The short video spoofs all the eras of The Beatles including *A Hard Day's Night*, *Sgt. Pepper* and the *Yellow Submarine* animated film.

The only thing that isn't great about this is that Ringo's moustache is even less convincing than it was in *John & Yoko: A Love Story*, but this is forgiven, as it's a comedy sketch and not a serious dramatisation!

Robot Chicken (2009)

Written By - Seth Green, Matthew Senreich and Mike Fasolo
First Broadcast - August 23rd 2009
Running Time - 25 Minutes

Robot Chicken is a US comedic stop-motion animated sketch series for adults, which usually satirises pop cultural icons and crosses them over with something else eg. Bugs Bunny and Elmer Fudd doing a rap battle in the style of the Eminem movie *8 Mile*. It has been running since 2005, and continues to do so to this day. It's a really fun series, though their version of *Toy Story 4* will completely ruin your childhood!

In the season 4 episode 'Due to Constraints of Time and Budget', the famous *Yellow Submarine* movie is parodied with The Beatles encountering the Blue Meanies in the Blue October - the sketch was a crossover between *Yellow Submarine* and *The Hunt For Red October*, and was actually pretty funny.

Nowhere Boy (2009)
Directed By - Sam Taylor-Wood
Written By - Mark Greenhalgh
Release Date - October 29th 2009
Running Time - 98 Minutes

Inspired by the book written by Lennon's sister, Julia, *Imagine This: Growing Up With My Brother John Lennon*, this is a surprisingly good biopic movie about the teenage years of John Lennon spanning from 1955-1960, mainly focusing on his relationship with his mother Julia and his Aunt Mimi.

Reception to the film was mostly positive, though the script had to be altered for the consent of Paul McCartney and John's widow, Yoko Ono, as they believed that the portrayal of Aunt Mimi was too strict. The actors playing the leads are very convincing, and don't come across as shallow caricatures, not to mention getting age appropriate actors for John, Paul and George rather than, as in other biopics, men in their mid-30s. The actress who played Aunt Mimi (the highly regarded Kristin Scott Thomas) portrayed her in a sympathetic fashion, and was nominated for a BIFA (British Institute Film Award) for the Best Supporting Actress role.

As far as biopics go, this is arguably the best one, with good acting with a lot of heart, and plenty of emotion too. If this one is available to stream, it's definitely worth a watch.

Beatlefacts

* Like *A Hard Day's Night*, the word 'Beatles 'isn't said once in the entire film.
* The movie's score was provided by the electronic dance act Goldfrapp - a rather unlikely choice, but it works really well.

Lennon Naked (2010)

Directed By - Edmund Coulthard
Written By - Robert Jones
First Broadcast - June 23rd 2010
Running Time - 82 Minutes

A BBC TV drama that focuses on John Lennon's life circa 1967-1971 (with a bit of 1964 thrown in at the beginning).

John is played by none other than the famed Christopher Eccleston. While he does an excellent job at portraying John, Eccleston was 46 when the film was made, which was older than John was when he died, and in the film, he is meant to be 27-31! Because of his strong performance, you forget about the age difference.

Overall, this is a pretty good TV movie, and certainly a step up from other Beatles biopics in terms of quality. It does however mainly focus on the darker and more unpleasant side of Lennon's character, which might put you off John, but remember, this is a partially fictionalised drama - it even says so in the beginning! Oh and you do get to see Lennon naked (maybe a little more than we need to) so the title of the movie is not misleading. It also makes a nice companion piece and a good compare-and-contrast to the Yoko approved version of John's life as presented in *John & Yoko: A Love Story*.

Beatlefacts

* Christopher Eccleston (John Lennon) is the second actor to be both Doctor Who and a Beatle. Previously, Peter Capaldi, who would play the 12th incarnation of The Doctor, played George Harrison in the aforementioned *John & Yoko: A Love Story*.

* The original TV broadcast version of this film used actual recordings of Beatles and John Lennon songs in the soundtrack - because of clearance issues, these were replaced with rock & roll standards on the DVD version, but the Lennon solo songs remained.
* Speaking of *Doctor Who*, David Tennant, who played the 10th Doctor, introduced the film when it was shown on PBS in the USA.
* Rory Kinnear, who plays Brian Epstein, is the son of Roy Kinnear, who had acted with the real John Lennon in both *Help!* and *How I Won The War*.

Paul McCartney Really Is Dead: The Last Testament of George Harrison (2010)

Directed By - Joel Gilbert
Release Date - September 1st 2010
Running Time - 95 Minutes

A no budget spoof documentary about the infamous 'Paul Is Dead 'rumour told through the testimony of George Harrison. The story goes that in the summer of 2005, a package arrived from London at the Hollywood offices of Highway 61 Entertainment, without a return address, which contained two cassette tapes from December 30th 1999 labeled 'The Last Testament Of George Harrison'. An actor doing an unconvincing George Harrison voice tells the infamous "story" of how Paul was killed in a car crash in November 1966 and was replaced by a double named William Shears Campbell. We later learn that British Intelligence MI5 was forced to cover up Paul's death to prevent the mass suicide of Beatles fans, and we also learn about a man named "Maxwell" - the Beatles 'MI5 handler, and that John's assassination in 1980 happened because he was about to reveal that Paul was an imposter.

Directed by Joel Gilbert, who has directed many spoofs of sensationalist documentaries, such as *Elvis Found Alive* and others with a more political theme, the "rockumentary" didn't get good reviews, mostly from people who didn't realise the irony behind it.

Harry and Paul (2010)

"Yeah, yeah we're The Beatles/Still having fun/we never took no drugs/not even one/we're still together/50 years on/Oooh!"

225

Written By - Harry Enfield and Paul Whitehouse
First Broadcast - April 13th 2007-May 25th 2014
Running Time - 30 Minutes

Originally known as *Ruddy Hell! It's Harry & Paul*, this was a UK comedy sketch show starring Harry Enfield and Paul Whitehouse, and was the successor to the immensely successful *Harry Enfield And Chums* - one the biggest TV shows of the 1990s. While not as successful as *Chums*, *Harry And Paul* had some very funny skits and some memorable characters. In the show's third series in 2010, there was a new reoccurring sketch called The Silver Haired Beatles, which is an alternate universe reimagining of the Fab Four still together in 2010 - they had never taken drugs and never been in any real controversy - and both John and George are still alive.

In this universe, they are permanently stuck in the *A Hard Day's Night* era, and are chased around by knicker throwing geriatric ladies, and are still as successful as they were during the height of Beatlemania. Harry Enfield plays John Lennon, Paul Whitehouse is George Harrison, Lewis MacLeod is Paul McCartney, Kevin Elson is Ringo Starr and George Martin, while John Henshaw plays their new manager. Bob Dylan (played by Phil Cornwell) appears in some of the sketches offering the boys some drugs, only to get turned down.

This is a really funny series of sketches, and is available on the *Harry and Paul* Series 3 DVD.

Playhouse Presents - Snodgrass (2013)

Directed By - David Blair
Written By - David Quantick
First Broadcast - April 25th 2013
Running Time - 24 Minutes

I've always been a fan of alternate history, and in this short we learn about a "what if" scenario, where John Lennon left the Beatles in 1962 over a dispute of having 'How Do You Do It '(which later went to Gerry and The Pacemakers) as their debut single instead of 'Love Me Do 'and it was The Hollies that became the biggest band of all time.

Created for the Sky Arts TV series *Playhouse Presents*, and based on a novella by Ian R MacLeod, the story takes place in 1991, where a 50-year-old Lennon (played by Ian Hart AKA Professor Quirrell in *Harry Potter*, who previously played Lennon in 1992's *The Hours And Times* and 1994's *Backbeat*) is unemployed in John Major era Britain, reduced to being on the dole, and The Beatles themselves are just a "middle of the road" group playing for

226

the nostalgia circuit. He eventually finds work as a man who simply folds letters and puts them in envelopes for a local firm - not exactly rock & roll. He has a fear of becoming a "snodgrass" (a person who only cares about work and nothing else) and has become a very bitter person, but he still maintains his dark, cynical sense of humour. For *Doctor Who* fans, you may recognise the actress Annette Badland, best known for being the Chief Slitheen in the Christopher Eccleston era, playing an ageing fan who Lennon snubs.

While not perfect, it's worth a watch if you can find it, and "imagine" how things might have been.

The Tonight Show Starring Jimmy Fallon (2014)

First Broadcast - February 24th 2014
Running Time - 60 Minutes

A popular US comedic talk show featuring interviews, celebs and sketches presented by, who else... Jimmy Fallon!

In an episode broadcast on the 24th February 2014 to coincide with the 50th anniversary of The Beatles 'first appearance on *The Ed Sullivan Show*, we get an "unearthed, never before seen" clip of them that took place right after their performance of 'I Want To Hold Your Hand 'that showed how "ahead of their time" they were.

In this sketch, John Lennon (played by Jimmy Fallon himself, and Ringo, played by Fallon's good friend, Fred Armisen) thank the audience and tell them *"don't forget to 'like' us on Facebook"* and *"You can follow us on Twitter at @TheRealBeatlesUK"*, with the Twitter account being superimposed on screen (this is not the real Beatles Twitter account, if you're wondering!) and John then later shouts out the group's account name on Instagram too, which includes an underscore, so fans ensconced in Beatlemania can also enjoy their "throwback Thursdays" too. It ends with the band doing a selfie. A pretty funny sketch, and a good send-up of the social media obsession of our times.

Beatlefacts

* Paul McCartney is played by an uncredited Gerard Bradford, who is an actor, as well as a producer and a writer for the show.

Rubber Soul (2014)

Ten Years, Two Interviews, One Lennon

Directed By - Jon Lefkovitz
Release Date - March 11th 2014
Running Time - 84 Minutes

An interesting hybrid of a documentary and a biopic, centred around two interviews with John Lennon and Yoko Ono conducted ten years apart (1970 and 1980, one after the fall of The Beatles and the other before his assassination). John is played by Joseph Bearor and Yoko is played by Denice Lee, and these reconstructions are adapted from available transcripts and audio with the two interviews being juxtaposed to explore the dynamic nature of John's identity over time.

Jimi: All Is By My Side (2014)

Directed By - John Ridley
Written By - John Ridley
Release Date - June 12th 2014
Running Time - 118 Minutes

Andre 3000 from the legendary hip-hop duo Outkast plays Jimi Hendrix in this critically divisive biopic film about his early years. Paul McCartney (played by an uncredited Ger Duffy) and George Harrison (played by another uncredited actor) make small cameo appearances in the audience when Hendrix covers 'Sgt. Pepper's Lonely Hearts Club Band 'at one of his gigs.

Cilla (2014)

Directed By - Paul Whittington
Written By - Jeff Pope
First Broadcast - 15th-19th September 2014
Running Time - 45-47 Minutes Each

An ITV mini-series about the early life of fellow Liverpudlian singer (and future light entertainment star), the late Cilla Black, who was a friend of The Beatles back in the day and was managed by Brian Epstein. The Beatles make appearances (played by actors, of course!) in the first and third episode, with John being played by Jack Farthing, Kevin Mains as Paul, Michael Hawkins as George and Tom Dunlea as Ringo. Brian Epstein and George Martin also show up played by Ed Stoppard and Elliot Cowan respectively.

The mini-series was a critical and commercial success, with the programme gaining a National Television Award for Best Drama Performance for Sheridan Smith, who played Cilla, and this led to the real Cilla having a career resurrection. Sadly, the real Cilla died in August 2015, and this led to the series being repeated on TV.

Minions (2015)

Directed By - Kyle Balda and Pierre Coffin
Written By - Brian Lynch
Release Date - June 26th 2015
Running Time - 91 Minutes

The Beatles make a small CGI animated cameo appearance in a scene where minions Stuart, Kevin and Bob come up out of a sewer on Abbey Road in London, in the middle of the famous Abbey Road zebra crossing, and you see the legs of the Fab Four walking across (with Paul barefoot like in the album cover), while a few bars of 'Love Me Do 'play in the background.

As well as introducing kids to the wonders of 1960s pop music, the end credits feature The Beatles song 'Got To Get You Into My Life', and after the credits have rolled, the cast of the movie do a dance off to a cover of 'Revolution 'sung in Minionese. A great film for the young and young at heart.

Vinyl (2016)

Directed By - Jon S. Baird
Written By - Riccardo DiLoreto and Michael Mitnick
First Broadcast - March 27th 2016
Running Time - 60 Minutes Each

Not to be confused with a low-budget but very enjoyable film from 2012 based on a musical hoax by the punk band The Alarm. This was a 2016 HBO television series created by an all-star team consisting of Mick Jagger, Martin Scorsese, Rich Cohen and Terrance Warner. The show is set in the gritty times of the 1970s and features a New York music executive who is hustling to make a career out of the city's eclectic music scene. John Lennon (portrayed by Stephen L. Sullivan) appears in the episode 'E.A.B'. It's set during his 'Lost Weekend 'period of 1974, showing him attending a Bob Marley gig with his temporary partner, May Pang (played by Celia Au). This is not historically accurate as John and May never attended a Bob Marley concert, but he did however attend a Jimmy Cliff concert at Carnegie Hall in November 1974.

John (along with his old pal, Ringo) did attend a Bob Marley concert in 1976. Sadly, John and Bob never collaborated together, as that would have been awesome.

The Lennon Report (2016)

Directed By - Jeremy Profe
Written By - Jeremy Profe and Walter Vincent
Release Date - April 6th 2016
Running Time - 87 Minutes

An indie movie about the horrible day of December 8th 1980 when John Lennon was gunned down by an insane fan outside the Dakota Apartment in New York. This dramatisation follows the untold, true-to-life story of those people who were part of his attempted recovery and who were witness to the human cost of tragedy. The movie received positive reviews, with several awards including one from film critic and book author Jack Garner, who said it was *"a potent drama . . . superbly crafted"*, and it won several prestigious film awards, including the Newport Beach Film Festival, the Boston International Film Festival and the High Falls Film Festival.

John Lennon is played by Gregory Barr, while Karen Tsen Lee plays Yoko Ono.

More Popular Than Jesus (2018)

Directed By - Paz Greemland
Release Date - July 22nd 2018
Running Time - 5 Minutes

Brazilian comedy short dealing with the 'Bigger Than Jesus 'controversy. This film was directed by an Israeli filmmaker called Paz Greemland, who was only 17 when the film was made, and who is diagnosed with Asperger's syndrome.

Paul Is Dead (2018)

THIS IS NOT A TRUE STORY

Directed By - George Moore
Written By - George Moore, Ben Bovington-Key and Stuart Armstrong
Release Date - August 18th 2018
Running Time - 14 Minutes

As you would guess from the title, this fictionalised comedic short about The Beatles is based on the 'Paul Is Dead 'myth of 1969. The plot revolves around John, George and Ringo retreating to the Lake District in the UK, back in 1967, where they convince a man named Billy Shears, a doppelgänger for Paul, who they meet in the local pub, to replace Paul McCartney after his death of a drug overdose. While braving the task of going up a perilous mountain top to bury the real Paul at the summit, they must face up to their inner conflicts and shortcomings if they are going to make it though the journey and stop The Beatles from falling apart.

The inspiration for the film came from a drunken taxi ride with director George Moore and screenwriter Ben Bovington-Key, who thought it would make a funny film, and it was filmed on a cold February, despite the sun being out throughout filming. A snowstorm hit after filming wrapped, so everything was done just in time.

The short film got positive reviews, and it is a really fun little skit. A highlight of this would have to be the cinematography, which is beautiful - the Lake District sure does look pretty!

Chapter Thirteen
Movies and TV Shows Inspired By The Beatles

The world of film and television has had its fair share of Beatle-inspired motion pictures and TV shows.

These range from parodies of The Beatles, to movies and TV shows where The Beatles, or the music of The Beatles, play an integral part in the storyline. This isn't an exhaustive list, as it would take forever to watch everything, but here are the most relevant ones I've found after extensive research.

Pinky and Perky (1957-1972, 2008)

Created By - Jan and Vlasta Dalibor
First Broadcast - 1957-1972, 2008
Running Time - 14 Minutes

Pinky and Perky are a pair of anthropomorphic pig marionette puppets, who were one of the biggest names in children's comedy in the UK back in the 1960s.

As well as covering the hits of The Beatles on their iconic show, also appearing were a combo of crows appropriately named The Beakles (obviously spoofing our Fab Four), who also appeared on the front cover of their 1965 EP 'Pinky & Perky's Beat Party'.

In 2008, the show received an obligatory all-CGI reboot, and the Beakles reappeared again in the episode 'Meet The Beakles'. In this programme, Pinky and Perky try to reunite the band, who haven't spoken in decades, and who refuse to perform together again.

Beatlefacts

* At the height of Pinky and Perky's fame, they received almost as much fan mail as The Beatles themselves - we are not making this up!
* The Beatles actually shared the bill with Pinky and Perky on *The Ed Sullivan Show* on 23rd February 1964.

Petticoat Junction (1964)

Directed By - Donald O'Connor
Written By - Paul Henning and Mark Turtle
First Broadcast - March 24th 1964
Running Time - 26 Minutes

Popular US sitcom from the 1960s about a trio of sisters called Bobbie Jo, Billie Jo and Betty Jo Bradley, who live with their Uncle Joe, who owns a family hotel, and is always coming up with some crazy ideas. It was a spin-off of *The Beverly Hillbillies*, which was then succeeded by *Green Acres*.

In the 1964 episode 'The Ladybugs', which was broadcast a month after The Beatles 'appearance on *The Ed Sullivan show*, Uncle Joe wants to make some money, and he recruits the Bradley sisters (and their friend, Sally Ragsdale) to form their own Beatle-inspired band called The Ladybugs.

Pinoy Beatles (1964)

Directed By - Artemio Marquez
Release Date - October 5th 1964
Running Time - Unknown

This was an unlicensed Tagalog musical, made in the Philippines. It was released three months after *A Hard Day's Night* and directed by Artemio Marquez, whose credits include the unofficial James Bond/Batman crossover film *James Batman*. This movie was made by Ambassador Productions, with the leading characters wearing Beatles style wigs, and featured appearances from other rock & roll bands.

The Flintstones (1965)

Created By - William Hanna and Joseph Barbera
First Broadcast - January 22nd 1965
Running Time - 25 Minutes

Very popular classic US animated series about the misadventures of a modern Stone Age family led by their bumbling father, Fred Flintstone. In the fifth season episode 'The Hatrocks and The Gruesomes', The Flintstones annoy the Hatrock family by playing 'bug music 'popularised by a group called The Four Insects, with the song 'She Said Yeah, Yeah, Yeah!', a take-off of The Beatles hit 'She Loves You'. Yabba-dabba-dooooo!!!!!

The Girls On The Beach (1965)

Directed By - William N. Witney
Release Date - May 12th 1965
Running Time - 80 Minutes

A teen beach party movie about a group of girls from Alpha Beta, who raise $10,000 in two weeks to save the sorority house. When three guys arrive at the beach with the eye for love, and brag that they know The Beatles, the girls plan a concert, with The Beatles as the main attraction (they don't show up!).

The movie featured appearances from The Beach Boys, as well as a group that helped inspire the real Beatles - The Crickets. The movie got a tepid reception from critics.

Gilligan's Island (1965)

Directed By - Steve Binder
Written By - Sherwood Schwartz and Brad Radnitz
First Broadcast - December 9th 1965
Running Time - 30 Minutes

A very famous US sitcom about seven men and women who are stranded on an uncharted island following a torrential storm. In the 1965 episode 'Don't Bug The Mosquitoes', a band named The Mosquitoes (who are of course, inspired by The Beatles) consisting of Bingo, Bongo, Bango and Irving arrive onto the island. They throw an impromptu concert and perform the song 'He's A Loser '(very loosely inspired by 'I'm A Loser 'from the *Beatles For Sale* LP). They eventually manage to leave the island via helicopter the following day, and leave behind an unsigned copy of their album *The Mosquitoes at Carnegie Hall* for Gilligan.

The Jungle Book (1967)

Directed By - Wolfgang Reitherman, James Alger and Jack Kinney
Written By - Rudyard Kipling, Larry Clemmons, Ralph Wright, Vance Gerry and Bill Peet
Release Date - December 24th 1967

Walt Disney's wonderful (if not-so-faithful) adaptation of Rudyard Kipling's Mowgli stories, which is still beloved by audiences to this day. In the film, Mowgli encounters some vultures named Buzzie, Flaps, Ziggy and Dizzy who help cheer him up; their voices sound very similar to The Beatles. Originally, Brian Epstein approached Disney about having the boys appear in the film, and Uncle Walt even had his animators make sure that the vultures had a resemblance to our Fab Four, but when Epstein took the idea to The Beatles, John Lennon wasn't keen, and told Epstein that they should hire Elvis instead!

The Gumby Show (1967)

Created By - Art Clokey
First Broadcast - December 27th 1967
Running Time - 30 Minutes

Not to be confused with the dimwitted characters from the Monty Python series, *Gumby* was an American stop-motion claymation series featuring a stretchy green clay figure called Gumby, who was a very popular character with American children in the 1960s. In an episode called 'Piano Rolling Blues 'broadcast in 1967, we meet a pianist called Paul Plunk, who is very obviously based on Paul McCartney. Despite only featuring in one episode, his appearance resonated with fans of the show.

The character of Paul Plunk would reappear in the *Gumby* comic book series in 2017, 50 years after his initial appearance.

Sesame Street (1969-Present)

Created By - Jim Henson
First Broadcast - November 10th 1969-Present
Running Time - 60 Minutes

Beloved US pre-school television series featuring Jim Henson's famous Muppet characters, such as Big Bird, Elmo, Bert, Ernie and Oscar The Grouch, teaching numbers, the alphabet and other subjects with fun and games. In 1981, the show saw the debut of a band called The Beetles - a group of four musical beetle Muppets, who sang hit songs such as 'Letter B '(Let It Be) and 'Hey Food '(Hey Jude). Previously, songs of The Beatles have been sung on the show by various Muppet cast members.

In 2012 during the Queen's Diamond Jubilee, Paul McCartney shared the stage with none other than Kermit the Frog himself!

I Am The Walrus (1971)

Directed By - Paul Scully
Release Date - 1971
Running Time - Unknown

Super-obscure animated short by a man named Paul Scully, which is presumably about the classic Beatles song from the *Magical Mystery Tour* film. The only information about this film is in the 1984 book *Beatlemania - An Illustrated Filmography* by Bill Harry.

All This And World War II (1976)

Directed By - Susan Winslow
Release Date - November 12th 1976
Running Time - 88 Minutes

A documentary movie about the Second World War that juxtaposes cover versions of Beatles songs with WWII clips and films from the 20th Century Fox back catalogue. Because of the film's negative reception, it only lasted for two weeks in cinemas. The movie has never seen an official home video release, but it did get distributed in bootleg circles, though a revised edition was made in 2016 entitled *The Beatles And World War II*, which used alternate footage and a revised soundtrack.

The original soundtrack for the film contained a massive ensemble of big artists of the time period covering the Beatle classics such as The Bee Gees, Elton John, Rod Stewart, Jeff Lynne, The Four Seasons, Frankie Valli, Tina Turner and Peter Gabriel.

Beatlefacts

* The film's soundtrack actually grossed more than the film itself!

The Rutles: All You Need Is Cash (1978)

Me with the legendary Neil Innes, who played Ron Nasty in The Rutles, and who was a good friend to both The Beatles and The Pythons.

Directed By - Eric Idle & Gary Weis
Written By - Eric Idle & Neil Innes
First Broadcast - March 22nd 1978
Running Time - 76 Minutes
Beatle Involved - George Harrison

"A legend that will last a lunchtime!" The Rutles were pretty much the de-facto affectionate spoof of our beloved Fab Four. Originally a skit in Eric Idle's (of Monty Python fame) TV series *Rutland Weekend Television* in 1975, made in collaboration with Bonzo Dog Doo-Dah Band member (and honorary Seventh Python) Neil Innes. The sketch parodied 'A Hard Day's Night 'era Beatles with a song called 'I Must Be In Love '(in itself, a take-off of the aforementioned song). It was later shown on *Saturday Night Live* in America to a rapturous reception (this was during a time when Beatle reunion rumours were rife), and this gave Idle and Innes the motivation to commission a feature length "mockumentary" entitled *All You Need Is Cash*.

Inspired by the unreleased Beatle documentary *The Long And Winding Road* (which later evolved into *Anthology*), the *All You Need Is Cash* TV movie was shown on NBC in the US and BBC2 in the UK, charting the rise and fall of the Prefab Four - Ron Nasty (not John Lennon, played by Innes),

Dirk McQuickly (not Paul McCartney, played by Idle), Stig O'Hara (not George Harrison, played by former Beach Boy, Ricky Fataar, who is, in fact, Indian, and is literally the quiet one, as he doesn't have a single line in the film) and Barry Wom (not Ringo Starr, played by John Halsey).

If you love both The Beatles and Monty Python, as well as *Spinal Tap* (this film preceded it), then you will adore it! In fact, the Beatles themselves endorsed this parody with George Harrison himself making a cameo in the film as an interviewer, and he even said that it is one of the most accurate Beatles biographies ever made! It also has an all-star cast of some really big names including Mick Jagger and Paul Simon as themselves, both Blues Brothers (John Belushi and Dan Ackroyd), two Ghostbusters (Bill Murray and of course Dan Ackroyd), two Rolling Stones (Mick Jagger, who I mentioned before, and Ronnie Wood), Roger McGough, Cleo Rocos and best of all, George Harrison playing an interviewer.

The success of this TV movie led to The Rutles becoming an actual live act (with other people replacing Idle due to his other commitments), and they recorded an album of new songs called *Archeology*, spoofing the Beatles *Anthology* documentary and albums. In 2002, a sequel to *Cash* was made called *The Rutles 2: Can't Buy Me Lunch* - critical reception was more mixed, as there wasn't much new footage, and it mainly recycled the plot from the original. Sadly, Neil Innes, who played Ron Nasty (the Rutles 'John Lennon), passed away on the 30th December 2019 aged 75, ending the Rutles story for good, with tributes coming from the likes of John Cleese and Stephen Fry.

Definitely worth getting for all Beatle fans with a good sense of humour.

Beatle ahem . . Rutlefacts

* None of the Beatles objected to the film - according to Eric Idle, George Harrison was very supportive, so much so that he actually appeared in it playing an interviewer who talks to Eric Manchester (Michael Palin), who is based on Beatle buddy and press agent, Derek Taylor. Paul had some reservations (mostly due to how his Rutle counterpart, Dirk, was portrayed in the 'Let's Be Natural 'sequence), but his wife Linda loved it. Ringo liked the happy scenes, but felt the scenes which spoofed the sadder times were too close to home. John (as well as Yoko) however loved it (despite the Rutles version of Yoko being Hitler's daughter), and they refused to return the videotape and soundtrack which he was given for approval.

* George and Ringo considered forming a band with Eric Idle and Neil Innes, but this never came to be - in a very meta sense of fate, George and Ringo surprised Eric and Neil one day by singing 'Ouch!'.

* In the 'I Am The Walrus 'parody 'Piggy In The Middle', you hear a backwards voice that says *"Tekraaam ot tnew eiggip elttil siht"* or *"This little piggy went to maaarket"* - that is supposedly George Harrison!

* When George Harrison and Michael Palin shared screen time together, it was the first time they met. Ironically, according to Palin, he was a surprisingly enthusiastic talker, contradicting the stereotype of him being "the quiet one".
* John Lennon warned The Rutles that 'Get Up And Go 'sounded too similar to 'Get Back'. He was right, as Neil Innes was sued for copyright infringement by ATV Music, the people that looked after the publishing of The Beatles' back catalogue at the time. He settled with ATV out of court for 50% of the royalties.
* The *Yellow Submarine* parody 'Yellow Submarine Sandwich 'was animated by several of the people who worked on the real *Yellow Submarine.*

Sgt. Pepper's Lonely Hearts Club Band (1978)

Directed By - Josh Raskin
Release Date - July 21st 1978
Running Time - 113 Minutes

As the title suggests, this movie is based on The Beatles 'classic 1967 album of the same name. It is a musical featuring many big celebrities of the time, such as The Bee Gees, Peter Frampton, Steve Martin, Aerosmith, Alice Cooper, Earth Wind & Fire, George Burns and Billy Preston, who you may remember from the final two Beatles albums *Let It Be* and *Abbey Road*. Serving as musical director was none other than The Beatles 'own producer George Martin, and, as to be expected, it contains cover versions of songs from the *Sgt. Pepper* album, as well as songs from *Revolver*, *Abbey Road* and *Let It Be*. The film contains no spoken dialogue, save for a narrator at the beginning of the film (George Burns).

Despite Universal Studios claiming that the film would end up being this generation's *Gone With The Wind*, the movie ended up getting almost universally negative reviews, and was nominated for Worst Picture at the 1978 Stinkers Bad Movie Awards. The film, however, was a modest earner commercially, making $20million against a budget of $13million.

Despite the negative reception, it does have something of an ironic cult following, and over the years has seen multiple DVD releases, and even a Blu-Ray release.

Beatlefacts

* Paul and Ringo both attended the movie's premiere, and slammed the film, while John and George refused to see it!
* The Bee Gees wanted to bail out of the film two weeks into its production.

Alas Smith and Jones (1984-1998)

Written By - Mel Smith and Griff Rhys-Jones
First Broadcast - January 31st 1984-October 14th 1988
Running Time - 25 Minutes

Alas Smith and Jones was a popular UK sketch series starring alternative comics, Mel Smith and Griff Rhys-Jones. One sketch features Smith and Jones nostalgically discussing *Sgt. Pepper* and the 1960s, which is then succeeded with a funny mock-documentary called 'It Was 20 Years Ago Today', which is quite similar in tone to The Rutles. The highlight would have to be when the Mal Evans parody, Barry Tank Crithley (played by Smith) claims that 'Lucy In The Sky With Diamonds 'doesn't really spell out LSD, but LITSWD, which is in fact a village in Wales which Lennon used to visit on holiday.

The sketch was later voted online as being Mel Smith's No.1 Finest Comedy Moment on July 20th 2013, in memory of Smith after his passing the day previously.

Yesterday (1985)

Directed By - Radoslaw Piwowarski
Written By - Radoslaw Piwowarski
Release Date - June 10th 1985
Running Time - 87 Minutes

Not to be confused with the more well-known 2019 film of the same name, this 1985 Polish drama is about a quartet of high-school kids facing graduation day in the 1960s, and becoming a Beatles covers group. They don't have the amps, so they put together some makeshift equipment, which unfortunately leads to one of the members being electrocuted! It was selected as the Polish entry at the 58th Academy Awards for Best Foreign Language Film but it wasn't accepted as a nominee.

Joanie Loves Chachi (1986)

Directed By - John Tracy
Written By - Lowell Ganz and Harry K. Marshall
First Broadcast - February 2nd 1986
Running Time - 30 Minutes

240

Unsuccessful short-lived spinoff of the famous sitcom *Happy Days* made after the show "jumped the shark" focusing on the romantic misadventures of Joanie Cunningham and Chachi Arcola, and their pursuits into the music industry in Chicago. In the episode 'Beatlemania' broadcast in February 1986, Joanie is convinced she saw Paul McCartney while visiting her nurse friend in a hospital (it was a lookalike called Marvin O'Pizika!). To be honest, the show lacks the Fonz (aayyyee!), and it disappeared faster into the wilderness than Brother Chuck Cunningham.

Beatlefacts

* Ron Howard (Richie Cunningham) from the original *Happy Days* would later direct the Beatles documentary *Eight Days A Week* in 2016.

Prick Up Your Ears (1987)

Directed By - Stephen Frears
Written By - John Lahr and Alan Bennett
Release Date - April 17th 1987
Running Time - 111 Minutes

A biopic on the late Joe Orton, with Gary Oldman playing the main role. The final act of the film features the him being commissioned to write a screenplay for The Beatles (*Up Against It*, mentioned in this book), which ultimately never materialised. The movie received positive reviews, and Oldman's performance earned him a Best Actor award, and Vanessa Redgrave received a BAFTA and a Golden Globe for her supporting role as Peggy Ramsay.

Concrete Angels (1987)

Directed By - Carlo Liconti
Release Date - September 1987
Running Time - 97 Minutes

The year is 1964, and our Fab Four are going to perform in Toronto, Canada. There is also a group called the Concrete Angels, who enter a "Battle Of The Bands" competition, and the prize is to open for none other than The Beatles at Maple Leaf Gardens. Tony Nardi, who plays the character Sal, received a Genie Award nomination for Best Supporting Actor.

Red Dwarf (1988-Present)

Me with my friend, Actor, DJ, Poet, TV Presenter and Comedian, Craig Charles, promoting my previous book 'The Little Big Beat Book' at the BBC.

Created By - Rob Grant and Doug Naylor
First Broadcast - February 15th 1988-Present
Running Time - 30 Minutes

Beloved British sci-fi sitcom about the misadventures of Dave Lister (played by legendary fellow Liverpudlian actor, comedian, poet, DJ and presenter Craig Charles), the last human alive, and his friends Cat, Rimmer and Kryten, stranded 3 million years into deep space on the mining ship The Red Dwarf.

One of the lesser-known reoccurring characters in the show are a duo of artificial, electronic pet goldfish that Lister owns called Lennon and McCartney, obviously named in tribute to John Lennon and Paul McCartney. They are kept in a tank in the sleeping quarters Lister shares with Arnold Rimmer aboard the Red Dwarf ship.

In the episode 'Parallel Universe', Holly, Red Dwarf's computer, ponders an alternate universe where Ringo Starr was a really good drummer. That's mean, as Ringo is in reality proven to be a very good drummer without doubt!

There is also an episode in Series 7 called 'Tikka To Ride', which is named in tribute to The Beatles song 'Ticket To Ride'. This episode was about Lister accidentally preventing the assassination of US President John F. Kennedy, leading to a very bleak future - oh smeg!

Alvin And The Chipmunks (1988)

Written By - Steve Moore
First Broadcast - December 5th 1988
Running Time - 24 Minutes

1980s animated revival of the 1950s records, about a helium voiced trio of troublemaking anthropomorphic chipmunks - Alvin, Simon and Theodore. In this recap episode entitled 'Chipmunkmania '(the title is, of course a reference to Beatlemania), there is a press conference scene where Alvin infamously claims that The Chimpunks are more popular than Mickey Mouse, leading to mass controversy - yikes! This is of course a reference to John Lennon's "*more popular than Jesus*" quote from 1966.

Aaallllvvvvviiiiinnnnnn!!!!!!

Beatlefacts

* Fred Wolf, who produced the series, also produced the 1971 film *The Point*, narrated by Ringo Starr.

Hard Days, Hard Nights AKA Beat Boys (1989)

Directed By - Horst Konigstein
Written By - Peter Turner, Frank Gohre and Horst Konigstein
Release Date - 1989
Running Time - 103 Minutes

A German movie about a British rock & roll band from Liverpool descending onto Hamburg circa 1960, and forming romantic liaisons with the townspeople . . . this sounds awfully familiar doesn't it?

The Commitments (1991)

Directed By - Alan Parker
Written By - Roddy Doyle
Release Date - October 4th 1991
Running Time - 118 Minutes

Adapted from the 1987 novel of the same name, this excellent (but potty mouthed) film is about a group of working class young adults from Dublin forming a soul covers band, and their short-lived career. The eldest member of the band, the middle-aged Joey "The Lips" Fagan (played by Johnny Murphy) claims to have played saxophone on 'All You Need Is Love 'when auditioning for the band. It is later revealed in the film that he is known for telling many tall tales, with this claim being somewhat dubious.

Doug (1991-1999)

Created By - Jim Jinkins
First Broadcast - December 8th 1991-June 26th 1999
Running Time - 24 Minutes

Popular Nickelodeon cartoon series about the titular character, who meets friends, falls in love, and manoeuvres his way through school, writing all about it in his journal. He is also a fan of a Beatle-esque band called The Beets, who have appeared in five episodes in this iconic show. Consisting of Munroe Yolder (John), Chap Lipman (Ringo), Flounder (Paul) and Wendy Nespah (George), they have scored many hit albums such as 'Meet The Beets', 'Beets Me', 'Beet The Heat', 'The What Album 'and 'Let It Beet 'and have had many popular singles including 'I've Sneezed On My Face 'which is of course parodying 'I've Just Seen A Face'.

Dog City (1992-1994)

Created By - Jim Henson
Directed By - John van Bruggen
First Broadcast - September 26th 1992-November 26th 1994
Running Time - 60 Minutes

Created by Jim Henson, the man behind the beloved Muppets, this was a Muppets/cel animation hybrid series about a German Shepherd dog named Ace Yu (played by Kevin Clash) facing bulldog gangster, Bugsy Vile AKA The Dog-father. Some of the reoccurring characters that are occasionally seen are a "bark and roll" band named The Beagles, best known for their hit single 'I'm Your Doggy'. The song gets played frequently on the WFIDO radio station, and they have performed in the prestigious music venue The Dog City Water Bowl. Barking mad if you ask me!

Secrets AKA One Crazy Night (1992)

Directed By - Michael Pattinson
Release Date - December 3rd 1992
Running Time - 98 Minutes

A *Breakfast Club* clone starring Kylie Minogue's sister, Danni Minogue, and Noah Taylor. This film is set in 1964, and follows four Beatle megafans (and an Elvis fan, who hates The Beatles) who end up being locked in a basement of a hotel where the Beatles are staying during a tour. While locked in, they end up sharing some deep secrets with each other.

The film featured instrumental versions of many Beatle hits, but received criticism for including songs beyond the Beatlemania period. Willa O'Neil, who plays Vicki, was nominated for the Australian Film Institute Award For Best Supporting Actress for her performance in this film.

Animaniacs (1993-1998, 2020-Present)

Produced By - Stephen Spielberg
First Broadcast - September 13th 1993-November 14th 1998, November 20th 2020-Present
Running Time - 24 Minutes

Classic 1990s cartoon set in 1930s Hollywood, produced by the legendary Stephen Spielberg, which brought back the spirit of the classic Warner Bros. *Looney Tunes* and *Merrie Melodies* shorts, centring around a trio of siblings known as The Warners. The voice of Wakko Warner (Jess Hartnell) is clearly based on Ringo Starr's distinct Liverpudlian accent. There is also an episode in the series entitled 'A Hard Day's Warners', which of course is a shout-out to the Beatles movie and album *A Hard Day's Night*. They also walk across the Abbey Road crossing in one of the show's opening titles.

Eek! The Cat (1995)

Directed By - Jamie Whitney
First Broadcast - October 7th 1995
Running Time - 30 Minutes

Eek! The Cat, also known as *Eek! Stravaganza*, is an American/Canadian cartoon series created by Savage Steve Holland and Bill Kopp that ran from 1992-1996. It revolved around a happy-go-lucky housecat named Eek, whose optimistic attitude gets him into trouble - kind of like a feline Charlie Brown. In the episode 'OutbrEek 'broadcast in 1995, about an outbreak of deadly fleas, there is a *Hard Day's Night* movie parody featuring the song 'Can't Stop The Bugs', which is a funny spoof of 'Can't Buy Me Love'. Thankfully, the flea epidemic is over by the end of the episode!

Timon & Pumbaa (1995)

First Broadcast - October 7th 1995
Running Time - 24 Minutes

A spin-off TV series from the beloved 1994 Disney animated classic *The Lion King*, focusing on the comic relief characters - Timon, who is a meerkat, and Pumbaa, who is a warthog. In the episode 'Rocky Mountain Lie', they come across a stinkbug with blue skin and a Beatle moptop called Stinky, who is based on Ringo Starr. He used to be the drummer in a band with three other bugs, but was fired because he was smelly. He later befriends Timon and Pumbaa (who was close to eating him) and the three other members of the bug band apologise. He then re-joins the band, only to be kicked out again! Later in the episode, after telling a nasty lie about Stinky being captured, Timon and Pumbaa are taken hostage by some bears and are about to be toast, but thanks to a giant sneeze, because of the cold, Stinky comes in to save the day, scaring the bears off! At the end of the episode, Timon and Pumbaa apologise for their behaviour, and are left very hungry so, at Stinky's suggestion, they eat the rest of the band - gross, especially considering it's a kids' programme!

South Park (1997-Present)

"You know, I learned something today!" Kyle Broflovski

Created By - Trey Parker and Matt Stone
First Broadcast - August 13th 1997-Present
Running Time - 25 Minutes each

One of the funniest (and most controversial) animated television series for adults is *South Park*, which debuted all the way back in 1997, created by Trey Parker and Matt Stone. It follows the misadventures of four school kids from a quiet little mountain town called South Park in Colorado.

The Beatles have been referenced quite a few times in this iconic animated series. In the episode 'Ike's Wee Wee '(the one where Mr. Mackey, the school counsellor, says *"Drugs are bad MMkay!"*) he mentions that LSD was popularised by John Lennon and Paul McCartney and that it is bad (mmkay!). In the episode 'Chef Aid', Jerome McElroy, the school chef (voiced by soul singer Isaac Hayes, who previously covered 'Something') shows a picture in his photo album of him and The Beatles from his time in the rock business to Cartman and the boys.

Probably the most controversial Beatle-related reference in the show is in the 2010 episode 'The Tale Of Scrotie McBoogerballs 'in which Mr. Garrison gives the book *The Catcher In The Rye* as a homework assignment, and because of the book's controversial nature, the boys (especially everybody's favourite evil bastard, Eric Cartman) get very excited about reading it. This leads the usually nice and mild-mannered Butters Stotch take on the desire to kill John Lennon, until his dad comes in to tell him he's already dead!

Yoko Ono makes an appearance (voiced by co-creator Trey Parker) in the episode 'Worldwide Recorder Concert 'presenting the aforementioned concert, and she gets very angry when 4 million 3rd graders don't know how to play 'My Country 'Tis Of Thee'; there is also a Beatles poster in Mr. Garrison's parents' house in the same episode. A Blue Meanie from the *Yellow Submarine* film also makes a cameo in the 2008 three-part special 'Imaginationland'.

Pinky and the Brain (1997)

Written By - Bill Matheny, Charles M. Howell IV and Earl Kress
First Broadcast - September 17th 1997
Running Time - 24 Minutes

Spin-off of the Warner Bros. animated series *Animaniacs* about a genius mouse (The Brain), who sounds like Orson Welles, and his bumbling sidekick (Pinky), thinking of schemes to take over the world. In the episode 'All You Need Is Narf', set in 1960s India, Pinky becomes a guru known as the Mousarishi (a spoof of the Maharishi), and befriends a group called The Feebles (a

Beatles parody, duh!), who are known for their hit songs 'All You Eat Is Lunch 'and 'I Am The Cheesebag'. The Feebles are Jim (John), Fred (Paul), Steve (George) and Bongo (Ringo) and The Brain introduces The Feebles to a lady named Yoyo Nono - an Asian lady with a strange singing voice (a not-so-affectionate parody of Yoko Ono). Jim Lemon, the lonely Feeble, is immediately smitten by her. They end up doing a demonstration to teach people not to wear trousers by singing 'What We Are Saying is Take Off Your Pants '- a parody of 'Give Peace A Chance'. Their eventual marriage leads to the end of The Feebles.

Beatlefacts

* The episode's title is of course a reference to 'All You Need Is Love'.
* A Beach Boys parody also makes an appearance in this episode.
* Bongo was also the nickname the real Ringo was given by Eric Morecambe in The Beatles 'appearance on the series *Two of A Kind*.
* In the very end of the episode after the fade to black, Pinky yells *'I GOT BLISTERS ON MY FINGERS!'* referring to Ringo's famous line in 'Helter Skelter'.

Mr. Show with Bob and David (1997)

Written By - Bob Odenkirk and David Cross
First Broadcast - October 10th 1997
Running Time - 28 Minutes

Highly influential US dark sketch comedy series that connected together like an episode of Monty Python. In a programme broadcast in 1997 ('Flat Top Tony and the Purple Canoes'), an unseen band called The Beetletown Players perform the very Beatle-eque instrumental piece 'Got A Good Thing Going ' in a sketch that parodies *A Hard Day's Night*, directed by Famous Mortimer (who is later played in the show by comedian Patton Oswalt).

CatDog (1999)

Created By - Peter Hannan
First Broadcast - July 29th 1999
Running Time - 15 Minutes Each

Popular Nickelodeon cartoon series about a conjoined cat and dog, who have very different personalities, similar to shows such as *Ren And Stimpy*. In the episode 'House of CatDog', there is a brief scene where a Beatles lookalike band (with the ears of actual Beetles) come out of an airplane and ask where Shea Stadium is. The title of a previous episode is 'All You Need Is Lube ' (broadcast October 6th 1998), which is a reference to 'All You Need Is Love', and there is also an episode entitled 'Squirrel Dog '(broadcast October 14th 1998) which contains a reference to 'I Am The Walrus'.

Family Guy (1999-Present)

Written By - Seth MacFarlane
First Broadcast - January 31st 1999-Present
Running Time - 25 Minutes

The Beatles have been referenced many times in this very popular and controversial animated series for grown-ups about a dysfunctional family from Rhode Island, USA, who are being thrown into crazy scenarios. The show is also known for its cutaway gags.

In the episode 'The Thin White Line 'Peter Griffin (the dad character) is revealed to have been a security guard for George Harrison back in 1999, which unfortunately led to his near fatal stabbing. Another episode called 'Ready, Willing and Disabled 'we find out that Stewie Griffin (a talking baby with a British accent) was the one that got John Lennon together with Yoko Ono. Ringo also appears in a cutaway gag, where a girl says she had a crush on Ringo during a sleepover when the other girls noted their love for various members of The Beatles. When Ringo appears before her, she quickly denies it (poor Ringo!).

They have been referred to many more times in the show's history.

Futurama (1999-2013)

Created By - Matt Groening and David X. Cohen
First Broadcast - March 28th 1999-September 4th 2013
Running Time - 25 Minutes

Underrated animated sci-fi sitcom from the creator of *The Simpsons*, about a pizza delivery boy called Phillip J. Fry who is accidentally frozen on New Year's Eve 1999, and wakes up in the year 2999.

Matt Groening is a massive Beatles fan, and managed to sneak a few Beatle references into the show. There is a reoccurring character called the No.9 Man (a reference to John Lennon's obsession with the number nine), who appears predominantly in the special 'Into The Green Yonder', as well as a nod to the *Yellow Submarine* film with the Planet Express ship redecorated like the Yellow Submarine for the intro of the special 'Bender's Game'. There is also a 2011 episode called 'Fry Am The Egg Man', which is obviously a reference to the line *"I am the Eggman"* from the song 'I Am The Walrus'.

Paul Is Dead (2000)

Directed By - Hendrik Handloegten
Release Date - January 27th 2000
Running Time - 75 Minutes

As expected from the title, this film is based on the infamous 1969 rumour of Paul McCartney's "death". This is a German film that's set in the year 1980, and a 12-year-old boy named Tobias is having a summer holiday, but is finding it boring, until one day, his attention is drawn to a strange man driving a white Volkswagen Beetle. Tobias is convinced that he has seen it before, and he looks at the album covers of several Beatles albums, and swears he saw it on the cover of *Abbey Road*. Tobias then discovers the 'Paul Is Dead 'legend, and is convinced he is close to Paul's killer, who he believes is his English teacher, who was seen driving the VW Beetle. When he finds out that Paul's "death" was nothing more than a hoax created by a radio DJ, there is a feeling of anticlimax, but soon afterwards, his English teacher leaves Germany to go to New York City. One night, Tobias 'brother wakes him up to tell him the awful news about John Lennon's assassination in New York.

The Million Dollar Hotel (2000)

Directed By - Wim Wenders
Written By - Nicholas Klein and Bono (of U2 fame)
Running Time - 122 Minutes
Release Date - April 28th 2000

A star-studied tragicomedy mystery set in a rundown hotel in America which plays host to mentally ill people too poor to afford medical insurance. The character of Dixie (Peter Stormare) believes that he is the uncredited fifth Beatle, and wrote all The Beatles' back catalogue! He even sings an unusual version of 'I Am the Walrus'. He is still waiting for his royalty payments, as well as his recognition.

The Powerpuff Girls (2001)

Directed By - John McIntye and Craig McCracken
Written by - Craig McCracken
First Broadcast - February 9th 2001
Running Time - 24 Minutes

AKA Craig McCracken's love letter to all things Beatles.

As stated previously in the book, Ringo Starr once appeared in the cartoon TV series *The Powerpuff Girls*, created by a Beatles mega fan, which lasted from 1998-2005 for Cartoon Network, but has since been revived several times.

February 2001 saw the broadcast of the episode 'Meet The Beat Alls', which is about the baddies of the series, Mojo Jojo, HIM, Princess Morbuck and Fuzzy Lumpkins teaming up as a band called The Beat Alls to finally defeat The Powerpuff Girls once and for all, and the episode is riddled with endless Beatles references. The Beatles themselves make animated appearances in this episode, both in the Dennis Marks mid-1960s cartoon form and George Dunning's *Yellow Submarine* designs.

i am sam (2001)

Directed By - Jessie Nelson
Release Date - December 18th 2001
Running Time - 132 Minutes

A heartbreaking 2001 drama about a mentally challenged man named Sam (Sean Penn), who fights for custody of his 7-year-old daughter (Dakota Fanning), whose homeless mother has abandoned them both, and in the process, teaches his cold-hearted lawyer (Michelle Pfeiffer) the value of love and family. The film's Grammy Award nominated soundtrack consists entirely of Beatles covers from the likes of The Black Crowes, Nick Cave, Stereophonics, Sheryl Crow, Rufus Wainwright and many more. As the film was shot and produced with the original recordings, the artists recorded their covers in the same tempo as the original Beatles tunes.

The movie didn't get a good reception from film critics, but was a commercial success, grossing $97.8million against a $22million budget, and Sean Penn did receive a nomination for Best Actor at the Academy Awards in 2002. Dakota Fanning was also nominated for a Screen Actors Guild Award.

A Hard Day's Day - A Day In The Life Of A Beatles Tribute Band (2002)

Directed By - David Kessler
Written By - David Kessler and Quinton Flynn
Release Date - September 2002
Running Time - 7 Minutes

A really fun short film, which is a comedic look at the life of real world Beatles tribute band The Mop Tops (which includes Joe Stefanelli as John, who had previously voiced him in *Forrest Gump* and portrayed him in 1996's *Dark Skies*), who are in search of finding a new Ringo Starr (as the current one didn't present the right image), in time for their biggest concert. After plastic surgery, Ringo looks more like Ringo, and they end up doing a big show... in a Bar Mitzvah!

The idea for the short came about around 2000, when the film's director, stand-up comic David Kessler, saw a Beatles tribute band in the real world and wondered if they *"kept up the accents off stage"*. He thought the idea was hilarious, and that it would make a great film, but realised it didn't carry much weight for a feature, but was a great concept for a short subject. The film premiered on the website iFilm in 2002 to a positive reception, becoming one of the highest rated comedy shorts on the site. When iFilm closed its doors in 2008, the film was getting very hard to find until 2011, when screenwriter Quinton Flynn put it up on Youtube, albeit in low quality.

The Rutles 2: Can't Buy Me Lunch (2002)

Directed By - Eric Idle
Written By - Eric Idle
First Broadcast - November 9th 2002
Running Time - 56 Minutes

Not really a true sequel as such to the fantastic first Rutles film *All You Need Is Cash*, but rather, as Eric Idle puts it in an interview for *Entertainment Weekly*, a *"remake supplement"* - and it shows! While the new interviews from David Bowie, Billy Connolly, Carrie Fisher, Steve Martin, Salman Rushdie, Tom Hanks, Bonnie Raitt, James Taylor etc. are all very amusing, they don't really add anything, and the bulk of the film consists of outtakes from the original Rutles movie. The film would have been a lot better if it had had more involvement from Innes, Fataar and Halsey, and maybe it could have focused on what The Rutles did next after they split up. More like a DVD extra than a proper film.

Teen Titans (2004)

Directed By - Michael Chang
Written By - John Esposito
First Broadcast - October 16th 2004
Running Time - 22 Minutes

2000's animated series set in the *Batman* universe, featuring Robin, Starfire, Cyborg and Raven, which ran from 2003-2006. The 2004 episode 'Revolution 'contains many references to The Beatles. The villain in the episode, the stereotypically British "Mad Mod", replaces the busts of the US Presidents at Mount Rushmore with those of The Beatles, and in his final confrontation with the Titans, he adopts the shape of a Blue Meanie from the *Yellow Submarine* film. The character of Beast Boy also plays a Rickenbacker 325 classic, which was John Lennon's guitar of choice, and the episode contains the almost mandatory (and somewhat clichéd in any cartoon that references The Beatles) famous Abbey Road crossing featuring the Teen Titans.

Holy Beatlefacts!

* The episode's title shares the same name as the Beatle song, which is more than likely intentional.

American Dad! (2005-Present)

Created By - Seth MacFarlane
First Broadcast - February 6th 2005-Present
Running Time - 23 Minutes Each

Adult animated series created by Seth MacFarlane, best known for *Family Guy*, which has been running since 2005. It's about a family known as the Smiths (led by CIA agent Stan Smith), and the show is known for being very satirical and politically charged, though nowadays is best known for its surrealism and absurdity.

There is an episode entitled 'I Am The Walrus', which is, of course, a shout-out to the Beatles song of the same name, and the 2012 episode 'Dr. Klaustus 'features the alien character of Roger adopt the pseudonym of Sgt. Pepper when he gets sent off to fight in Iraq. His alias is, of course, a reference to the Beatles album of the same name.

I Met The Walrus (2007)

Directed By - Josh Raskin
Release Date - March 22nd 2007
Running Time - 5 Minutes

A short 5 minute animation directed by Josh Raskin, who is best known for *Kids & Explosions*. This is based on an interview with John Lennon by Jerry Levitan in 1969, who was then 14 years old. The story goes that Levitan tracked Lennon to his hotel room in Toronto's King Edward Hotel after a rumour was floating around that he had been sighted at Toronto Airport. After finding him, Lennon agreed to be interviewed, and the original 30 minute recording was cut down to five minutes. In the interview, Lennon expresses his thoughts on capitalism, as well as his attitudes towards promoting world peace.

A very well made short with some great animation, which won many awards such as a 2009 Daytime Emmy, Best Animated Short at the American Film Institute and the Middle East International Film Festival, as well as a nomination for an Academy Award for Best Animated Short Film by the Academy of Motion Picture Arts And Sciences.

The success of this film led to it being adapted into a book authored by Jerry Levitan and published by Harper Collins in 2009.

Drake & Josh (2007)

Directed By - Josh Peck
Written By - Dan Schneider and Matt Fleckenstein
First Broadcast - April 15th 2007
Running Time - 24 Minutes

A Nickelodeon live action sitcom for kids about two teenagers named Drake and Josh, who become step brothers - one of them is an awkward geek but the other is a popular musician; it lasted from 2004-2007. In the 2007 episode 'Battle Of Panthatar', the duo of Drake and Josh get an invitation to Thornton the cool kid's 16th birthday party. In this story, Drake offers Thornton his autographed copy of The Beatles album *Abbey Road* in exchange for entrance to the party, but Thornton doesn't welcome them, taking the album and going back inside to the party, leading to Drake and Josh trying to sneak in to "get back" the signed copy of *Abbey Road*.

Beatlefacts

* Josh Peck, who directed the episode, also plays the character of Josh.

Across The Universe (2007)

Directed By - Julie Taymor
Written By - Dick Clement and Ian La Frenais
Release Date - September 28th 2007
Running Time - 133 Minutes

Another jukebox musical like 1978's *Sgt. Pepper's Lonely Hearts Club Band*, but this one was a lot more successful. Starring Jim Sturgess as Jude, a poor Liverpudlian artist, and Evan Rachel Wood as Lucy, a rich American girl (both obviously named after the songs 'Hey Jude 'and 'Lucy In The Sky With Diamonds'), it's a romantic comedy set in the 1960s with events from the time period serving as the film's background, such as the Vietnam War and the political tensions of the time. In true *Let It Be* style, the movie climaxes with a rooftop concert.

Thirty-four Beatles songs are featured in the movie, all sung by the film's cast.

While not getting amazing reviews, this movie was much better received than *Sgt. Pepper's*, and was praised for its cast and music numbers, but received criticism for the plot and direction. The film did however get a Golden Globe nomination for Best Motion Picture - Musical Or Comedy, and an Oscar Nomination for Best Costume Design. The movie also received praise from Paul and Ringo, as well as John and George's widows, Yoko and Olivia. A sequel, taking place in the 1970s, was announced in October 2020.

Beatlefacts

* As well as Lucy and Jude, other Beatle-related named characters in the film include Sadie (Sexy Sadie), Jo-Jo (Get Back), Prudence (Dear Prudence), Daniel (Rocky Raccoon), Molly (Ob-La-Di, Ob-La-Da), Martha (Martha My Dear), Teddy (Teddy Boy), Bill (The Continuing Story of Bungalow Bill), Doctor Robert (Doctor Robert, obviously!), Mother Superior (Happiness Is A Warm Gun), Mr. Kite (Being For The Benefit Of Mr. Kite!), Rita (Lovely Rita) and Bang Bang Shoot Shoot (Happiness Is A Warm Gun).
* Cast members Carol Woods and Timothy T. Mitchum performed as part of a special Beatles tribute at the 50th Grammy Awards in 2008.

The History Of The World Backwards (2007)

Written By - Robert Newman
First Broadcast - October 30th 2007
Running Time - 96 Minutes

A BBC4 comedy mock history programme written by Robert Newman, set in a world where time flows forwards, but history flows backwards. One of the episodes features a Beatles tribute band, who are stranded in a Brazilian rainforest in Mato Grosso. It was Newman's first TV project for 14 years.

The Bootleg Beatles - Vox And Rugs And Rock & Roll (2007)

Directed By - Ian Penman and Jackie Scollen
Release Date - 2007
Running Time - 53 Minutes

A documentary on the history of the long-running acclaimed Beatles tribute band The Bootleg Beatles. Originally formed from the UK cast of the Beatles musical *Beatlemania* in 1980, over 40 years on, The Fab Faux are still performing and selling out venues today, though their line-up has changed a few times since then.

Vipo: Adventures Of The Flying Dog (2008)

Written By - Ido Angel
First Broadcast - January 5th 2008
Running Time - 11 Minutes

An Israeli CGI animated series about a flying dog named Vipo and his friends, Betty (a toy cat) and Henry (a stork), travelling to various locations around the world. The programme ran from 2007-2008. In an episode called 'The Missing Windmill 'broadcast on the 5th January 2008, they come across a band of storks named The Beakles.

Wonder Pets (2008)

Written By - Josh Selig
First Broadcast - April 21st 2008
Running Time - 24 Minutes

Wonder Pets is a cute pre-school animated series, with animation using cut-outs in a style not too dissimilar to that which Terry Gilliam used in the Monty Python cartoons. It ran from 2006-2016, and followed the adventures of Turtle Tuck, Linny The Guinea Pig and Ming-Ming Ducking, who save the day by using teamwork (*"What's gonna work? Teamwork!"*).

In the 2008 episode 'Save The Beetles', the Wonder Pets travel to Liverpool to save a band of four mop-top haired Beetles (obviously based on our Fab Four), when their Yellow Submarine gets stuck in Kelp! and is in need of "Fixing A Hole". The Wonder Pets save the day, and go to their concert at the end of the episode at the Octopus 'Garden - a really nice show for the little ones.

Beatlefacts

* The Beetle members Wingo (the Ringo parody), Jack and Pete (John and Paul), are voiced by Lenie Colacino, who was a star of the Broadway musical *Beatlemania*, with Greg (George) being voiced by Tom Teeley, another veteran from the *Beatlemania* musical.

Quantum Of Solace (2008)

Directed By - Marc Foster
Written By - Paul Haggis, Neal Purvis and Robert Wade.
Running Time - 106 Minutes
Release Date - October 31st 2008

The second James Bond movie to star Daniel Craig as 007 centres around him trying to stop a mysterious organisation from destroying a country's most valuable resource. Bond being Bond he likes to sleep with many beautiful women, with one of them being an MI6 Agent called Strawberry Fields (played by Gemma Arterton) - obviously, her name is a shout out to The Beatles' song 'Strawberry Fields Forever'.

Beatlefacts

* Bond isn't a fan of The Beatles - in the 1964 film *Goldfinger*, he said to a lady in a bedroom, while replacing champagne, *"My dear girl, there are some things that just aren't done, such as drinking Dom Perignon '53 above the temperature of 38 degrees Fahrenheit. That's as bad as listening to the Beatles without earmuffs."*
* Gemma Arterton and Paul McCartney shared the screen together in the *Some Mothers Do 'Ave 'Em* TV special in 2016.
* Paul McCartney tipped Amy Winehouse to sing the theme song to this film - it eventually went to Alicia Keys and Jack White.

K-On! (2009-2011)

Created By - Kakifly
First Broadcast - April 3rd 2009-March 16th 2011
Running Time - 24 Minutes Each

A popular Japanese manga series created by Kakifly, which was later adapted into an anime. It is about an all-female teenage rock group called The Houkago Teatime Band. Fans have speculated that the core cast is a female version of The Beatles: Yui is believed to be based on John Lennon and is the guitarist, Ritsu the drummer is believed to be based on Ringo Starr, Mio the bassist is believed to be based on Paul McCartney (and is also left handed), and Mugi is the quiet one, like George Harrison (unlike The Beatles, they do have a fifth member called Azusa). In the show, Yui was taught how to play guitar from scratch by Mio, paralleling The Beatles 'early days, as John was taught to play the guitar by the left handed Paul McCartney.

In the film spin-off (2011's *K-On! The Movie*), they do the famous Abbey Road crossing, as well as performing a re-creation of The Beatles 'final rooftop concert on their classroom's tabletop.

Detective Conan - The Raven Chaser (2009)

Directed By - Yasuichiro Yamamoto
Written By - Gosho Aoyama
Release Date - April 18th 2009
Running Time - 111 Minutes

Movie adaptation of the very long-running anime and manga series *Detective Conan*. There is a brief scene in the movie which parodies various Beatles album covers such as *Please Please Me, With The Beatles, A Hard Day's Night, Beatles For Sale* and *Help!* featuring characters from the anime. The movie grossed more than 3.5. billion Yen in the Japanese box office.

Turn Me On Dead Man (2009)

Directed By - Adam Blake Carver
Written By - Adam Blake Carver and Tyler Knell
Release Date - June 18th 2009
Running Time - 22 Minutes

A fictionalised account of the 'Paul Is Dead 'myth using expys (exported characters) of our Fab Four. This film explores the accidental death of Blake Connolly, the expy of Paul McCartney, and in an attempt to keep their fame going, the band choose to cover up the tragic event by replacing Blake with a lookalike/soundalike hoping that their millions of fans won't be able to tell the difference.
The music for the film was provided by a band named The Bumblebees.

Beatlefacts

*   The title is based on a backmasked sample used in 'Revolution 9 'where 'Number Nine, Number Nine 'sounds ambiguously like 'Turn Me On Dead Man, Turn Me On Dead Man', which fuelled the real 'Paul Is Dead 'myth.
*   Adam Blake Carver, the film's director, isn't really much of a Beatles fan, but said he was inspired by playing *Let It Be* backwards, and hearing *"He's dead, He's dead"*. The film's producer, Tyler Knell, is actually a fan, and even enjoys playing The Beatles' music forwards.

Norwegian Wood (2010)

Directed By - Tran Anh Hung
Written By - Haruki Murakami
Release Date - December 11th 2010
Running Time - 133 Minutes

Based on the novel of the same name, this is a Japanese romantic film about life in the 1960s when Toru's friend, Kizuki, committed suicide and Toru grew close to Kizuki's girlfriend, Naoko, and another woman named Midori. In the beginning of the film, the character of Toru hears an orchestral cover of The Beatles' song 'Norwegian Wood (This Bird Has Flown) 'from the *Rubber*

Soul album during a trip to Hamburg, which makes him feel nostalgic, as it was the favourite song of the character Naoko.

Femmine Contro Maschi (2011)

Directed By - Fausto Brizzi
Written By - Fausto Brizzi
Release Date - February 4th 2011
Running Time - 98 Minutes

A sequel to 2010's *Maschi Contro Femmine*, this is an Italian comedy movie known in English as *Women vs Men* about a lady called Anna who loves opera and French literature, while her husband, Piero, loves football and other women. In the film, we briefly see an Italian Beatles tribute band perform 'Twist and Shout' in one scene. Not much to say, but just wanted to point that out.

Phineas and Ferb The Movie: Across the 2nd Dimension (2011)

Directed By - Robert Hughes and Dan Povenmire
Written By - Jon Colton Barry, Dan Povenmire and Jeff "Swampy" Marsh
First Broadcast - August 5th 2011
Running Time - 78 Minutes

A TV movie spin-off of the popular Disney animated series *Phineas and Ferb*, a show about two boys on a summer vacation doing the impossible, while their pet platypus fights a mad scientist - crazy stuff if you ask me!

In this film, the main baddie of the franchise, Heinz Doofenshmirtz, and his self from an alternate reality, visualises himself as a number of famous duos including John Lennon and Paul McCartney of The Beatles. A very brief scene, but it's nice to see a Beatles reference in this fun kids' flick.

Beatlefacts

* An episode of the TV series was entitled 'A Hard Day's Knight 'which is a shout-out to The Beatles movie *A Hard Day's Night*. Another episode of the series also sees Phineas and Ferb form a band called The Bajeatles.
* Disney, of course, distribute the 2021 documentary film *The Beatles - Get Back*.

The Doo's - Kidology (2012)

Directed By - Stevie Riks
Written By - Stevie Riks
Release Date - March 12th 2012
Running Time - 14 Minutes

Funny mini-parody documentary about the Unfab Four - Dom Lemon, Saul McHardley, Jorge Harikrishna and Caringo "No Autographs" Barr AKA The Doo's. While not a particularly original spoof, it is however very well done, and the jokes, for the most part, work. It is available for free online on YouTube.

Playing The Moldovans At Tennis (2012)

Directed By - Tony Hawks and Mikolaj Jaroszewicz
Written By - Tony Hawks
Release Date - June 22nd 2012
Running Time - 100 Minutes

Adapted from the 2007 book of the same name, this is a comedy featuring UK comic Tony Hawks (not to be confused with the American skateboarder of the same name) setting a challenge of beating at tennis all 11 of the Moldovan international footballers, who lost 4-0 to England at Wembley. There is a scene in the film where Tony visits a Beatles convention in Liverpool in 1998, and we get to see a Beatles tribute band perform. Tony meets the band after the show.

The Disappearance of Eleanor Rigby (2013, 2014)

Directed By - Ned Benson
Written By - Ned Benson
Release Date - September 9th 2013 and May 14th 2014
Running Time - 96 Minutes, 205 Minutes and 123 Minutes

A trilogy of films starring James McAvoy and Jessica Chastain, about a couple trying to reclaim the life and love they once knew, and pick up the pieces of a past that may be too far gone. Not much to say Beatles-wise, other than that the Jessica Chastain's character, Eleanor Rigby, is of course named after the Beatles song of the same name.

Living Is Easy With Eyes Closed (2013)

Directed By - David Trueba
Written By - David Trueba
Release Date - October 31st 2013
Running Time - 108 Minutes

The winner of six Goya Awards including Best Film, Best Director, Best Original Writing and Best Leading Actor, *Living Is Easy With Eyes Closed* is a Spanish "dramedy" set in 1966 during the filming of *How I Won The War*, where a hardcore Beatle fan and English teacher named Antonio (Javier Camara) goes on a road trip to Almeria, where *HIWTW* is being shot, in the hope of meeting John Lennon. On the way, he picks up two hitchhikers, and the trio follow their dream and look for their own freedom.

The movie received positive reviews from critics, and ironically received much better reviews than *HIWTW* itself!

Beatlefacts

* The film's title comes from a lyric from the Beatles song 'Strawberry Fields Forever'.

Portlandia (2014)

Written By - Jonathan Krisel
First Broadcast - April 3rd 2014
Running Time - 23 Minutes

A sketch show about life in Portland in Oregon, USA that ran from 2011-2018. In the episode 'Bahama Knights', Fred Armisen has an idea of doing a documentary about The Beatles, only for Carrie to say it's been done a million times, as everybody knows the story so well. He perseveres, and attempts to clear the rights for using Beatles music for a modest sum of $50, even travelling all the way to Apple HQ in London - only to be turned down flat, as they demand $1 billion for licensing their music!

Beatles (2014)

Directed By - Peter Flinth
Written By - Lars Saabye Christensen and Axel Hellstenius
Release Date - August 29th 2014
Running Time - 114 Minutes

An adaptation of Lars Saabye Christensen's bestselling 1984 novel with the same name, about four boys from Olso in the 1960s and their love of The Beatles. This coming-of-age story set in Norway follows the adventures of Kim, Gunnar, Ola and Seb pretending to be The Beatles, and they start their own band called The Snafus. Like many teenage dreams, this one doesn't get realised, but the need to save up for musical instruments ends up becoming the drive behind what they do during their adolescence; struggling with out-dated textbooks and elderly teachers, discovering the opposite sex, being beaten up by rival gangs, experimentations with booze, and eventually becoming political activists.

Beatlefacts

*   The film's soundtrack was composed by Magne Furuholmen, a former member of A-Ha.
*   The band's name, The Snafus, might be a reference to the military slang, SNAFU, which means "Situation Normal, All F***ed Up". In the 1940s, Warner Bros made animated military propaganda films with a buffoonish character named Private Snafu.

Bob's Burgers (2014)

Directed By - Chris Chong
Written By - Steven Davis and Kelvin Yu
First Broadcast - December 7th 2014
Running Time - 22 Minutes

Cult 2010s US animated sitcom about a burger joint that's described as a crossover between *The Simpsons* and *Home Movies*. In the episode 'Father Of The Bob', we see Bob make a creative burger entitled 'Baby, You Can Chive My Car', which is, of course, a shout-out to the Beatles song 'Drive My Car', and the burger is made to impress Henry, a friend of his dad, Big Bob.

Come Together: A Beatles Tribute (2015)

Directed By - Stephen Ison and John Schofield
Release Date - February 3rd 2015
Running Time - 53 Minutes

A documentary focusing on the ever-growing phenomenon of Beatles tribute bands. Hosted by John Lennon's sister, Julia Baird, this film is shot during International Beatles Week, which is hosted every year in Liverpool. We get to see a variety of Beatles tribute bands from all around the world, and we also learn that there are at least 8000 worldwide, who do their absolute darnedest to look and sound like their idols and, for the most part, they succeed.

Danny Collins (2015)

"Being rich doesn't change your experience in the way you think"
John Lennon

Directed By - Dan Fogelman
Written By - Dan Fogelman
Release Date - May 29th 2015
Running Time - 106 Minutes

The directorial debut of Don Fogelman, this star-studded comedy-drama is based on the true story of British folk musician Steve Tilston, to whom John Lennon penned a letter of support in 1971, having read an interview with Tilston conducted by Richard Howell for *ZigZag* magazine, in which Steve feared that wealth and fame might affect his songwriting in a negative way. John's letter, which he sent to Howell at the magazine to pass on to Steve, was not delivered. (Steve believes that someone at the magazine must have sold it). It ended up in the hands of an American Beatles memorabilia collector in 2010, who then contacted Steve to verify the letter's authenticity.

In this fictionalised version of the story, Steve Tilston is renamed Danny Collins, and is played by the legendary Hollywood actor, Al Pacino, and in this version, Danny Collins is an American rock musician rather than a British folk singer, and it is his manager who gives him the letter rather than a collector. Because of this, Collins gives up his hard-living ways and decides to change course and embarks on a heartfelt journey to rediscover his family and begin a second life.

It received mostly positive reviews from critics and *Entertainment Weekly*'s Chris Nashawaty named the film *"one of 2015's overlooked gems"*. The film's soundtrack also contained many iconic tunes from Lennon's solo years such as 'Imagine', 'Instant Karma!', 'Love', 'No.9 Dream 'and 'Beautiful Boy'.

My Little Pony - Friendship Is Magic (2015)

Directed By - Jim Miller and Jayson Thiessen
Written By - Lauren Faust and Bonnie Zacherle
First Broadcast - June 27th 2015
Running Time - 22 Minutes

Very popular 2010s animated spin-off series of the 1980s toy franchise My Little Pony by Hasbro (Transformers, G.I. Joe etc.) about cute, colourful cartoon ponies, who go on adventures and learn about the power of friendship.

The episode 'Party Pooped 'features a flashback of the character of Pinkie Pie joining a group called The Travelling Band, whose lineup consists of George Horrsen, Liam T. Walrus, Paul McCartneigh and of course Pinkie Pie, who plays the role of their Ringo. They are known for their hit singles, which include 'He Is The Stallion 'and 'It Would Be Fun', and the episode shows a slideshow of photos of their rise and fall, which pays homage to various stages in The Beatles 'career including their big break, *Abbey Road* and their iconic album 'Sgt. Pinkie's Lonely Hearts Club Band'. Like the real life Beatles, they do unfortunately disband.

The episode 'Magical Mystery Cure 'is of course a reference to the Beatles TV movie and EP/LP *Magical Mystery Tour* and the title of the episode 'Eery Little Thing She Does 'is a nod to 'Every Little Thing '- a song from the *Beatles For Sale* album.

Beat Bugs (2016-Present)

Created By - Josh Wakely
First Broadcast - August 3rd 2016-Present

A very charming CGI animated series for young children, set in a garden and based around a group of insects who sing Beatle songs, created by Josh Wakely and streamed through Netflix. The project was in development for six years, as Wakely tried to get the rights to the music, with a deal that reportedly cost around $10million. Its objective is to teach young children life lessons in a calm and gentle manner, with a little help from our friends, known as Beatles tunes! As of writing, the series is currently in its third season, with a special being broadcast in 2017.

Aimed at the 5-7 year old market, the main characters are Jay (possibly named after the song 'Blue Jay Way'?), a curious, ambitious and impulsive beetle (ahem, Beatle!), Crick, a grasshopper who's also an inventor, Walter Walrus, a slug with a theatrical personality, but who's very fearful, Buzz, a young optimistic and enthusiastic fruit fly, and Kumi, a confident and imaginative ladybug. The cover versions of Beatle songs in the show are provided by very famous recording artists such as P!nk and Sia.

Because of the show's success, a stage show called *Beat Bugs: A Musical Adventure* began in 2018, and a feature film *Beat Bugs: The Movie* is currently in development. It received an AWGIE Award in animation for an episode script, and an AACTA Award for best children's programme, as well as a Daytime Emmy award in 2017.

This is the perfect way for tykes to get into the world of The Beatles, with likeable characters and tasteful cover versions of Beatle classics. As it's a show aimed at young children, some of the lyrics have been sanitised, so any lyrics about sex or death are censored - for example, the line *"but of all these friends and lovers"* is replaced by *"but of all of all these friends la la la"* in 'In My Life', though oddly they get away with singing 'Why Don't We Do It In The Road?'!

A further show has been made with the same creator, for Netflix, called *Motown Magic* using a similar concept.

Beatlefacts

* In the show's setting, there is an octopus sprinkler in the garden - obviously referencing the rather divisive song 'Octopus 'Garden 'from the *Abbey Road* album.

Sausage Party (2016)

Directed By - Greg Tiernan and Conrad Vernon
Written By - Seth Rogan, Even Goldberg and Jonah Hill
Release Date - September 2nd 2016
Running Time - 89 Minutes

One of the first CGI animated films for grown-ups, about a sausage named Frank, striving to discover the truth about his existence. There is a minor character in the film called Sergeant Pepper, whose name is obviously a shout-out to The Beatles album *Sgt. Pepper's Lonely Heart's Club Band*. He is voiced by the co-creator of the film, Seth Rogan.

The Boss Baby (2017)

Directed By - Tom McGrath
Written By - Marla Frazee and Michael McCullers
Release Date - April 1st 2017
Running Time - 93 Minutes

Based on the novel by Marla Frazee, a fun and very successful CGI movie by Dreamworks (*Shrek*) about the titular Boss Baby, who wears a suit and carries a briefcase, and is voiced by the famous actor Alec Baldwin. One of the minor reoccurring plot elements of the movie is none other than the Beatles song 'Blackbird', which is sung to the secondary protagonist, Tim Templeton, and his brother, the Boss Baby, as a lullaby by their parents, and appears throughout the film.

Beatlefacts

* Ringo Starr and Alec Baldwin have both played the character of Mr. Conductor in the Thomas The Tank Engine spin-offs *Shining Time Station* and *Thomas & The Magic Railroad*.

Yesterday (2019)

Directed By - Danny Boyle
Written By - Richard Curtis
Release Date - June 25th 2019
Running Time - 116 Minutes

What if the Beatles were never famous? This is the story!

This is a tale of a struggling singer-songwriter named Jack Malik (played by Himesh Patel). One day, the whole world suffers a total blackout, and Jack gets knocked over by a bus. After recovering, he sings 'Yesterday 'to his friends but, much to his surprise, nobody recognises it: history is now messed up, as in this universe, The Beatles never took off. Seeing as nobody knows about them, Jack passes the songs off as his own, and gives a demo tape to a producer, and because of this, ends up opening for Ed Sheeran (playing himself) in Moscow. Jack's fame grows from here, and he records his debut album (entitled *One Man Only* - as we all know, most chart music nowadays is created by a large team of people) consisting of The Beatles' back catalogue.

The movie was a big hit. It's a very entertaining, innocent, inoffensive romp for a rainy Sunday afternoon, which has a good message about the soullessness of fame, and how it's lonely being at the top. It does however suffer from being something of an unintentional period piece of late 2010s popular culture, with Ed Sheeran playing himself, a cameo from James Corden, and references to current trends, such as the flossing dance from the Fortnite video game. The movie did however receive praise from Paul McCartney himself, and was nominated for several awards, and even won an award for World Cinema at the Monclair Film Festival in America.

Beatlefacts

* Writer Richard Curtis asked Paul to approve the film's title - Paul liked it, but jokingly suggested that it be called 'Scrambled Eggs', a reference to the placeholder name that the song 'Yesterday 'was given while Paul was working on it.
* Paul and Ringo, as well as the estates of John and George, approved the film, despite them having no creative input.
* Some of the characters are named after Beatle songs. Rocky, the temporary manger, is named after 'Rocky Racoon', Ellie, the love interest, is named after 'Eleanor Rigby', and her roomie, Lucy, is of course named after 'Lucy In the Sky with Diamonds'.
* Ed Sheeran, who appears in the film, says that The Beatles are his biggest influence.
* Debra (Kate McKinnon) compares Jack in one scene to Jesus, calling him the messiah, alluding to the "bigger than Jesus" controversy of 1966. Jack is not the messiah, he's a very naughty boy!
* The studio where Jack records his music is the EastWest Studios in Hollywood, where Paul McCartney recorded his solo album *Egypt Station* in 2018.
* In the film, Jack was also supposed to meet George Harrison and Ringo Starr in a pub, but the scene was cut out, as it was felt that it would lessen the impact of his meeting with John Lennon.
* Cigarettes don't exist in this alternate universe, so not everything is bad in the Beatleless universe!

Lucy In The Sky (2019)

Directed By - Noah Hawley
Written By - Brian C. Crown, Elliott DiGuiseppi and Noah Hawley
Release Date - December 6th 2019
Running Time - 124 Minutes

Sci-Fi thriller starring Natalie Portman. The film's title is obviously inspired by The Beatles' song 'Lucy In The Sky With Diamonds'. Lucy does go into the sky, but doesn't come across any diamonds!

The Day I Met Sir Paul McCartney

Me, with my VIP lanyard, moments before meeting Paul McCartney! Because of copyright reasons, unfortunately, I'm not able to include the photos of us together, as they are owned by MPL.

To end this book, I wanted to finish with the story of the day I actually met Paul McCartney, which was on the 14th December 2018 (the day before my birthday); undoubtedly, one of my greatest moments ever! I've been a fan of his all my life. I'd had an email from Paul's team in London inviting me to meet him backstage during his December 2018 short tour in the UK. I could choose either Glasgow, Liverpool or London for the meeting, and I opted for Glasgow, as my dad's family live there, and I thought I could combine it with a Christmas visit. I was also able to take Mum and Dad as my guests.

We travelled to Glasgow on the Thursday afternoon, and stayed in Dad's old home town of Milngavie (pronounced Mull Guy), which is on the outskirts of the city. We had been getting a little concerned, as it was a bit of a military operation arranging this meeting together, and we had been talking to Macca's people, as we were supposed to have received an email with all the meeting details, but nothing had arrived. They promised to chase everything up, but reassured us that everyone was aware we were going to be there. Luckily at 7:30pm the evening before the concert and meeting, we got a call from Macca's 'right-hand man', a super lady, who reassured us again that all was in hand, and we were invited to arrive at the SSE Hydro for 3:30pm on the Friday afternoon for the initial soundcheck.

The following day, we arrived at the venue in the afternoon about 3pm to queue up for the soundcheck. About 200 people had paid a fortune to have a special package for the day, which included the soundcheck and a decent seat for the show. About 70% of the fans in the queue were very fanatical fans from Japan (one had been to see Macca 139 times, one had been to his tour in Canada, Oslo, Liverpool and was going to London as well! There was one fan who was at Shea Stadium all those years ago.) There was my dad, who saw The Beatles in Glasgow back in 1965!

They had all travelled all the way to Scotland to see Macca (which was weird for the Japanese, considering he was already in Japan the previous October and November). There were Americans and lots of Europeans. Dad got chatting to a lady from Glasgow and it seemed as if they were the only Scottish people in the queue! Some had even come dressed as Paul, and I had a photograph with a Japanese lady, who was in Sgt. Pepper regalia, who turned out to be actually something of a celebrity in Japan, appearing there on television many times.

After waiting in the cold, we finally entered the venue around 3:30pm. Then there was a mess-up with the seat tickets, as we had some special tickets to pick up, which had mistakenly been given to some Japanese fans, but we managed to secure them eventually!

Once inside, we were all given a special merchandise package of a beautiful fleece blanket, woven with 'Paul McCartney - Freshen Up 2018'. We spoke to a lot of people who worked for him - he has an army of hundreds of people putting these tours together. They all said what a great guy he is and a pleasure to work for, and how honoured we were to be meeting him, as he usually only meets family and friends backstage before the show. Then we piled in for the soundcheck, which started at around 4:15pm.

It was just like having an intimate Paul McCartney show to about 200 die-hard (mainly Japanese) fans! He played some old rock & roll and Beatle standards, as well as tunes like 'Ram On 'from my favourite Beatles solo album *Ram*, which he said Kiera Knightley had asked to be played at her wedding, and the beautiful 'I Don't Know 'from his album *Egypt Station*. All the tracks were different (except 'Lady Madonna') from the ones he performed on the actual show, so it was great having an extra intimate Macca Show!

Then after the soundcheck, Paul's "right-hand lady", who looked after us, gave us our VIP lanyards to wear, and then took us away to the VIP suite, which was all beautifully decorated in black drapes, velvet sofas and chairs, mood lighting, glorious flowers in bowls with soft classical music playing. For what seemed like ages, we waited and waited, and waited and waited - more people came in who were friends and family of the band, and the band themselves came in. Then around 7:45pm, our host returned, and finally, we were taken away through the maze of corridors to the room where I would finally meet the Beatle legend...

We went up in a lift, and then I stood next to a nice purple hippie tapestry type backdrop, waiting for the main man to arrive, and got introduced to the lovely professional photographer, who was going to take our photographs. About 7:50pm, out of the green room comes Paul McCartney, looking fantastic and dressed for the show... and he was the nicest possible guy you could expect to meet. We immediately shared big hugs, and he asked how far we had travelled and, when we told him where we live (Yorkshire), he said *"What are you doing here then?"* and I said *"It's my birthday tomorrow, and we've come just to see you!"* and we all laughed. Mum then chatted with him a little bit about myself, my music, my *Autism & Me* film, and then I gave him a copy of my *Little Big Beat Book*, which he was really taken with - he leafed through it, and couldn't believe I managed to write such a comprehensive book - *"very impressive"* he said. I had written a special inscription for him. We then had some photographs of just the two of us together, as well as some with me, Mum, Dad and Macca. As we were leaving, he said to me *"Come on, let's hug it out again!"* which we did, and we all thanked him. He called Mum *"Sweetheart"*, which was really nice, and told us to look after ourselves. We were told the photographs would be posted to us in about six weeks, and then our host took us to finally see the show, which started around 8:15pm. It was quite something, the three of us emerging from backstage, when the arena was full and all eyes were on us, as we were shown to some of the best seats in the house. Dad always looks like a bit of a rock star anyway (well, he was one!), and a few people asked him if he was in music.

We took our seats, and within five minutes, the concert had started - and it was the greatest concert I've ever been to. This is actually my third Paul McCartney show (the first was at the O2 in London in 2009 and the second was at the Manchester Arena in 2011) and he did his repertoire of Beatles classics, Wings classics, solo classics, and songs from his *Egypt Station* album. He sounded amazing, the band were out of this world, the lights and visuals were spectacular, and he was on stage for three hours! When he played 'Birthday', he said *"This is for everyone who has a birthday today"* and then pointed to me and said *"or tomorrow!"* So, including the soundcheck, we saw him for four hours that day! What an amazing amount of energy he has.

The show ended about 11pm, and we were all very, very tired. We travelled away from the Hydro, and then we went back to Milngavie... and barely slept (again, which is understandable, as I'd only just met the legend that is Paul McCartney!).

References

[1] https://faroutmagazine.co.uk/the-beatles-earliest-known-footage-paul-mccartney-john-lennon/

[2] https://en.wikipedia.org/wiki/A_Hard_Day%27s_Night_(film)

[3] https://www.beatlesagain.com/breflib/cartoons.html

[4] http://tittenhurstlennon.blogspot.com/2009/07/self-portrait-1969.html

[5] https://www.imdb.com/title/tt0701077/trivia

[6] https://www.beatlesbible.com/1968/11/15/george-harrison-smothers-brothers-comedy-hour/

[7] https://www.academia.edu/11958096/STUART_SUTCLIFFE_A_MYTH_IN_THE_MAKING

[8] *The Beatles on Film* by Roland Reiter (Transcript Film, 2008)

[9] https://www.beatlesbible.com/1964/02/11/live-washington-coliseum/

[10] https://madelinex.com/2019/01/04/yoko-film-no-6-rape/

[11] http://www.beatlesinterviews.org/db1967.1227.beatles.html

[12] http://www.beatlesinterviews.org/dbmovies.html

[13] https://www.youtube.com/watch?v=xmFDcZVDopE

[14] https://www.youtube.com/watch?v=teJIZGCfiMA

[15] https://www.youtube.com/watch?v=kbrYRvzNgao

[16] https://www.youtube.com/watch?v=LYzSbRYFaPQ

[17] https://www.youtube.com/watch?v=r2lGS_f5Bqo

[18] https://www.youtube.com/watch?v=TxE8YlTYx7k

[19] https://www.youtube.com/watch?v=JDMZ_PHxtuo

[20] https://www.youtube.com/watch?v=axgW--rphgk

[21] http://ctva.biz/Music/US/HollywoodDiscotheque.htm

[22] https://www.beatlesbible.com/1963/04/13/television-625-show-beatles-first-national-tv-appearance/

[23] http://www.beatlesinterviews.org/db1963.0622.jukebox.jury.john.lennon.html

[24] https://www.beatlesbible.com/1963/10/30/television-drop-in-stockholm-sweden/

[25] https://calendar.songfacts.com/january/3/675

[26] http://www.todayifoundout.com/index.php/2015/12/the-many-unrealized-beatles-film-projects/

[27] *Beatlemania - An Illustrated Filmography* by Bill Harry.

[28] https://en.wikipedia.org/wiki/Oh!_Calcutta!

[29] https://tvtropes.org/pmwiki/pmwiki.php/Script/OurShowForRingoStarr

[30] https://www.amazon.co.uk/50-Greatest-Movies-Never-Made/dp/031220082X

[31] https://www.imdb.com/title/tt8268962/

[32] https://www.imdb.com/title/tt2381333/

[33] https://lostmediawiki.com/Yellow_Submarine_(partially_found_cancelled_CGI_remake_of_animated_film;_2010-2011)

[34] https://sonarent.com/news/sonar-entertainment-to-develop-the-fifth-beatle-as-event-series

About The Author

Rory Hoy is a multi-award-winning music producer/DJ, author and film maker. He has released eight albums on various worldwide labels and hundreds of singles, EPs, remixes and collaborations.

In 2018, he wrote the guide to the late 1990s dance music movement, big beat, with *The Little Big Beat Book*, published by New Haven Publishing, to critical and commercial acclaim, in which he interviewed 120 artists from the time, including Fatboy Slim and The Prodigy. A bookazine edition called *The Story of Big Beat* followed a year later.

He has DJ-ed at many major festivals in the UK and his tracks have been used as syncs for the likes of Disney, Google, Sony BET TV, ITV, Costco, Buzzfeed Yellow, FOX TV and Audi.

He is also a film maker, with the multi-award-winning film, *Autism & Me*, about his own personal experiences living on the autistic spectrum, released on DVD by Jessica Kingsley Publishers. He goes into schools and organisations where they show his film and he talks about autism.

He was the winner of the Yorkshire Young Achiever of the Year Award, hosted by ITV, in the Arts category, which he won alongside actor Mikey North from *Coronation Street*. He won a Film 4 Youth Award, presented by film director Guy Ritchie at the showing of his *Autism & Me* film at the Waterfront Hall in Belfast. He was nominated for a Royal Television Society Award, has a UNICEF Award, 4Front Award and Wavemakers Award among others. He's Youth Patron of the London based charity Resources for Autism, and in this capacity was invited to a special reception at the House of Lords. He was a Centenary Ambassador for the national charity UK Youth, and featured in their promotional film. He continues to be an Ambassador for them. He was invited to be a Royal Commonwealth Associate Fellow. He is also an Ambassador for the charity Henshaws, which supports people with sight loss and other disabilities to go beyond expectations - something we should all strive to achieve.

Lightning Source UK Ltd.
Milton Keynes UK
UKHW020625030621
384854UK00004B/15